636.088   Guthrie
GUT

Home book of animal care.
148612

Date Due

JUN 1 4 1988		
FEB 1 3 1991		
NOV 2 2 1993		
OCT 2 4 1994		
DEC 2 7 1994		
JUL 2 1 2010		

HOME BOOK OF ANIMAL CARE

HOME BOOK of ANIMAL CARE

BY

ESTHER L. GUTHRIE

WITH THE TECHNICAL ASSISTANCE OF

ROBERT C. MILLER

HARPER & ROW, PUBLISHERS

NEW YORK and LONDON

CONTENTS

PART I

MAMMALS

BIRDS

AMPHIBIANS

REPTILES

SPIDERS AND OTHER ARTHROPODS

v

INSECTS

PART II

THE VIVARIUM

PART III

HOW TO GROW AND PREPARE FOOD FOR CAGED PETS

PART IV

DESIGNS FOR CAGES

PREFACE

OF THE innumerable questions that come to natural history museums, zoological gardens, and public aquariums—by mail, by telephone, or by inquirers who present themselves in person—the most familiar and recurrent have to do with the care and feeding of animals. The people on the receiving end of these questions gradually come to think of their metropolitan area as a kind of large, disorganized zoo; any house or apartment may contain a baby alligator brought back from Florida, a horned toad picked up in Arizona, a pet turtle that won't eat, a bowl of goldfish that aren't doing too well, a tropical aquarium that has been so taken over by algae that the owner can't see the fish, or even such unusual pets as chipmunks, flying squirrels, toads, frogs, or snakes.

Man's interest in his animal neighbors is universal. One theory of the domestication of animals is that first they were kept as pets and that only thereafter was their usefulness discovered. At all events, the keeping of pets is found at every level of culture, whether advanced or primitive. Australian aborigines, whose only domesticated animal is the native dog or dingo, are in the habit of catching small animals and birds and keeping them as pets, or at least as playthings. Since they have never learned how to feed and care for them, these unfortunate captives soon die—an example of what all too often happens to animals through misguided human interest.

The purpose of this book is to provide directions on how to take care of animals, so that they will be well fed, healthy, and comfortable under indoor conditions. It tells how to make a terrarium, how to keep an aquarium, how to provide for the needs of small mammals, birds, reptiles, amphibians, and fish—almost any animal that one is likely to want to keep (excepting, of course, large or exotic animals which usually can be kept only in zoos).

Esther Guthrie was a teacher of long experience, who concluded a highly successful career in secondary education by serving many years as science supervisor in the Sacramento (California) City schools. She had a great deal of firsthand experience in keeping alive in the classroom, for student observation, the animals of which she wrote. Regrettably the senior author died unexpectedly while her manuscript was in the hands of the publisher. She had the satisfaction of knowing that her book would be published, and that it would carry into the future her love of animal pets and her special knowledge, obtained through years of study, of how to care for them.

Her book fills a long-recognized need, and will be welcomed by all people who like to keep unusual animals as pets; by parents whose offspring bring home unusual guests such as turtles, snakes, frogs, toads, or lizards and expect them to be entertained under the parental roof; and by teachers, who not only have the problem of keeping animals alive for observation in the classroom, but the further problem of answering—for pupils or parents—questions concerning the diet and health of everything from tadpoles to parakeets and hamsters. This book provides the answers.

ROBERT C. MILLER
SENIOR SCIENTIST
CALIFORNIA ACADEMY OF SCIENCES

San Francisco, California
October 1, 1965

ACKNOWLEDGMENTS

NO PIECE of writing is ever brought to fruition without interest, advice, encouragement, and assistance from authorities, friends, and other writers in the fields of endeavor. This book has been no exception in this respect; hence acknowledgments are due the many who have been of assistance during its writing.

My appreciation and my thanks are extended to those authorities on the staff of the California Academy of Sciences who gave generously of their crowded time to check the text for accuracy. They are: Dr. Robert T. Orr, curator; Mrs. Jacqueline Schonewald, assistant, and Mrs. Dorcas McClintock, research associate, of the Department of Birds and Mammals; Dr. Alan E. Leviton, curator of herpetology, whose criticisms were excellent and especially helpful; Dr. C. Don MacNeil, assistant curator, and Hugh B. Leech, associate curator, of the Department of Entomology; Dr. Earl S. Herald, curator, and Robert P. Dempster, associate curator, of the Steinhart Aquarium; Harriet Exline (Mrs. Don L. Frizzell, Rollo Gardens, Rollo, Missouri), research associate, whose suggestions on arthropods were excellent.

To the General Biological Supply House, Inc., Chicago, Illinois, I am most grateful for data which they offered and for their permission to quote from their Turtox leaflet on the salt water aquarium.

My thanks are also extended to the kindly, helpful people in the Division of Systematic Biology, Stanford University, especially for the liberal use of the library; also to the many authors whose texts I used freely to check data.

To Dr. Laurence M. Klauber, internationally known herpetologist of San Diego, California, I give my profoundest gratitude for his interest, advice, and criticisms on the sections on amphibians and reptiles, which began with the first draft and closed many years later

with the final writing; and to him "that is last but shall be first,"—
Dr. Robert C. Miller, senior scientist of the California Academy of
Sciences, Golden Gate Park, San Francisco—I give my heartfelt
thanks and deep appreciation. Without his generous assistance, constant interest, and unfailing enthusiasm this material would never
have reached the stage of publication.

In conclusion I give my sincerest thanks, respect, and appreciation
to my typist, Mrs. Susan S. Kramer, whose interest, diligence, patience, excellent editing, and forbearance as well as determination to
hold me to the rugged path have been of immeasurable value; and
to Mrs. Jayne McCracken my thanks for giving generously of her
time to read through the final manuscript for clarity.

E.L.G.

INTRODUCTION

THE purpose of this handbook is to give ready information to a child, a parent, or a teacher on the care and handling of both familiar and sometimes strange animals that fall into the hands of children and often die from lack of knowledge on the part of the owners. Generally speaking, the information given about each animal is brief, but it covers the questions that are usually asked by those who come into the possession of some pet unfamiliar to them. This is followed by the information deemed most essential for the proper establishment and maintenance of various kinds of pets in captivity.

Included are many animals that the average adult would not consider as pets; yet children would consider them so. For example, a tarantula that has become used to handling will tolerate hours of being carried about on a child's sleeve or shirt front, yet it can respond in no way as a cat or dog would under similar circumstances. Also, many creatures among the lower animal forms have economic importance; some are beneficial to man; many are injurious. Common examples of these animals occur throughout our country. They are interesting, they should be recognized, and they should be understood. These creatures afford excellent material for lessons in natural science.

An attempt has been made to embrace those larger areas of the animal kingdom in which the more conspicuous and more common forms of animal life occur throughout the United States, since these are the animals that most often appeal to children. These are the mammals, birds, amphibians and reptiles, insects, spiders, and their relatives. There is also a general discussion of the various vivaria (such as the terrarium and aquarium), their establishment and care, plus detailed cage diagrams for specific animals, and information on how to grow and prepare food for captive pets.

This handbook is planned as a ready reference for children, parents, and teachers. A brief but general description of the phylum is given first. This is followed by a more detailed but also brief description of the order to be discussed. One or more specific species belonging to the order are then described. This is followed by information on housing and feeding the pet.

There are many instances where there are several species detailed before the information on housing and feeding is given. This is because the entire group may be maintained in the same manner, and it is so stated. Sometimes there are minor differences in the food, or the nest, or some trait of the animal. In this case the specific animal is named, and the difference in treatment is designated.

I have referred, in the paragraphs above, to the terms phylum, order, species, and so on. These are common terms which are used in our system of classification, a system which is necessary in order to keep scientific information accurate, clear, and universally understood.

The classification of plants and animals began in the middle 1700s with the great Swedish naturalist Linnaeus, who devised a system of short scientific names in an attempt to make classification a generally understood language. Well-known animals always have common names, but these names vary according to different localities and different languages. Often a specific common name is transferred to a similar-*looking* species in a new locality but is definitely a different species. For examples, Easterners who moved West in the early days were familiar with their eastern "yellowhammer," or flicker, and immediately applied the name to a western flicker of an entirely different species.

Linnaeus's system makes it possible to avoid such mistakes. He devised a plan of two-word names in either Latin or Greek. Since these two languages were taught in all schools in those days, these names were familiar to all naturalists of the world in Linnaeus's time.

This system proved so useful that it has been continued through the centuries. Common names are still applied and accepted, but a scientist will always use the scientific name, which generally gives one or more characteristic traits of the specimen itself. It is a simple system. The scientific names seem difficult and unwieldy only because Latin and Greek are no longer common knowledge to the layman. In modern practice, words from other languages, or place names or personal names are often used, but must be in Latinized form.

The system of classification may be explained as follows:

The living world is divided into two kingdoms—the plant kingdom and the animal kingdom. Since we are interested in the animal kingdom at the moment, we shall use it for illustration and explanation. The kingdoms are then divided into groups, each of which is called a phylum, which, in Latin, means race or tribe.

Let us take the phylum to which man belongs, the phylum Chordata, the word referring to a cord running along the back. The one characteristic common to all members of Chordata is that at some stage in life they have a notochord (from the Greek word *notos* meaning back). In most chordates this notochord becomes surrounded by a column of bone made up of a series of joints called vertebrae, from the Latin word meaning a joint; hence all animals with a backbone are placed in a subphylum, Vertebrata.

Classification continues further by taking characteristics that the vertebrates may have in common and which then place them together in a class. Selection of similar traits continues, and an order is formed, followed perhaps by a suborder, then a family, and a genus; finally the species is reached, which has characteristics that belong to it alone.

Now, let us classify the African lion. We know, of course, that it has a backbone, which immediately places it in the phylum Chordata and subphylum Vertebrata. We also know that it nurses its young. This places it in the group with all those animals that produce milk to nurse their young. They are called mammals and belong to the class Mammalia. Next we know that it is a meat eater, with teeth specialized for biting and tearing prey. This puts it in the order Carnivora. Then scientists tell us that the lion belongs to the family Felidae, meaning catlike. Since it is a cat, the genus is *Felis*, but the particular species which is like no other cat is a lion, *leo*. In outline it is like this:

Phylum: Chordata (Latin—a chord)—all have notochords
  Subphylum: Vertebrata (Latin—a joint)—all have jointed backbones
    Class: Mammalia (Latin—breast)—all nurse their young
      Order: Carnivora (Latin—flesh-eating)—all are flesh eaters
        Family: Felidae (Latin—cat)—all are catlike
          Genus: *Felis* (Latin—cat)—all *are* cats
            Species: *leo* (Latin—lion)—African lion, *Felis leo*

In many species there is a third name following the second which may add to the description of the species or may be the Latinized name of some scientist in whose honor the specimen is named. For example, the Tucson shovel-nosed snake is *Chionactis occipitalis klauberi*. This snake is named for a well-known herpetologist, Laurence M. Klauber.

As classification develops and more groupings become necessary, one finds that there are subclasses, suborders, subfamilies, and so on, all of which are necessary in order to keep the pattern clear and uncomplicated.

Since common names are used throughout the handbook, the scientific names have been used no more than necessary, and only as an aid to accurate information and to avoid confusion.

POINTS TO BE REMEMBERED IN HANDLING PETS

1. Most adult wild animals either do not tame readily or tame not at all.
2. Young (babies) of most animals tame readily.
3. Use patience and slow and gentle movements at all times when working with a pet.
4. Talk to pet in soft, low tones.
5. When picking up pet be sure to give it support for its feet.
6. Heat and moisture from human hands are not good for small rodents.
7. Avoid:
   a. Sudden jerky movements when working with pet.
   b. Sudden loud and unusual noises.
   c. Placing hands on or over back of pet.
   d. Unnecessary fright.
   e. Handling smaller animals, such as mice, rats, and chipmunks. Allow them to run over you, but they do not feel safe when confined by your hands.
   f. Picking up pets by ears, tails, or legs.
   g. Teasing, since it produces an irritable and bad-tempered animal.
8. It should be kept in mind that most animals will bite or try to bite when frightened. It is a wise precaution to wear heavy gloves when picking up animals that are of uncertain temper or unused to being handled. There is no point at all in handling venomous animals, such as black-widow spiders, centipedes, or scorpions. The snakes mentioned in this volume are nonpoisonous, but they can inflict an unpleasant bite. Many species become quite docile after getting accustomed to a home terrarium. Still, anybody who handles a wild animal does so at his own risk.

PART I

MAMMALS

THE members of the class of mammals differ from all other classes in the animal kingdom in that the young are nourished on milk produced by the mother's mammary glands. The young are usually born fully formed; and the majority of them are covered with hair or fur; all are warm-blooded.

Some mammals are susceptible to diseases which may be transmitted to humans, such as rabies, spotted fever, and bubonic plague. Many states have regulations which forbid the capture of some wild pets for this reason. One should ask local or state health departments about these regulations if a wild mammal is to be trained as a pet.

Children find more pets among mammals than any other group of animals, as they are creatures that respond in a greater or lesser degree to human attention and learn to adjust more or less satisfactorily to association with man and his ways.

Probably the most common pets come from the order of rodents (gnawing mammals) while the most popular and no doubt the most favored come from the order of carnivores (flesh-eating mammals). However, pets are also found among several other orders, but these will be discussed in whichever division they fall, as the group is divided into those pets which come from the wild and those that have been domesticated and are no longer found in the wild state.

The discussion takes up the animals in their biological order and begins with the more primitive forms.

PETS FROM THE WILD

Marsupials or Pouch-bearing Mammals

Marsupials are primitive creatures which carry their young in an external pouch or brood sac. Members of this order are found only in Australia and its neighboring islands, and in America. The best known example is the Australian kangaroo. In America there is but one example, the opossum, which is found scattered across the United States.

OPOSSUM: Genus *Didelphis*

VIRGINIA OPOSSUM: *Didelphis marsupialis*

Range: Most of the United States east of the Rocky Mountains, south into Mexico and Central America; introduced to the Pacific States

Description: Fluffy, grayish-white; small ears; long snout; long, almost naked, prehensile tail; eyes small and dark; feet black with 5 toes each, 1 opposable; stupid, slow-moving animal, nocturnal in habit; reaches length of 3 feet including 15-inch tail, and weight of 5 pounds

Habitat: Holes in hollow trees and stumps, in holes under roots of trees, in old ground dens, in old abandoned buildings, usually in vicinity of water, about swampy or wet lowlands

Reproduction: 1 or 2 litters a year, depending upon range; number of young may be as many as 20; born in embryonic state, about ½ inch long but able to find way, unassisted, through mother's fur to brood pouch; each embryo that finds a teat grasps it; those that do not, die; young remain attached until sufficiently developed to move in and out of pouch

Life span: May live to age of 8 years

Economic position: Used for food and trapped for fur in some sections of United States; destructive to fruits, vegetables, and poultry in some areas

The opossum is seldom, if ever, known to bite, although it bares its teeth and curls its lips in a threatening manner. Often it drops to the ground limp and helpless in a pretense of death, from which comes our phrase "playing 'possum." It may also hang by its tail, immovable, as though lifeless.

The greatest problem with a captive opossum, especially a young one, is food. It is difficult to maintain the perfectly balanced diet required to prevent the development of a disease similar to rickets.

Opossums are not difficult to handle in captivity when properly housed and fed, and when not kept too long. An adult opossum does not become gentle but will tolerate handling. A baby opossum reacts much the same way. It is advisable to keep the creatures in captivity for short periods of time only, then liberate them in the area from which they were captured.

HOUSING

As plenty of room is required, use large cage (see Part IV). Comfortable retreat is necessary for sleeping quarters. Obtain a large, old, hollow stump; fasten high up in cage. When stump is not available, use roomy wooden box with entrance hole cut in one side. Place several bunches of dry grass or clean, soft hay in sleeping hole. Opossum spends greater part of day in sleeping hole, but may be coaxed out in mornings by offering bits of food.

A captive opossum usually chooses one corner of cage in which to place its droppings, returning to same corner each time for this purpose. Place a flat container in one corner; partially fill with mixture from bottom of cage to facilitate cleaning. Remove wet portions of sawdust each day; replace with fresh, dry sawdust.

Allow out of cage daily. Place large, many-branching limb which reaches from floor to ceiling in one corner of room, for opossum to climb about on limbs.

FOOD

In wild state opossum is an omnivorous feeder, consuming anything of both animal and vegetable nature. Hold to restricted diet in captivity.

REQUIRES DAILY: *Fruits*—Offer any which are in season and those which opossum seems to prefer; in winter months give apples, bananas, and oranges. *Greens*—Offer variety of vegetables and their tops; must be fresh and clean. *Milk*—Essential to diet, liked by pet; use large bottle and clean daily. *Water*—Must always be available.

REQUIRES OCCASIONALLY: *Meat*—Feed once per week or in very small quantities 2 or 3 times per week. Give fresh beef, fresh chicken heads, young birds which have fallen from nest, fresh fish, especially minnows, of which it is extremely fond. Do not overbalance diet with meat as young opossum develops rickets easily. *Dry food*—Offer several times per week; give dry, stale bread soaked in milk; stale, butterless bread; cooked cereal such as oats. *Meal worms*—Essential to diet. If opossum refuses to take meal worms from fingers or a dish, put them in bread and milk mixture.

NOTE: Since the opossum is nocturnal and prowls during the night, it should be provided with some food for that time. It should also have something for activity. Provide it with a fresh bone from which all fat and most of the meat has been removed.

Edentates or Toothless Mammals

This group of mammals is made up of some of the most curious creatures to be found in nature. In it are the anteaters, animals native to the American tropics, with a tubelike mouth through which a sticky tongue works collecting insects from the ground; sloths, also native to the tropics, which spend their lives hanging by their toes from limbs of trees in which they live; and the armadillo, an animal which lives encased in its own armor. All belong to the order Edentata which means toothless. However, all are not completely toothless, as the armadillo does have a set of peglike teeth.

Out of this group, the armadillo is the one that becomes good pet material, as it tames easily.

ARMADILLO: Genus *Dasypus*

NINE-BANDED ARMADILLO: *Dasypus novemcinctus*

Range: A tropical American species that has extended its range into Texas along the Gulf Coast to Florida and north to Kansas and Missouri

Description: Skin developed into heavy, shell-like armor which covers upper part and sides of body; middle section of armor made up of 7–9 movable joints; armor covered with thinly scattered, bristlelike hairs sensitive to touch; head hung low; ears long and pointed, but hearing varies; eyes small, vision very poor; snout long and sharp; has keen sense of smell; 4 toes on front feet, 5 on hind feet; reaches length of 28 inches, which includes 12-inch tail; weight may reach 15 pounds; good swimmer; can even walk under water and remain for some minutes; largely nocturnal although may be found abroad during day

Habitat: Areas where there is cover of low woods, thick brush, tall grass, and rocky areas where there are caves and crevices; digs burrows from 2 to 12 feet under ground; sometimes found in groups of varying numbers

Reproduction: Breeds July–September; young born February–April; 4 or 8 young, of 1 sex, as there are 4 per fertilized egg born at a time; born with eyes open, but armor soft and flexible; armor hardens as animal grows

Life span: Not known

Economic position: Destroys many insects and snakes; has keen sense of smell, and can detect insects 6 inches underground; may also damage melon crops in some areas; known to eat chickens on occasion

The armadillo may be easily captured by hand as its sight is extremely poor. When suddenly startled it can run with great speed, but its usual defense is to roll into a tight, iron-clad ball. It is easily maintained as a pet as it adjusts itself readily. However, it cannot be kept comfortably in a school. It is advisable to make the pet a daily visitor for observation only. When no longer wanted as a pet, the animal should be returned to the area from which it was captured.

An armadillo is easily maintained in captivity when properly fed and treated.

HOUSING

Requires plenty of room, so that it can move about freely. Place in yard or garden where it can dig and make its own burrow. Once it becomes adjusted and receives food from one source, it will not wander away from area.

FOOD

In wild state, armadillo eats large variety of insects, snakes, and, on rare occasions, chickens. Feed as many insects as available. Always include meal worms, both larvae and adults. Also, feed canned dog food, bits of horse meat, melons in season. Once a week, give stale dark bread soaked in milk and squeezed dry.

Rodents or Gnawing Mammals

There are probably more rodents in America than any other order of mammals. They are found all over the continent. They vary in size from the beaver, which may weigh sixty pounds, to a little mouse that weighs less than an ounce.

The chief characteristic of rodents is the possession of two incisor (chisel-like) teeth on the upper jaw, and two on the lower, and the absence of canine teeth. As the incisors, which are the gnawing teeth, are worn away by constant use, growth occurs continuously from the roots.

Children probably find more pets among rodents than among any other mammals. This is due to their abundance and to their general hardiness in captivity as well as to their interesting reactions to humans.

SQUIRRELS AND RELATED SPECIES

Squirrels and their relatives make up a rather large family in the order of Rodentia. The squirrels themselves naturally fall into three groups—those that are terrestrial or ground dwellers, those that are arboreal or tree dwellers, and those that fly. They are discussed under this grouping as follows:

Ground Squirrels

Ground squirrels are busy, active creatures, some beautifully patterned, others plain in color. Their claws are usually developed for digging, and of course, their incisors for gnawing. The majority are bushy-tailed and have bright, beady eyes.

PRAIRIE DOGS: Genus Cynomys

Prairie Dog: *Cynomys ludovicianus*

Range: From North Dakota to central Texas, west to northern Mexico, Arizona, Utah, and western Montana

Description: Stout-bodied; head broad and rounded; ears low and rounded; tail 3 inches long, flat but well-haired; reddish brown, flesh colored, or gray with pale muzzle; reaches length of 14½ inches including tail; diurnal in habit

Habitat: Dry open country with clay soil; digs burrows to length of 16 feet; lateral burrow near entrance; large mound built around burrow entrance

Reproduction: 1 litter a year; 2–10 young; born April–June. Reach maturity at 2 years

Life span: To 8 years

Economic position: Destroy great quantities of prairie grass on cattle ranges, especially in those states where large herds of cattle are run over grazing lands

Prairie dogs are closely related to the ground squirrels and belong to the same family as all squirrels. They were once widely distributed across the plains of the United States but are now greatly reduced in numbers due to the expanded settlement of our once open country.

Prairie dogs are best known, perhaps, for the so-called "dogtowns" they build, as they live in groups or colonies and tunnel close to each other. For protection they descend into their burrows with the speed of lightning.

One dog in a colony apparently acts as a sentinel. When danger appears, it emits a sharp, piercing note or whistle. This sends all the members of the colony scurrying into the nearest burrow.

Prairie dogs may be captured by flooding them out of their burrows. They must be handled with gloves, as they bite. A young dog is a happy, active creature, but when it reaches maturity it loses its gay spirit. It is naturally a gregarious animal at all times. When full grown it should be returned to its home "town" and freed among its own kind.

Prairie dogs are hardy in captivity and easily tamed when taken as babies. They do not like to be handled or fondled, but are full of curiosity, playfulness, and have a wonderful zest for keeping busy, which makes them interesting as pets.

HOUSING

Since prairie dog cannot be confined in ordinary cage for more than a few hours, use or build a heavy packing box 5′ × 3′ × 3′ with a screened, hinged top (see Part IV). Fill box two-thirds full of *damp, firmly packed* soil. A 1'-wide glass panel may be placed across front. Place pen where it will receive maximum sunlight each day. When prairie dog is two-thirds grown, it will need more space; at this point, it should be liberated.

FOOD

In wild state, prairie dog consumes stems and roots of forage plants such as grasses, grain, and alfalfa, as well as native fruits, grasshoppers and, sometimes other animals. Feed clover, alfalfa, lettuce, celery tops, carrots and carrot tops, any kinds of greens pet seems to like, apples, and meal worms. Feed live grasshoppers whenever possible. All vegetables must be *fresh, crisp,* and *clean.*

GROUND SQUIRRELS: Genus *Citellus*

FRANKLIN'S GROUND SQUIRREL: *Citellus franklini*

Range: Indiana, Illinois, Wisconsin, Minnesota, Iowa, Missouri, the Dakotas, Nebraska, and Kansas
Description: Uniformly grayish-white to darker above; slight suggestion of stripes and dots; tail black and white and quite bushy; grows to length of 14 inches including 4½-inch tail
Habitat: Edges of woodlands and fields; spends most of time in burrows under ground; forages only few yards away from burrow; does not appear above ground before April
Reproduction: 4–11 young; born May–June
Life span: Not recorded
Economic position: Does a great deal of good in destroying insects but also damages forage and farm crops

GOLDEN-MANTLED GROUND SQUIRREL: *Citellus lateralis*

Range: Eastern borders of mountains of British Columbia, south to near Mexican border, except close to coast; east through central Montana, Colorado, and Wyoming, into Arizona and New Mexico.
Description: Broad dark and light stripes down back; head and neck golden; no stripes on face; tail fairly bushy; reaches length of 12 inches including 4½-inch tail
Habitat: In bushy areas of mountains, among fallen trees or rocky

rubble where it digs short, simple burrows; always found in public camp sites where it becomes tame and begs for food

Reproduction: 1 litter a year; 2–8 young; born May and June.

Life span: Not recorded

Economic position: No economic importance

ROCK SQUIRREL: *Citellus variegatus*

Range: Eastern California, Nevada, through most of Utah, much of Colorado, through southwest Texas, and almost all of Arizona and New Mexico

Description: Grayish-brown to blackish; under parts lighter gray; tail bushy; may reach length of 20 inches including 10-inch tail

Habitat: Prefers rocky slopes and canyons; also found in rocky fields, along roadsides, where it perches on top of rocks and fence posts

Reproduction: May be 2 litters a year, 5–7 young; born May–June to August–September

Life span: 10 years

Economic position: Does some damage to forage crops

THIRTEEN-LINED SPERMOPHILE OR THIRTEEN-LINED GROUND SQUIRREL: *Citellus tridecemlineatus*

Range: Central Ohio to southern Alberta, south to Texas and Arizona

Description: Alternating dark brown and dirty white stripes down back; light spots in dark stripes; tail somewhat bushy; animal sits erect with nose pointed straight up; reaches length of 11 inches including 4½-inch tail

Habitat: Prairies—and home garden lawns!

Reproduction: May be 2 litters a year; 5–7 young; born May–June

Life span: Not recorded

Economic position: Probably does more harm than good to crops

Ground squirrels usually make excellent pets when they are captured young. It is wise to use gloves when pet is first handled. Be sure to move slowly and handle gently.

As a rule squirrels are hardy in captivity when properly maintained. Sometimes, however, a squirrel does not tame readily. It may be a little too old. If so, it should be liberated in the area where it was captured. At other times a pet as it grows older may develop a tendency to bite, especially if it has been teased. Such a squirrel should be returned to its natural habitat as the habit of biting cannot be broken.

Baby Squirrel

Housing: Line small, strong cardboard box with plenty of soft, warm cloths; protect pet from chilling at night.

Food: Give milk warmed to body temperature, using medicine dropper; feed every hour if pet is very young. As pet develops, feed by teaspoon; lengthen time between feedings, and add stale bread soaked in warm milk. When gnawing teeth come through, add stale bread or dry, *butterless* toast to milk diet. Later add a little bird and melon seed.

HOUSING

After gnawing teeth are in use, place pet in large animal cage (see Part IV). Reproduce forest floor as closely as possible: Fill cage with 12–14 inches of clean, moist soil, preferably mixed with leaf mold; moisten soil from time to time; change once a year; put piece of old tree stump against one side of cage for pet to sprawl on; scatter 2–3 flat rocks about for it to dig under, as well as *old* bark and layers of dead pine needles and dry leaves. Provide bunches of clean, dry grass, sweet hay, old furniture stuffings such as clean kapok for nesting, but *do not use cotton*. Pet should have freedom of the room during the day; leave cage door open so that it can come and go at will. If pet must be confined to cage, place cage in direct sunlight each morning and move to cool, shady part of room when weather becomes warm.

FOOD

In the wild, adult squirrel feeds on plant life, insects, small birds, frogs, garden crops, seeds, grains, plant buds, birds' eggs, and baby mice; needs similarly balanced diet in captivity in order to remain healthy.

Requires daily: *Seeds*—Use prepared hamster mix, which can be bought in pet stores. *Fruits*—Offer berries, cherries, grapes, melons in season; apples and oranges in winter. *Green food*—Variety necessary; offer young growth of buds of plants, trees, and shrubs; clover and alfalfa blossoms; green seeds and weeds such as mallow or common cheese weed; carrot tops and young carrots; lettuce; young weed growth that comes up after early rains. *Water*—Must be fresh, clean, and always available; use water bottle.

REQUIRES OCCASIONALLY: *Nuts*—Feed a few pine nuts or other *hard*-shelled variety, one at a time, *once* only per week. *Meat*—Feed weekly; offer meal worms 4 or 5 at a time; vary with piece of fresh bone of young animal from which all fat and most of meat have been removed.

GNAWING MATERIAL: Keeps pet's teeth in good condition; offer hard-shelled nuts such as black walnuts (sparingly), old, weathered limbs, chunks of plaster, pieces of rock salt or salt brick; salt is good for pet and may be kept in cage at all times; salt brick can be purchased at feed stores. As captive squirrels grow old, their gnawing teeth sometimes grow too long; should be trimmed, using sharp clippers, by pet expert or veterinarian.

CHIPMUNKS: Genus *Tamias*

EASTERN CHIPMUNK: *Tamias striatus*

Range: From the Dakotas through Illinois; Wisconsin, Minnesota, Michigan, Iowa, and east to the Atlantic; south almost to the Gulf Coast

Description: Small, usually with 5 conspicuous black stripes which alternate with lighter chestnut or buffy stripes; stripes run along back to base of tail; head rounded; face striped; ears short and rounded; underparts soft buff; well-developed cheek pouches; only 1 premolar in upper jaw; reaches length of 9½ inches, including 3½-inch tail

Habitat: Primarily terrestrial; often climbs trees short distances; climbs into shrubs to obtain nuts, seeds, and berries; found in forested areas, in plains and flat lands, always where plenty of natural food is available

Reproduction: May be 2 litters a year; 4–5 young; born in soft nests in holes in ground in spring, time depending upon geographical location

Life span: To 7 years

Economic position: Chipmunks appear to be harmless in every way; they are entertaining to campers and excellent as pets

LEAST CHIPMUNK: Genus *Eutamias*

LEAST CHIPMUNK: *Eutamias minimus*

Range: West from Great Lakes to southern Alaska; most western states

Description: Well-defined dark and light stripes along back; fainter stripes on face; well-developed cheek pouches; 2 premolars in upper jaw; tail black above, light underneath; underparts white; reaches length of 9 inches including 3½-inch tail

Habitat: Terrestrial but does climb to some extent for safety and for food; found on mountains, rocky slopes, in wooded areas, up to elevation of 11,000 feet; also on plains and flat lands

Reproduction: May be 2 litters a year; 4–5 young; born in soft nests in holes in ground in spring, time depending upon geographical location

Life span: To 7 years

Economic position: No different from the preceding species

Chipmunks are hardy in captivity and make interesting pets. Usually several may be caged together, and often an adult will become tame with the gentlest of treatment. These attractive little creatures never like to be picked up and handled, but once their confidence has been gained they like to climb into one's hands or lap, run over one's arms, and they quickly learn to search through one's pockets for goodies hidden there.

BABY CHIPMUNK

HOUSING: Line small, strong cardboard box with plenty of soft, warm cloths; protect pet from chilling at night.

FOOD: Give milk warmed to body temperature, using medicine dropper; feed every hour if pet is very young. As pet develops, feed by teaspoon and teach it to lap from spoon; lengthen time between feedings and add dry, stale bread soaked in warm milk. When gnawing teeth come through, add stale bread and dry, butterless toast to milk diet. As teeth develop, add a little bird seed and nuts. Nuts must be finely chopped; feed sparingly, once a week only.

HOUSING

After gnawing teeth are in use, place pet in chipmunk cage (see Part IV), but give plenty of freedom in room. Fill cage with 12–14 inches of leaf mold or other clean, rich soil (soil from forest floor is best); moisten soil when it becomes dusty, but do not allow it to get wet. Change soil at least twice yearly. Scatter several large, flat rocks about for pet to burrow under.

NEST: In the wild, is made in ground in hollow rotting log or stump. Obtain log or stump from woods and place in cage; log or stump should have hole at either end or in sides. Supply leaves; dry, clean grass; soft, clean hay; and old furniture stuffing such as kapok. *Never use cotton or wool floss.* These cling to pet's claws; may become wound around its body and choke it; and hold moisture, which makes them unsanitary. Nesting boxes are unsanitary, too.

WHEELS: Should be of lightweight material and should turn easily; place where they can turn freely. May be omitted if pet is not confined to cage for long periods; does give pet entertainment and exercise and will always be used.

FOOD

In the wild, chipmunk consumes grass seed, nuts, berries, and acorns, plus such animal foods as insects, birds' eggs, and baby mice.

REQUIRES DAILY: *Seeds*—Use prepared hamster mix, which may be bought in pet stores. *Fruits*—Essential; offer all berries, melon seeds, melon rinds, also mushrooms, in season; apples in winter. *Green food*—Essential; variety necessary; offer young growth of plants, buds, trees, and shrubs; blossoms of clover and alfalfa; green weed seeds; carrot tops, spinach, lettuce; young weed growth; all greens must be fresh, crisp, and clean. *Water*—Must be fresh, clean, and always available; use bottle.

REQUIRES WEEKLY: *Nuts*—Feed pine nuts, hazelnuts, acorns, beechnuts, and others sparingly; hard-shelled varieties must be cracked. *Meat*—Offer meal worms, 3 or 4 at a time; grasshoppers and beetles when available; vary with fresh bone of young animal from which all fat and flesh have been removed or, occasionally, *small* piece of cooked lean meat and a little raw egg. *Treat*—Offer a little bread soaked in milk, dry bread crust, toast, or a little dry cereal.

GNAWING MATERIALS: Keep pet's incisors in good condition.

Place in cage piece of old, weathered limb, medium soft-shelled nuts (but see Nuts, above), evergreen bough, or chunk of plaster.

Tree Squirrels

The term tree squirrel implies that these rodents spend their lives in trees, which is not entirely true. They use trees for their nests and rearing of young, but they also spend much time on the ground in search of food. However, they never search too far afield, as trees provide them with their greatest protection.

Tree squirrels usually are not patterned but are beautifully colored. They have large, bushy tails and large bright eyes.

TREE SQUIRRELS: Genus *Sciurus*

EASTERN GRAY SQUIRREL: *Sciurus carolinensis*

Range: From Maine to the Dakotas, south to central Texas and Gulf; when food shortages occur, which happens periodically, squirrels migrate, hence seem to disappear from given areas for some time, to return again much later in greater numbers

Description: Upper parts blackish gray; hairs tipped with white over black, buff, and gray; albinos and black varieties occur in this species also; tail long and bushy; cheek pouches present; reaches length of 18 inches, half of which is tail

Habitat: In forested areas, in large parks; common visitor at bird-feeding stations where often considered pest

Reproduction: May be 2 litters a year; 1–6 young; born in bulky nest made of twigs and leaves, placed in crotch of tree or in hollow of rotted tree trunk; born through summer months

Life span: Recorded at 15 years

Economic position: Excellent agent in reforestation

FOX SQUIRREL: *Sciurus niger*

Range: From Rhode Island through southern New York to Minnesota and South Dakota, south through central Texas to Gulf of Mexico; east and south to the Atlantic, with related forms in the West

Description: Largest of tree squirrels with variable color pattern;

may be gray, buff, or black; nose and ears white; reaches length of 2 feet including 1-foot tail

Habitat: In forested areas, especially in oak belts where it hunts on ground for acorns

Reproduction: May be 2 litters a year; 2–5 young; born in early spring

Life span: More than 6 years

Economic position: Especially effective as an agent of reforestation, as it habitually buries nuts which then germinate

WESTERN GRAY SQUIRREL: *Sciurus griseus*

Range: From central Washington through western Oregon and most of California (except southern coast belt), to northern Lower California, Mexico

Description: Large, pale gray squirrel, with large, handsome bushy tail; upper parts finely speckled with white, sometimes with yellowish cast to back; white ring around eyes; under parts white; reaches length of 22 inches including 11-inch tail

Habitat: In forested areas where conifers and oaks abound; only few squirrels occur at a time in a given locality

Reproduction: One litter a year, 3–5 young; born February–June

Life span: Assumed same as Eastern Gray—recorded at 15 years

Economic position: Reforestation agent

RED SQUIRRELS AND CHICKAREES: Genus *Tamiasciurus*

RED SQUIRREL: *Tamiasciurus hudsonicus.*

Range: Most of North America except the prairies and the extreme south and southwest

Description: Rusty red from top of head to tail; sides gray; tail flat and bushy; ears fairly long; reaches length of 12 inches including 4½-inch tail

Habitat: Coniferous and oak forests

Reproduction: May be 2 litters a year; 3–6 young; born May–June

Life span: Up to 12 years

Economic position: Considered a predator because of number of birds preyed upon

CHICKAREE: *Tamiasciurus douglasii*

Range: West of Rocky Mountains
Description: Under parts rusty reddish and tail fringed with yellowish or white
Habitat: Coniferous and oak forests
Reproduction: May be 2 litters a year; 3–6 young born May–June
Life span: Up to 12 years
Economic position: Considered to be predators because of number of birds and their young preyed upon

The chickarees are the smallest of all the tree squirrels. Regardless of range a chickaree can always be recognized first by its size, second by its noisy defiance of anything strange, and third by the reckless manner in which it slithers, dangles, and leaps through the trees.

Tree squirrels, like ground squirrels, are hardy in captivity and make excellent pets when it is possible to capture them as babies. An adult seldom becomes tame, and since it has been free in the wild state it will not be happy confined in a cage. A baby squirrel will know only the life associated with the owner. It will become gentle and make a most satisfactory pet. However, pet squirrels must be housed and trained alone.

BABY SQUIRREL

HOUSING: Line small, strong cardboard box with plenty of soft, warm cloths; protect pet from chilling at night.

FOOD: Give milk warmed to body temperature, using medicine dropper; feed every hour if pet is very young. As pet develops, feed by teaspoon; lengthen time between feedings and add stale dry bread soaked in milk. When gnawing teeth come through, add stale dry bread or dry *butterless* toast to milk diet. Later add a little bird and melon seed.

HOUSING

After gnawing teeth are in use, pet should be placed in regular squirrel cage (see Part IV) for its headquarters. Place cage where it receives direct morning sunlight; move cage to cool, shady part of room in warm weather. Fill cage with 12–14 inches of good leaf mold or other clean, rich soil—soil from forest floor is best; moisten soil when it becomes dusty, but do not allow it to get wet; change soil twice yearly. Squirrel does little burrowing, but soil is necessary to keep fur clean and free of parasites.

CLIMBING SPACE: Pet should be given plenty of freedom in room. In one corner of room place large, heavy, branching limb that reaches from floor to ceiling; this is an excellent playground for pet and gives it sufficient exercise.

NESTING BOX: In wild, nest is made in tree holes or is constructed of twigs and leaves placed in crotch of tree. In captivity, usually nests on shelf in cage. Place wooden box 12″ × 12″ × 6″, with one end open, on shelf (see squirrel cage diagram, Part IV). If pet does not take to box, remove it. *Nesting materials*—Supply dry grasses, thin, loose bark, lichen-covered twigs, and bits of kapok; pet mixes these and constructs own nest. Supply fresh materials several times yearly.

FOOD

In the wild, tree squirrels feed on young green cones, fungi, nuts, buds, seeds, berries, some insects, birds' eggs, and young birds. In captivity, well-balanced diet absolutely essential.

REQUIRES DAILY: *Seeds*—Offer sunflower seeds, whole oats, wheat, melon seeds, corn and seed mixes prepared for any of the larger birds; hamster mix may be used. *Fruits*—All kinds, especially melons, in season; apples and oranges in winter; cultivated mushrooms. *Green food*—Must be varied; offer young growth or buds of plants, trees, and shrubs; blossoms of clover and alfalfa; green weed seeds; carrot tops and *young* carrots; lettuce and young weed growth. *Water*—Must be fresh, clean, always available; use water bottle.

REQUIRES OCCASIONALLY: *Nuts*—Pine nuts and acorns excellent plus any hard-shelled nuts; give sparingly. *Meat*—Weekly; give 4–5 meal worms at a time; vary with piece of fresh [veal] bone from which *all* fat and *most* flesh have been removed.

GNAWING MATERIALS: Hard-shelled nuts, old weathered limbs, chunks of plaster, pieces of rock salt keep teeth in good condition; salt brick good for pet; buy at pet or feed store.

Flying Squirrels

The flying squirrel is a small, soft, lovely creature that does not fly but glides through the air with such speed, and for such distances, that it seems to fly. It is able to do this because of extensible folds of skin or membranes on each side of the body which reach from the ankle of the hind leg to the wrist of the fore leg. Also there is a small process of cartilage on each wrist which helps to extend the membranes. When the squirrel launches into space it extends all four legs straight out from its body. This action immediately spreads the membranes and they become perfect gliders. Speed, course, and angles of flight are all controlled by tensions in the membranes. In addition, the tail is used as a rudder and a stabilizer. The flying squirrel is found throughout North America with the exception of the Great Plains. This squirrel is completely nocturnal.

There are but two species of flying squirrels—the *sabrinus,* found in the north; and the *volans,* found in the south.

FLYING SQUIRRELS: Genus *Glaucomys*

NORTHERN FLYING SQUIRRELS: *Glaucomys sabrinus*

Range: From central Alaska to Labrador, south to southern California, Minnesota, Maryland, and Appalachian Highlands to Georgia

Description: Softly furred creature, drab-colored above, dirty white underneath; eyes large; ears small; tail broad and flat; reaches length of 12 inches, including 6-inch tail

Habitat: Dens in hollow trees and in old buildings

Reproduction: Probably but 1 litter a year; 2–6 young born March–April

Life span: Not recorded

Economic position: No economic importance

SOUTHERN FLYING SQUIRRELS: *Glaucomys volans*

Range: East from Minnesota and central Texas; south of a line from Minnesota to southern Maine

Description: Softly furred above, drab to pinkish cinnamon; fur slate-colored at base; head grayish, ears light brown; hind feet brown, toes white. Reaches length of 9½ inches, including 4½-inch tail

Habitat: Dens in hollow trees and in old buildings

Reproduction: Probably but 1 litter a year; 2–6 young born March–April

Life span: Not recorded

Economic position: Harmless creatures; appear to have no destructive habits; much too small to be considered good game

Flying squirrels are hardy in captivity, tame readily, both as adults and young, and make lovely pets for the home. Young and adults live happily together and are more interesting with several in a cage. They soon become friendly and affectionate. However, all their activities take place during the night, which does not give the owner many hours in which to enjoy them.

BABY SQUIRREL

HOUSING: Use small, snug box well-filled with warm, soft cloths; protect pet from chilling at all times.

FOOD: Give milk warmed to body temperature, using medicine dropper; feed every hour. As pet grows, feed by teaspoon and lengthen time between feedings. When gnawing teeth come through, add stale bread or dry *butterless* toast to milk. Later, add bird seed, prepared hamster mix, and melon seed.

HOUSING

When baby becomes active, transfer to large animal cage (see Part IV). Cover cage bottom with 12 inches of good soil well mixed with leaf mold. Freedom of movement essential; leave cage door open at night. Provide cage-high, heavy, branched limb or old hollowed stump for hiding in and climbing; if screened porch is available, provide pet with tall, heavy, branching limb as playground.

NEST: In the wild, nests in woodpecker holes, knot holes, tree hollows, old stumps, bird boxes, dovecotes, attics, cupboards, boxes, and in such nooks in occupied or unoccupied houses within or at borders of its woods; may also make leaf nest lined with fibrous bark, grass, moss, lichens, ferns, and other soft materials and placed in crotches of trees. Some northern flying squirrels use tree cavities in winter and tree-top nest in summer. In captivity, nests in box placed on cage shelf (see Part IV). *Nesting materials*—Supply leaves, shredded bark, moss, dry grass, bits of old fur; drop on floor of cage; pet makes own nest; supply fresh materials from time to time.

FOOD

In wild, flying squirrels feed on nuts, seeds, berries, plant buds, and some insects. Well-balanced diet essential in captivity.

Requires daily: *Seeds*—Prepared hamster mix; buy at pet shop. *Fruits*—Melons and all other kinds of fruit in season; apples and oranges in winter. *Green food*—Must be varied; offer young plant buds, blossoms of clover and alfalfa, green weed seeds, carrot tops and young carrots, lettuce, and very young weed growth. *Water*—Must be fresh, clean, available at all times; use water bottle.

Requires occasionally: *Nuts*—Weekly; small amount at a time; offer pine nuts and other hard-shelled varieties. *Meat*—4–5 meal worms (adult and larvae) once or twice a week.

Gnawing materials: Hard-shelled nuts such as black walnuts (but see Nuts, above), old, hard, weathered limb, or piece of salt brick (buy at pet or feed store) necessary to keep incisors in condition.

GOPHERS

Many species of gophers with great variations in size are scattered across the United States, but all are similar in characteristics and habits. All are solitary creatures that spend their lives underground and are seldom seen, but their work is in constant evidence.

Before man made so much food easily available to gophers, they were a great benefit in nature as they continually carried subsoil to the surface and buried quantities of humus in its place.

POCKET GOPHER: Genus *Geomys*

Plains Pocket Gopher: *Geomys bursarius*

Range: In the Plains, mostly west of the Mississippi River. (There are other species scattered throughout the West, Southwest, and Southeast, but the above is typical)

Description: Forefeet modified and developed for digging; incisors yellow and visible; 2 grooves down front of incisors; external, reversible, furlined cheek pouches; tail almost naked, shorter than body; head broad, neck short; eyes and ears small; fine, soft, light reddish brown fur; reaches length of 12 inches including 3½-inch tail

Habitat: Below ground surface; burrows where plant growth abundant

Reproduction: 1 or more litters a year depending upon range and species; 2–8 young born in April

Life span: Not recorded

Economic position: Highly destructive as they tunnel through dikes and ditches, injure roots of trees and garden plants, and destroy truck crops

VALLEY POCKET GOPHER: *Thomomys bottae*

Range: Throughout the southwestern United States

Description: Forefeet modified and developed for digging; incisors yellow and visible, frontal groove lacking; external, reversible, fur-lined cheek pouches; tail almost naked, shorter than body; head broad, neck short; legs short; eyes and ears small; fine, soft, reddish brown fur; reaches length of 10½ inches including 3½-inch tail

Habitat: Below ground surface; burrows where plant growth abundant

Reproduction: More than 1 litter a year; 4–8 young born in spring

Life span: Not recorded

Economic position: Highly destructive as they tunnel through dikes and ditches, injure roots of trees and garden plants, and destroy truck crops

A captive adult gopher must be handled with heavy gloves as it is a vicious creature and bites readily. It cannot be tamed, but a baby gopher is seldom ill-tempered and usually develops into a gentle and interesting pet which is hardy in captivity when properly maintained. However, when a pet gopher matures it is wise either to have it destroyed or to liberate it, as it requires a greater space in which to tunnel and is unhappy in confinement.

HOUSING

Use prairie dog cage (see Part IV); must be made large enough to allow ample room for burrowing. Provide firmly fastened screen top; otherwise, pet pushes it out during night. Cover cage bottom with rich, damp, firmly packed soil; keep soil damp. *Baby gopher* can be housed temporarily in 10-gallon aquarium tank.

NEST: Nest is made at end of burrow and lined with plant fibers. Supply bunches of dry grass for lining.

FOOD

In wild, gopher is strictly vegetarian; feeds on tubers, bulbs, roots of garden vegetables; roots and succulent top growth of clover, alfalfa, and grain; roots of fruit trees such as apples, pears, figs.

REQUIRES DAILY: *Vegetables*—All kinds; must be fresh and crisp; feed with tops; push down into soil. *Clover and alfalfa*—Transplant into cage. *Succulent top growth*—Necessary; push unglazed flower pot saucer into soil in one corner of cage and fill with water; water seeps through porous saucer and keeps soil moist; plant wheat, corn, other grains in moistened area. *Dry foods*—Must always be available; offer such seeds and grains as wheat, corn, and sunflower seeds; place on soil away from moist area. Water not required except as explained above.

NOTE: Pet can learn to take food from owner's hand. It is fun to watch it stuff and empty its pouches on top of soil as long as food is offered.

MICE

Numerous species of wild mice are scattered over the greater part of the United States. Most of them are nocturnal in habit, though some are diurnal, and a few are crepuscular (active at twilight).

POCKET MICE: Genus *Perognathus*

SPINY POCKET MOUSE: *Perognathus spinatus*

Range: Deserts of southern California and northern Lower California

Description: Upper parts drab brown; under parts buffy white; hind legs long; poorly developed forelegs; conspicuous spinelike hairs on rump; ears small and rounded; external fur-lined cheek pouches. Small animal—3½ inches long with a 4½-inch tail

Habitat: Essentially desert dweller but sometimes found in woods or cultivated fields; lives in burrows which it digs in desert soil; burrow usually ends in grass-lined den; comes out at dusk to forage

Reproduction: Breeds at any time but usually only 2 litters a year; 2–8 young

Life span: Not known

Economic position: There are a few recorded occasions where pocket mice have done some damage to farm crops

There are more than twenty-four species of pocket mice. The smallest of all the rodents are in this group. None of the species is ever large. The smallest is the little Silky pocket mouse which is 4½ inches long (including tail) and weighs one-third of an ounce. The largest member is the Hispid pocket mouse which measures up to 9 inches (including tail) and weighs one to one and two-thirds ounces.

Pocket mice are seldom seen as they remain in their burrows during the day. However, they are attractive and interesting visitors about a camp. When food is placed in certain spots they soon learn to come each evening to get it.

KANGAROO RATS: Genus *Dipodomys*

DESERT KANGAROO RAT: *Dipodomys deserti*

Range: In Colorado and Mohave desert regions and adjoining areas

Description: Head large; eyes large; external fur-lined cheek pouches; small, poorly developed forelegs; large, well-developed hind legs; front feet do not touch ground; hops or leaps along, kangaroo fashion, on large hind legs; hind feet with soft, furred soles; tail long and tufted on end; fur soft, long, and silky; reaches length of 13 inches including 7½-inch tail

Habitat: Arid regions where soil is dry, loose, and sandy; burrows extensively; remains in burrows during day; comes out at dusk to feed

Reproduction: 1 litter a year; 2–4 young born in April; do not breed readily in captivity

Life span: Not known

Economic position: No economic importance

Kangaroo rats are unique creatures because of their physical characteristics. They are the handsomest of all North American rodents. There are many species which cover a wide range in North America; from Washington to Manitoba, and south to Panama. Probably the greatest number of species are to be found in the arid Southwest.

The kangaroo rat usually develops into a friendly pet, but it is advisable to handle it with gloves until it becomes gentle as it defends itself by striking with its hind legs and biting. Once the pet becomes tame it is interesting to hide caches of food about in a room, and then watch the pet seek them out. Remember that it does not become active until nightfall. It should be given freedom at that time.

Pocket mice and kangaroo rats make attractive pets as the adults become gentle after capture, but they must be properly maintained if they are to remain hardy. Note that kangaroo rats cannot be caged together; they will fight until one kills the other.

HOUSING

Use small, sturdy, well-built animal cage (see Part IV). Fill cage with 12–14 inches of clean, sandy, damp soil; pack down firmly; sand must have body so that burrows, in which pet nests, will not cave in on it; change soil as soon as it becomes dry and pulverized. Protect pets from chilling. Place cage where it is away from drafts but receives some sunlight. *Nest*—In the wild, used for sleeping, hiding, rearing of young. Drop small bunches of dry grass and soft plant fibers such as kapok about cage for lining nest.

FOOD

In the wild, pocket mice and kangaroo rats feed on seeds, leaves of desert plants, and seedling cacti just appearing above ground. In captivity, feed seeds—sunflower, hemp, oats, unhulled rice; young cacti and succulents; and seeds just beginning to sprout; prepared seed mixes for parakeets, hamsters, others, may also be used; buy at pet store. Scatter food about on soil of cage. *Water*—Typical desert animal; body chemistry changes food starches into water during digestive process; however, advisable to offer water occasionally on hot days; use water bottle.

HARVEST MICE: Genus *Reithrodontomys*

Eastern Harvest Mouse: *Reithrodontomys humulis*

Range: Common in Southeast United States; related species in Middle and Far West

Description: Looks like common house mouse but feet always white; belly dusky; ears large; tail long; no cheek pouches; reaches length of 5 inches including 2½-inch tail

Habitat: Usually in damp areas with plenty of grassy vegetation and shrub growth

Reproduction: Breeds March–December; several litters a year; 5–9 young born in grasslike nests made of grass and other vegetation, placed on ground or high in some shrub

Life span: Not known

Economic position: Rarely damages crops; provides good food for many carnivores

DEER MICE: Genus *Peromyscus*

DEER MOUSE: *Peromyscus maniculatus*

Range: North America with exception of southeastern United States; numerous related species

Description: Dark brown with yellowish tinge above, clear white underneath; blackish about eyes; ears large, dark, and edged with gray; tail dark above, white beneath; feet white; grows to 7½ inches including 3½-inch tail

Habitat: Varies from sandy, rocky areas with little vegetation to open, flat country, bush lands, and mountain forests where burrows in soil or under forest debris; nocturnal

Reproduction: Breeds throughout summer; several litters a year; 3–7 young

Life span: More than 5 years

Economic position: Often damage bedding not properly stored in mountain cabins

GRASSHOPPER MICE: Genus *Onychomys*

GRASSHOPPER MOUSE: *Onychomys leucogaster*

Range: Western North America

Description: Sturdily built; tail short, thick, tapering, and tipped with white; forefeet well developed; hindfeet densely furred on soles; general color soft cinnamon or gray; under parts white; fur soft and silky; reaches length of 5 inches including 2½-inch tail.

Habitat: Prairie lands or desert areas, where it digs burrows; nocturnal

Reproduction: More than 1 litter a year; 2–6 young born during summer

Life span: Not known

Economic position: Beneficial to man because of its diet

The above species of wild mice usually adapt themselves readily to captivity and make interesting and friendly pets. They may be easily maintained when each pair is placed alone together, the habitat is made to resemble the natural wild one, and food comparable to that in the wild is supplied.

HOUSING

Use small animal cage (see Part IV). Reproduce pet's natural habitat: If pet comes from desert area, cover cage bottom with very sandy soil; if from wooded area, reproduce forest floor; if from open country, use grassy sods. Change soil when odor becomes noticeable (wild mice less odorous than domestic forms).

NEST: Used for sleeping, hiding, rearing of young. Supply lining materials: grasses, dry lichens, bits of old kapok. Pull kapok apart into small pieces and drop with other materials on cage bottom. *Never use cotton.*

PLAY: Wild mice are playful, need toys. Plant a stiff-branching shrub in corner of cage; pets like to race through it. Tie tightly twisted and knotted cord to top of cage and allow to dangle down. Provide chipmunk-type wheel. Many other items may be used (see cage diagram, Part IV).

FOOD

ALL SPECIES: *Water*—Should always be available; keep fresh and clean; use water bottle. *Meal worms*—Essential; give several (adults and larvae) twice weekly; place insects in shallow container; otherwise, they burrow into soil and disappear.

HARVEST AND DEER MICE: In wild, feed on seeds, grains, wild fruits, and green plant life. Give prepared canary or hamster mix plus berries, small fruits in season, and fresh seed growth; scatter seeds on cage bottom.

GRASSHOPPER MICE: In wild, feed entirely on small animal life, including insects, scorpions, mice, lizards. Give *live* insects, scorpions when possible, baby mice, and small lizards.

BREEDING

Most wild mice breed readily in captivity, especially the white-footed deer mice. Provide plenty of nesting material. Gestation period 3–4 weeks; young born pink, naked, and blind. As soon as young are able to feed alone, remove from parents to another cage.

HAMSTERS: Genus *Mesocricetus*

GOLDEN HAMSTER: *Mesocricetus auratus*

Range: Native to Syria
Description: Like a ball of fur—body small; fur soft, fine, and long; reddish golden above and white underneath; tail short and inconspicuous; front feet with 4 toes, hind with 5
Habitat: Found among rocks and rocky ledges, beneath which digs 6-foot burrows; nocturnal
Reproduction: Can have 1 litter per month; 7–15 young, born in soft, grasslined nests in burrows
Life span: Short-lived; usually average 2 years
Economic position: Now used in laboratories for study of diseases, nutrition, genetics, and as pets for children

Probably no other small rodent has risen so rapidly in popularity with children as has the small, soft, big-eared, velvety hamster. It was first introduced from England into the United States in 1938 for laboratory experimentation, at which time its use as a pet was frowned upon. Its quick temper and the speed with which it could inflict a fairly deep cut with its sharp teeth seemed to make it too dangerous for handling by children. However, before long people learned that a hamster taken as a baby would develop into one of the most interesting and entertaining of pets.

Hamsters are now used so extensively in laboratories and commercially as pets that in time they may be grouped with domestic animals which once had their origin in a foreign land.

Hamsters are hardy in captivity when properly caged and fed.

HOUSING

Needs plenty of room; use "apartment-type" cage with metal tray on bottom (see Part IV). Use gnawproof materials; pet can gnaw through cage wood. Pet likes to burrow; fill cage with 6 inches of good loamy soil; cover soil surface with 1–2 inches sawdust-shavings mixture. For bedding, supply *large* quantities of soft, dry grasses and short pieces of raffia; pet arranges these to suit self; sleeping box not desirable. *Cleaning*—Cage must never become moist from excretions, but only soiled areas of wooden cage need be cleaned daily; wash with solution of 3 tablespoons prepared chlorine bleach solution (such as Clorox) to 1 quart of water; rinse in clear water and let dry before giving pet run of area again. *Temperature*—Most important; hamster tends to hibernate at low temperatures; maintain moderate warmth (about 70°F); protect cage from all drafts, especially in winter; protect from colds, which pet can contract from humans; anyone with cold must exercise extreme care in handling or feeding pet.

FOOD

In the wild, hamster feeds mainly on wild seeds, grains, some grasses, and fruit; also eats insects, worms, birds' eggs, smaller mammals. Feed prepared hamster mix, lettuce leaves, dog biscuits, and corn purchased at pet shop. *Meal worms*—Essential, as they substitute for animal food obtained by pet in the wild (see Part III); feed 3–4 worms several times weekly; place in flat dish out of which worms cannot crawl. *Water*—Always available.

BREEDING

Close opening between two floors of cage so as to keep sexes separate; if housed together, they fight until one is killed. Female matures at 7 weeks; comes into heat every 9 days and remains in heat 3–4 days; during this time, place female in with male for half-hour each day; if female fights male, she is not ready to receive him and must be removed at once. *Caution*—Scoop up breeding animal in small can or box rather than lifting it by hand; always wear gloves when separating fighting pairs.

Baby hamster

Gestation takes 16 days; 7–15 in litter; young born pink, naked, and blind. Do not disturb young or mother for at least a week after birth; if disturbed mother will either kill and eat the young or neglect them and allow them to die. After 3 weeks, remove young from mother; otherwise, mother fights with them and often kills them. Sexes should be separated before young reach maturity at 43 days.

HOUSE MICE: Genus *Mus*

HOUSE MOUSE: *Mus musculus*

Range: Practically throughout the world
Description: Uniformly brownish-gray; under parts light; feet small; tail sparsely haired. Grows to length of 7 inches including 3½-inch tail
Habitat: Fields, occupied dwellings, barns; any place where food is available
Reproduction: Breeds throughout year; several litters a year; 1–12 young
Life span: Averages 5 years
Economic position: One of man's great problems, as a house mouse damages property, food, and clothing

It is thought that the common, unwelcome house mouse probably originated somewhere in Asia, but it has spread throughout Europe, America, and practically the entire world. The house mouse is always found accompanying man in every environment.

Although the house mouse is a pest, it does make an interesting and gentle pet. Also, by using the house mouse in selective breeding, man has been able to produce the attractively colored mice now available in most pet shops.

A house mouse is one of the easiest mammals to maintain in captivity. It does not need a large cage, and is easy to feed. It is a most entertaining pet.

HOUSING

Use regular mouse cage (see Part IV), which is designed to facilitate cleaning. Place so as to protect sleeping box from drafts; pet is sensitive to cold.

CLEANLINESS: Never allow cage to become moist from excretions or accumulations of food. Peculiar odor of mice comes from excretions; pet itself is extremely clean. To counteract odor, use any good commercial cage bottom cover, such as pitch pine shavings purchased at pet store; clean out cage as soon as odor becomes notice-able; watch sleeping box; clean out as needed. Mouse usually chooses definite corner for droppings; wash corner weekly with Lysol solu-tion or other effective deodorant.

SLEEPING BOX: One side must be removable to permit cleaning. Size varies with number of mice to be accommodated; 6" × 4" × 4" box with 2" entrance hole suitable for several pairs of mice. For bedding, supply plenty of clean, soft straw, paper shavings, or excel-sior; do *not* use cloth or cotton. These hold moisture, and cotton becomes tangled in pets' paws.

PLAY: Mice need toys; see Part IV for suggestions.

FOOD

In the wild, mouse is omnivorous; eats all human food and more besides. Restrict diet in captivity. Offer no more food than can be eaten at one time; pet hides surplus in bedding and all about cage. Serve all solid foods except seeds in small, glazed flower pot saucers, which can be easily washed.

REQUIRES DAILY: *Seeds*—Use patented feeder; give any prepared seed mixture, such as hamster mix, parakeet mix. *Green foods*—Needed; give any kind pet likes; all must be *fresh, clean,* and *dry.* Lettuce twice weekly only, as it causes diarrhea when fed often in large amounts. *Water*—Must be fresh, clean, and always available; use water bottle.

REQUIRES OCCASIONALLY: *Bread*—Whole wheat bread soaked in milk weekly; small pieces of whole wheat toast several times weekly. *Animal food*—Give meal worms, no more than 3 or 4 at a time, twice weekly. *Milk*—2 or 3 times weekly, in water bottle.

GNAWING MATERIALS: Pieces of dog biscuit keep incisors in good condition.

BREEDING

Best to keep together but 1 pair at a time for healthier stock. Female may nest anywhere in cage. Young are born pink, naked, and blind.

Carnivores or Flesh-eating Mammals

The carnivores are mammals that vary in size from small to large, but all have the following characteristics: Feet have claws; teeth modified for eating flesh—three incisors and one canine on each side of jaw, in addition to the molars; brain rather highly developed; food primarily flesh.

RACCOON: Genus *Procyon*

RACCOON: *Procyon lotor*

Range: From Gulf of St. Lawrence to southeast British Columbia, south to Gulf of Mexico and South America; not found in northern Rockies, Wyoming, Utah, Nevada, Colorado, New Mexico, and much of Montana

Description: Thick-set; head broad across jowls; ears prominent and erect; black band across face and eyes; tail fairly long, bushy, and ringed with black; fur long; fore and hind feet with 5 toes; reaches weight of 25 pounds

Habitat: Wooded areas along or near water courses; lives in dens in holes in trees or logs; sometimes in dens in ground burrows; nocturnal

Reproduction: Mates January–June; litter of 1–6 born 60–73 days later

Life span: May reach 13 years

Economic position: Does some damage to farm crops, especially corn; also destroys chickens; may carry rabies

Adult raccoons do not make good pets, but one taken as a baby makes an excellent one. It adjusts to captivity readily, and quickly becomes a lively and affectionate animal. However, when the pet grows older, it often tends to become cross and irritable. A pet raccoon should be liberated in its native area when it reaches full growth and maturity.

BABY RACCOON

HOUSING: Line roomy box with soft, warm cloths. Protect pet from chilling at night.

FOOD: Give cow's milk warmed to body temperature, using nursing bottle with small nipple. Feed every hour or two if pet is very young. When baby learns to drink by itself, add stale, dry dark bread soaked in milk; take care not to overfeed. As pet grows in size, adult diet may be gradually given.

HOUSING

Use large animal cage (see Part IV). Cover cage bottom with slightly damp soil; cover soil with thick layer of sawdust-shavings mixture; remove soiled portions of mixture each day and replace with dry sawdust.

SLEEPING: Box may be used, but basket is better because pet sleeps curled up. For young pet, half fill basket with soft, warm cloths and dry, soft hay or grass. For adult, use dry grass or hay only. Change bedding once weekly.

EXERCISE: Pet can be kept healthy only by giving it much freedom and exercise. Use cage as headquarters only; train pet to this use by placing food and water containers in cage. If pet must be shut up in cage at night, give it several bright toys, as it will be very active most of night; release pet in the morning. Place large, heavy, branching limb in one corner of room or enclosed porch for pet's entertainment and exercise. Provide toys, as a raccoon is playful: Tie bright or glittering trinkets to top and sides of cage and to the tree limb; a ball is liked, too. Pet also requires some petting and handling each day; this helps to gentle it.

FOOD

In the wild, raccoon is virtually omnivorous; feeds on fish, crayfish, birds and their eggs, frogs, snails, fruits, nuts, corn, and other foods; frequently washes food before eating it. Take care not to overfeed. Best to feed pet toward evening, although it can be trained to take food earlier in the day.

REQUIRES DAILY: *Meat*—Give raw fish, shell fish, frogs, eggs, fresh chicken heads when available, an occasional rat or mouse. Meal worms should always be in the diet (see Part IV). Do not feed raw beef; tends to cause irritability. *Dry food*—Dry, stale crusts of bread or dry, stale cake, *diced*. *Green food*—Any fresh vegetable pet likes, especially green corn, of which raccoons are intensely fond; all must be *fresh* and *clean*. *Water*—Essential; use large, deep container. Change water often; pet dirties it by washing food in it.

REQUIRES OCCASIONALLY: *Nuts*—Sparingly.

SKUNK: Genus *Spilogale*

Spotted Skunk or Civet: *Spilogale putorius*

Range: Most of United States west of the Mississippi, with exception of Montana and most of Wyoming; found also along Gulf Coast and up southern Appalachian highlands

Description: Small skunk with 4 white stripes along back sides and tail which appear not to be continuous; reaches length of 22½ inches including 9-inch bushy tail

Habitat: Varies greatly, although largely found in plains and deserts; some in forests on mountain slopes, in rocky canyons, cliffs, and rugged country

Reproduction: 2–10 young; born in mid-spring in hidden den or burrow often shared with other skunks

Life span: Not recorded

Economic position: Of great value as they kill many rats, mice, and insects, but are also known to kill chickens and to carry rabies; fur of poor quality but beautifully patterned

SKUNK: Genus *Mephitis*

Striped Skunk: *Mephitis mephitis*

Range: Southern half of Canada south through most of United States with exception of southern Florida and Coastal Plain

Description: Fairly large, heavy-bodied; head small, legs short; tail large and bushy; claws of forefeet developed for digging; glistening black with broad, white stripe from nape to shoulder, then continuing to base of tail as pair of lateral stripes; narrow white stripe along nose to nape patch; tail black and white; reaches length of 30 inches including 7½-inch tail; may weigh 10 pounds

Habitat: In woods and plains with loose soil; often near towns

Reproduction: 4–10 young; born April–May in a den which may be shared with other animals

Life span: Not recorded but can be several years

Economic position: Protected in some areas because they destroy rodents and insects

There are times when epidemics of rabies break out in skunk populations of a given area. When this occurs, state and county health departments issue regulations to control the use of skunks for pets. This is a safety measure to prevent the spread of rabies among humans who may be bitten by a rabid skunk. Check with state or local health board before obtaining a skunk for a pet.

A baby skunk makes a playful, affectionate, and responsive pet. It remains so even as an adult. Its scent glands may be left intact, as it does not use this defense upon those it knows. However if a kitten is to become a house pet, no doubt it will be given some freedom in the yard. This may expose it to stray dogs or some other frightening factor; hence it is advisable to have the scent glands removed. This is a minor operation from which the pet recovers quickly, and it may be performed by any competent veterinarian. It should be done when kitten is about six weeks old.

Skunks are hardy in captivity when properly housed, fed, and fondled.

Skunk kitten

Housing: Line box with soft, warm cloths. Protect pet from chilling at night.

Food: Give milk warmed to body temperature, using nursing bottle with small nipple if pet is too young to drink by itself; feed every 2 hours if pet is very young. After a few days, add dark bread soaked in warm milk and squeezed dry. In a few more days, add meal worms, 2 or 3 at a time.

HOUSING

Pet skunk may be kept healthy only by giving it much freedom. Do not confine to cage unless necessary, and then for short periods only. A pet skunk can be treated much like a house cat.

Sleeping box: Cage may be used as sleeping box in school room; should be left open at all times and proper approach should be built into it. Best choice at home is large wooden box or small barrel with entrance hole cut into side of box or end of barrel. Partially fill box or barrel with clean, soft hay for bedding. Always keep box in same corner of room and teach pet to use it.

Cleanliness: Pet can be housebroken. Place large box of packed dirt in out-of-way corner of room. Teach pet to use this box for its droppings. Renew soil often enough to prevent odors. Spread paper, old canvas, or oil cloth under box to protect surrounding floor from scattered dirt; skunk is a natural digger and may satisfy this urge by digging in box.

EXERCISE: If skunk is school pet, allow children to take it out to school yard for additional exercise and to dig. Guard it carefully against dogs and injuries, since skunks do not run from danger.

FOOD

In the wild, skunk consumes poultry, rats, mice, eggs, all kinds of insects, some fruits, berries, and so on.

REQUIRES DAILY: *Insect food*—Add grasshoppers, crickets, cockroaches, any other available insects to kitten's diet. Meal worms should always be included (see Part II). *Meat*—As pet develops, add young rats and mice reared for animal food; vary with an occasional fresh bone from which all fat and most of meat have been removed; offer chicken heads when available; raw eggs occasionally. *Fruits and vegetables*—Use any pet likes; fruits in season essential; all green food must be fresh, clean, and dry. *Water*—Must be fresh, always available; use water bottle.

REQUIRES OCCASIONALLY: *Gnawing material*—Fresh bone weekly helps keep teeth in condition; dog biscuit may also be used. *Milk*—Weekly only; adults exceedingly fond of milk, but it causes diarrhea when given too often; use water bottle.

DIURNAL HABIT

Skunk can be trained to come out during the day. Let it sleep for an hour or two in the morning. Then remove it from sleeping quarters and offer it choice bits of food. Fondle and pet it after it has eaten. It may then be kept out for a few hours each day. After a few days, pet has the habit.

PETS FROM DOMESTIC MAMMALS

Animals that originally existed in the wild state but were captured, bred, and developed for man's use are considered domestic animals. Those that are frequently children's pets—rabbits, dogs, cats, guinea pigs, colored rats and mice—are discussed here.

Harelike Mammals

Hares and rabbits are often thought of as rodents, but they belong to the order Lagomorpha, or harelike animals. The members of this group are characterized by two pairs of incisors (chisel-like teeth) on the upper jaw and one pair on the lower jaw. The upper and lower jaws oppose each other in such a way as to cause a lateral motion when food is chewed.

True rabbits bear young that are naked and blind, whereas hares are born fully furred and with their eyes open. This distinction is not observed in common usage; thus the Belgian hare is a rabbit, and the American jackrabbits are really hares.

None of our native hares or rabbits thrives or even lives any length of time in captivity. There are some records of a little success with the eastern cottontail, but it is not common. The best pet material comes from the domestic rabbits; hence these are the only ones discussed here.

The domestic rabbit originated from native rabbits of central Europe and the Carpathians, and now stands close to the dog in varieties of breeds developed. They have been developed for fur, food, and show. Out of the numerous breeds the albinos, the Dutch, and possibly the English produce the best pets, with the Dutch heading the list.

RABBITS: Genus *Orcytolagus*

EUROPEAN RABBIT: *Orcytolagus cuniculus*

Domesticated: Usually carried at pet shops

Description: Small; reaches weight of 6 pounds; background color white with rear half of body, head, and ears black, blue, or some other color; fur heavy and velvety; seldom shows any tendency to kill young should nest box be disturbed; exceedingly gentle; excellent pet for small children

Reproduction: Breeds throughout year, winter months possibly excepted; usually 3–9 young

Life span: Several years

Economic position: Bred for food, fur, pets, and show

A rabbit should never be picked up by its ears. This breaks the cartilage and causes the ears to hang in an ugly, floppy manner. Lift the rabbit by the skin of the back near the neck. At the same time place the free hand under the body to give support to its feet.

A rabbit's natural means of defense is to strike with its hind legs and to bite. Sometimes it will also scratch. A rabbit may demonstrate such tendencies when quite young, in which case it should not be used as a pet.

Domestic rabbits are hardy in captivity and easily maintained when properly housed, fed, and petted.

HOUSING

Cage is needed only for confinement at night and for mother with young. Pet at home may be given freedom in an enclosed yard but must be watched; otherwise, it will dig itself out of its yard. Pet in classroom should have run of rooms; confine to cage at night to protect it.

CLEANLINESS: Pet rabbit may be more easily housebroken than a kitten, since it picks out a particular spot in room in which to place its droppings and always returns to this spot. Place low, wooden box, such as fruit crate, filled with loose, damp soil or sawdust, in corner chosen by pet. Spread papers, oilcloth, or old canvas under box to protect surrounding floor from scattered dirt. Renew soil or sawdust of box every day or two to prevent odor. *Training*—Very occasionally, young pet must be placed in box several times until it learns.

FOOD

Use rabbit pellets in patented feeder. Green pellets are preferred as they contain all essentials. Supplement with alfalfa or clover hay and fresh young carrots. *Salt*—Place piece of salt brick where pet can reach it any time; buy at feed store. *Water*—Must be fresh, clean, and always available; use water bottle.

BREEDING

Advisable to obtain doe about to bear young. Use small animal cage (see Part IV). Cover bottom with 2–3 inches of sawdust or sawdust-shavings mixture. Provide wooden nesting box or a heavy carton 1½ feet square and 8–10 inches deep, depending upon size of doe. Half fill box with soft, clean hay. Doe makes nest in hay, lines it with fur pulled from her breast.

BIRTH: Gestation averages 31 days. Do not disturb doe for 2–3 days before expected birth date and 2–3 days after. Number in litter varies. Young are born blind, naked, and completely helpless. Eyes open at 9 days. At 3 weeks, usually able to come out of nest box.

At 6 weeks, may be weaned, but best to leave young with mother until they are 2 months old. Move family to larger quarters when young begin playing outside box. Advisable to place in outdoor pen or return to supplier of doe.

FOOD FOR DOE WITH YOUNG: In addition to regular diet, give doe bread crusts soaked in milk and squeezed dry plus fresh milk. As soon as young begin to feed themselves, give them bread and milk mixture. At 4–5 weeks, give them bran mixed with scraped carrots and oatmeal dampened with milk. *Water*—Must be fresh and always available; use water bottle.

Rodents or Gnawing Mammals

Rats, mice and guinea pigs are gnawing mammals or rodents. They belong to the order rodentia. The domestic rat has been developed from the wild Norway rat which reached America soon after the Revolutionary War. Through selective breeding the pure white and colored strains of domestic rats have been developed.

It is well known that in all mammalian life albino forms sometimes appear among the young. When this occurs the eyes are always pink. Man has taken albino forms that occur in wild Norway rats and bred them with other albinos until the strain has become fixed. To obtain black and white and other colors, the albino has been bred with the colored rat and the color strains selected out and further bred until the desired colors are obtained. The pure white is the first strain to have become fixed in rats. It is now a distinct breed. Next was developed the white with black head and shoulders, then the white with black head and spots along the back. The more recent colors developed are yellow, buffs, creams, blues, smokes, brindles, and blacks, but these are still not as common as white.

DOMESTIC RAT: Genus *Rattus*

WHITE RAT: *Rattus norvegicus* (albino form)

Domesticated: Usually carried at all pet shops
Description: Pure white with red eyes; feet small, tail long and sparsely haired; length 16 inches including 6-inch tail.

Reproduction: Breeds throughout year; number of young varies with size and age of female

Life span: 4–5 years

Economic position: Are among the most valuable animals used in the laboratory today for study of nutrition, disease, and genetics; in this respect they rank with hamsters, guinea pigs, and monkeys; are also bred for pets.

An adult rat, unless it was taken for a pet when a baby, will be nervous and tend to bite. One should guard against bites, as rat's teeth are extremely sharp and capable of inflicting a deep cut which can become infected. It is advisable to wear gloves until pet becomes accustomed to handling. Spend a little time with it each day. Be very slow and gentle in movements. Offer choice bits of food to give it confidence. In a short time it will be running over one's hands and arms. Handling should be in moderation, as moisture and heat from human hands are debilitating to pet rats.

Both the all-white and the colored rats are hardy in captivity when properly housed and fed. When taken young they become gentle immediately and are a great source of pleasure and entertainment.

HOUSING

Use "rat apartment" cage, which is large enough and so constructed as to facilitate cleaning (see Part IV). Cover bottom with 2 inches of sawdust-shavings mixture or any commercial cover such as pitch pine shavings, so as to counteract odor. Place cage where sleeping box is out of drafts.

SLEEPING BOX: Not needed in warm climate; 6″ × 4″ × 4″ box with 3½″ hole cut in one end suits 1 pair of rats. Place box in upper compartment of cage. *Bedding materials*—Supply generous amount of torn bits of paper toweling, clean, soft straw, paper shavings (excellent), or soft excelsior. In cold weather, add kapok; rats are very sensitive to extremes of temperature. Do not use cloth or cotton; these hold moisture and afford breeding places for mites. Pile bedding in cage; rats arrange materials to suit themselves.

CLEANING: Clean cage at least 3 times weekly; sooner if odor is noticeable. Watch sleeping box for odor; clean as needed. Never allow cage to become moist from excretions or accumulations of food.

FOOD

Rats are naturally omnivorous, but are much healthier when kept to restricted diet. Give no more food than can be eaten at one time; pet hides surplus in bedding. Serve all solid foods except seeds in small glazed flower pot saucers, which can be easily washed. Feed during late afternoon or evening; rats are more active from evening hours on through night.

REQUIRES DAILY: *Seeds*—Use patented feeder; give sunflower seeds, oats, wheat, prepared bird seed mixtures, and hamster mix (excellent). *Green food*—Any that pet likes; must be fresh, clean, and dry. Lettuce twice weekly only; causes diarrhea when given often in large amounts. *Water*—Must be fresh, clean, and always available; use water bottle.

REQUIRES OCCASIONALLY: *Bread*—Whole wheat bread soaked in milk weekly; small pieces of whole wheat toast several times weekly. *Gnawing materials*—Pieces of dog biscuit keep incisors in good condition. *Meal worms*—Rat's animal food; give no more than 3 or 4 at a time, twice weekly. *Milk*—2 or 3 times weekly, in water bottle.

BREEDING

Best to keep together but 1 pair at a time for healthier stock. Female may nest anywhere in cage. Close opening between floors of cage and keep male away from female when young are born.

BIRTH: Gestation averages 21 days. Number in litter varies with age and size of female. Young are born pink, naked, and blind. Eyes open in 10 days, after which young become active about cage. Rats mature at 3 months. Advisable to separate sexes when young are about one-third grown. Females may be left with mother, but males should be placed in separate cage; rats interbreed readily, but healthy stock is maintained only by mating mother with sons and father with daughters.

FOOD FOR MOTHER WITH YOUNG: Add whole wheat bread soaked in milk to regular diet; keep this in cage until young rats are removed from parent.

NOTE: Rats sometimes eat their newborn, especially if the nest with its litter is disturbed or moved about in the cage. The cause of this is not well understood, though several factors probably enter in, such as improper cage conditions, overcrowding, and a diet deficiency.

DOMESTIC MOUSE: Genus *Mus*

WHITE MICE: *Mus musculus* (albino form)

Domesticated: Usually carried by pet shops. Colored strains a little more difficult to obtain and often a little more expensive

Description: Pure white with pink eyes; feet small; tail long and sparsely haired; length 7 inches including 3½-inch tail

Reproduction: Breeds throughout the year; number of young depends on size and age of mother

Life span: Averages 3–4 years

Economic position: Used extensively in laboratories for the study of nutrition, disease, and genetics; also popular with children as pets

Adult mice usually become tame, with gentle handling, quite as easily as the young. One must be slow in movements, however, until the pets become used to one's presence. They can bite very quickly and do so when suddenly startled. The wound is not so deep as that from a rat, but it should be avoided even so.

Avoid holding mice for any length of time. The moisture and warmth from human hands affects the vitality of these delicate little creatures. Allow them to run all over you, but try to avoid too much holding in the hands.

White and colored mice are healthy and hardy in captivity when properly maintained and handled. They are a great source of pleasure and entertainment as they are extremely playful. When provided with the proper apparatus they become veritable clowns.

HOUSING

Use mouse cage (see Part IV), which is designed to facilitate cleaning. Protect cage from drafts; never place near window during winter.

CLEANLINESS: Peculiar odor of mice comes from their excretions. To counteract odor, cover bottom of cage with 2 inches of sawdust-shavings mixture or one of the treated commercial covers, such as pitch pine shavings. Clean cage every other day, or every day, if odor becomes objectionable. Never allow cage to become moist from excretions or accumulations of food. Mice usually choose definite corners in which to place droppings; wash these corners weekly with Lysol solution or any other effective deodorant.

SLEEPING BOX: Required. Use 6″ × 4″ × 4″ inverted box with hole at one end. *Nesting materials*—Provide paper shavings; if unavailable, use clean, soft straw or paper toweling cut into fine strips. In cold weather, add kapok; mice are extremely sensitive to cold. Do not use cloth or cotton; these become moist and afford breeding places for mites. Stuff some bedding material in sleeping box; pile remainder in cage; mice arrange material to suit themselves.

PLAY: Mice need toys, as they are exceedingly playful. See Part IV for suggestions.

FOOD

Mice are omnivorous, but are healthier when held to restricted diet. Offer no more food than can be eaten at one time; mice hide surplus in bedding. Serve all solid foods except seeds in small glazed flower pot saucers, which can be easily washed. Feed during late afternoon; mice are nocturnal, become more active late in day.

REQUIRE DAILY: *Seeds*—Use patented feeder; give variety of prepared bird seed, such as canary seeds, millet spray; also hamster mix. *Green food*—Dandelion leaves and clover tops are probably best, but *young* carrot tops are also good; all must be clean, fresh, and dry. *Gnawing material*—Dog biscuit must always be available; keeps incisors in good condition. *Milk*—Must be fresh daily; use water bottle; wash container daily. *Water*—Must be fresh, clean, and always available; use water bottle.

REQUIRE OCCASIONALLY: *Cooked foods*—Give puffed wheat, shredded wheat, whole wheat bread soaked in milk and squeezed dry; 2 or 3 times weekly. *Meal worms*—2 or 3 weekly; place in dish from which they cannot crawl.

BREEDING

Best to keep together no more than 2 pairs at a time for healthy stock. Female will probably make nest in sleeping box, but may nest anywhere in cage.

BIRTH: Gestation 21 days. Number in litter varies with size and age of female. Young are born pink, naked, and blind; mature at 3 months. Advisable to separate sexes when young are 6 weeks old; young males caged together must be watched as they tend to fight. Mice readily interbreed, but healthier stock is maintained when mother is mated with sons and father with daughters.

Food for breeding mouse: Add sunflower and turnip seeds to regular diet. Give only to mother with babies; too fattening for other mice.

Waltzing Mice: Mus musculus

Waltzing mice are found in pet shops occasionally and seem to appeal to some children. However, these small creatures are not hardy in captivity. They are extremely delicate and are a weak strain among the various mice which have been developed through selective breeding.

Waltzing mice are said to have been brought to America from either China or Japan, but their origin seems not definitely known. Their waltzing habit, for which the strain was deliberately bred, is caused by a defect in the mechanism of the inner ear which controls the sense of balance. They are smaller than the colored mice described above, and are deaf and very delicate. They are not recommended as pets, and so are not further discussed here.

GUINEA PIG: Genus Cavia

Guinea Pig: Cavia porcellus

Domesticated: Some still exist in Andes Mountains of South America; domesticated pigs available in pet shops

Description: Stocky, heavy body; head somewhat rabbitlike; ears small; hind legs relatively short; hind feet with 3 toes and large angular nails; forefeet with 4 toes; fur coarse and long; tail present but inconspicuous; reaches length of 11 inches and weight of 1 pound; domestic pigs have distinctive fur that determines breed, as follows: *English cavy*—hair smooth, short, and varied in colors; *Peruvian cavy*—hair long and silky; extends over head and rear; often called angora cavy; *Abyssinian cavy*—hair rough, short, but grows all over body in decided rosettes or whorls

Habitat: Burrows or rock crevices

Reproduction: Breeds throughout year; 4–12 young in litter; born fully developed; able to run about soon after birth

Life span: May reach 8 years

Economic position: Used for food in some countries; supplies children with pets; provides cavy enthusiasts with exhibition animals; greatest contribution is in field of science where it is used in study of disease, nutrition, serums, and heredity

The guinea pig or cavy originally came from South America where it was much favored by the ancient Incas, who raised it for food. There are still some known wild species in existence there today.

Guinea pigs are hardy in captivity when properly housed and fed. They are extremely gentle, as a rule, and safe for children to handle. Occasionally a pig will develop a tendency to bite and scratch. This one should not be bred or used as a pet.

HOUSING

Use any type of cage that can be cleaned easily and gives pet some running space; coarse-wire cage now used by pet shops is best (see Part IV).

SLEEPING BOX: May be wood or pasteboard carton without bottom; size depends on whether 1 or 2 pigs are to be housed. Cut entrance hole large enough to admit pet. *Sleeping materials*—practically fill box with clean, sweet, soft hay; pigs burrow under it for warmth.

WARMTH: Very important; pigs are extremely sensitive to low temperatures. Do not allow them to be chilled; protect them from drafts.

FOOD

Keep pigs on specific diet. Give generous amounts as they are real gourmands. Feed regularly.

REQUIRE DAILY: *Dry food*—Generous amount of sweet, clean hay, such as alfalfa, must always be available; pile in one corner of pen. *Pellets*—Give rabbit pellets; use patented feeder. *Green food*—Essential; any fresh vegetable tops, such as carrot tops, outer green leaves of lettuce, parsley, celery; fresh weed growth, such as dandelion, chickweed, wild lettuce, shepherd's purse; generous amount once daily. *Salt*—Excellent; place piece of salt brick in pen where pigs can lick it at will. *Water*—Must be fresh, clean, and always available; use water bottle.

REQUIRE OCCASIONALLY: *Wet food*—Give stale bread soaked in milk weekly. *Vegetables*—Small young carrots every few days; pigs are also fond of apples.

BREEDING

One pair averages 5 litters. When young are born, boar must be removed from sow and placed in another pen. Period of gestation 58–75 days. Young feed themselves shortly after birth; should be removed from mother when they are 4 or 5 weeks old. If boars are placed together, they must be watched carefully because they often fight.

FOOD FOR BREEDING MOTHERS: Add stale bread soaked in milk to regular daily diet; continue for 2 weeks after young are born.

Carnivores or Flesh-eating Mammals

DOGS: Genus *Canis*

DOMESTIC DOG: *Canis familiaris*

ORIGIN: The origin of the domestic dog is not really known, other than that it descended from some wild form. Many naturalists, influenced by the studies of Darwin, believe that it developed from wild wolves, jackals, and possibly dingoes, which are the wild dogs of Australia.

The consensus is that the domestic dog has descended from the common wolf which existed in several countries of Europe. This opinion holds because early evidences of domestic dogs have been found in those countries where the common wolf existed. It is well known that pups of some species of wolves tame readily and in fact, show many of the characteristics of the dog, but when mature they develop traits of the wild and are often not safe to keep as pets.

DOMESTICATION: Dogs were bred so long ago that only speculation can be made as to when and how it occurred. Long before there were any picture writings made by ancient man there is evidence that the dog was his close companion. There is also evidence that the dog was bred much as it is today; that is, for sport, companionship, and as a household pet. With no other domestic animal has man been able to produce so many and such varied breeds as he has with the dog.

TRAINING: Dogs are keenly sensitive and can be made to understand many things simply by changes in a person's tone of voice. Patience, plus encouragement, followed by much praise, and speaking in low tones while changing the temper of the voice is usually all that is necessary. A puppy can learn at once the meaning of a firm "no," provided the owner is consistent in his methods. So intelligent is the average dog that its actions are, like a child's, the reflection of the training of the parent. One should not shout at a dog or raise his voice when disciplining. The dog does not know it is doing something wrong and needs only to be taught what is desired. Dogs which are the victims of bad temper are cowed, and cowed dogs are the most unattractive of all animals. Patience, kindliness, and a gentle voice are the essentials if one desires a perfect pet.

EARS: Never punish a dog by pulling its ears. This is as ill-mannered on the part of the owner as shouting, kicking, or striking the animal. A dog's ears are extremely sensitive. They may be injured readily, often permanently, by pulling, jerking, or twisting. The dog is so intelligent that it deserves a show of intelligence on the part of its owner. The ears should be checked also for mites and foreign items such as foxtails, which cause much trouble. In bathing the dog, guard against any water getting into the ears.

PARASITES: Dogs are susceptible to many kinds of parasites, such as fleas, ticks, and mites, which are external, and to roundworms, tapeworms, hookworms, and whipworms, which are internal. These parasites are picked up through contact with other animals and with plants. Some may be transmitted to man. All effort should be made to keep a pet dog free from such parasites. The owner should also protect himself against them. Guard against allowing a dog to lick the face and hands. Wash hands with soap and water after playing with a pet dog as after handling any other animal.

Since there is such a variety of breeds of dogs used as pets, only general points of discussion as to care are considered here. There are training classes regularly available to dog owners. Numerous books and pamphlets containing excellent information on the many breeds of dogs and their care can be purchased at most pet shops.

HOUSING

PUPPY: At 6–12 weeks, puppy may be removed from mother; may need 2 or 3 nights to adjust to being alone. Use sleeping box that puppy can snuggle into; supply parts of blankets and shaggy rugs as bedding. Puppy misses cuddling against warm sides of mother and siblings; give it tightly corked hot water bottle wrapped in bedding to cuddle against; ticking clock tucked into bedding often adds comfort. *Housebreaking*—Puppies hard to housebreak because they have short memories; about 2 weeks of patient effort needed; administer correction at immediate moment; training lesson lost otherwise.

ADULT DOG: Needs kennel, box, or basket for sleeping; keep permanently in one location; pad of cedar shavings prevents fleas from breeding and gives a pleasant odor. Essential to keep sleeping quarters clean; change and wash pad covering frequently to prevent pests from breeding.

GROOMING

Bathing not necessary when daily care of quarters and daily brushing of coat given; daily brushing keeps hair in good condition. If pet must be bathed, use moderately warm suds and rinse in clean, warm water. Take every precaution to keep water out of pet's ears; keep pet out of drafts until it is thoroughly dry.

FREEDOM

All dogs need a great deal of exercise; provide yard space for running if possible; otherwise, exercise twice daily on leash. A dog tied up and left alone to fret and cry becomes a mean animal. If dog must be confined outdoors, use long leash with sliding ring over 50-foot wire, which gives freedom for running.

FOOD

PUPPY: Needs *plenty* of food; should have all it can eat at each meal. Feed pup at regular time each day. For first 3 months, feed 4 times daily—morning, noon, evening, and bedtime. Food needs vary with size and kind of dog; obtain information from person supplying puppy.

ADULT DOG: Many theories on feeding; all agree that overfeeding is unhealthy: healthy dog is trim, active animal. Get professional information for your breed and size of dog. Put all food in containers used for dog only. Wash food containers by themselves, not with household's dishes.

WATER: Essential at all ages; must be fresh, clean, and available at all times.

CATS: Genus *Felis*

DOMESTIC CAT: *Felis catus*

Cats are such common animals, both as pets and as strays, that one seldom gives a thought to their economic position or to their origin. Today many strange and interesting breeds have been introduced from foreign lands, yet little thought is ever given to the cat other than as a pet. In America the common tabby cat predominates and seems to be the favorite with children.

DOMESTICATION: There is little doubt that the cat was first domesticated to control the numerous rodents that destroyed man's chief food—grain. This took place in Egypt, which was a grain country, and before the cat was exalted to the position of a deity in Egyptian life.

ECONOMIC POSITION: In spite of long centuries of association with man, and training by him, the cat's fierce instinct to kill is little changed today. In the original wild state, its nature was to prowl and hunt largely at night. This habit remains unchanged. Its food originally consisted of smaller rodents and birds. This is still its favorite food. Hence the cat, today, still serves man in its control of rodents. Only as a predator in the destruction of birds does the cat become an economic problem. Birds are more important in their control of destructive insects than are cats as pets.

TRAINING: Cats are intelligent animals. They learn quickly and they do not forget. These qualities make it possible to train a pet cat *not* to stalk and kill birds. In teaching the pet, any method may be used which creates an association in the mind of the animal with the bird stalked. For example, a pet owner concealed himself in a retreat and watched his cat every morning when it was turned out in the orchard. As soon as the animal began stalking birds he peppered it with a handful of gravel, throwing it hard enough to sting. A few of these experiences caused the cat to associate stalking with the uncomfortable sensation of being pelted by pebbles. Cats have excellent memories and require few experiences to teach them new ways of acting.

FREEDOM: A pet cat should not be given freedom to wander out of doors through the night. A well-trained cat, kept in its quarters, is prevented from mixing with strays or other prowlers and bringing home "foreign" fleas and diseases. Freedom at night is neither necessary nor desirable when the cat is given the privilege of running free during the day.

DISEASES: Cats are susceptible to a number of diseases which may be easily transmitted to humans; hence, it is not wise to pick up stray cats promiscuously for adoption, especially if there are children in the family. This is also an argument for keeping a well-trained pet shut in during the night. A kitten should come from a healthy, well-trained, and well-cared-for mother. From the standpoint of the health of the child and for the comfort of the animal, no child under the age of five years should be allowed to possess a pet cat. When anything appears to be seriously wrong with the pet, it is advisable to take it to a veterinarian. If this is not possible, the children should be kept away from the animal, and if it shows no sign of improving, it should be disposed of humanely.

The following are a few of the more common breeds of domestic cats now in America, with their origins:

MALTESE: *Felis catus*

Origin: Originally came to America from the island of Malta where the strain was probably brought by early traders; origin clearly a mystery as there is no native blue wild cat on Malta; theories are that color was selected and bred until it became fixed, or that, being a particularly hardy breed, it developed naturally into a fixed strain

Description: Sturdy, short-haired, all blue strain, usually with yellow-green eyes

MANX CAT: *Felis catus*

Origin: Came to Britain and America from Isle of Man; hence the name; it is thought that the Manx landed on the Isle of Man from wrecks of the Spanish Armada, but its origin beyond that point is not known

Description: No tail; has tuft of fur where tail should be; forelegs short, while hind legs are long, causing animal to proceed by rabbit-like hops; sometimes called rabbit cat

PERSIAN-ANGORA: *Felis catus*

Origin: Persian from Far East, Angora from Turkey; descended from long-haired manul which is found in mountains of Central Asia and is a strain easily tamed

Description: Long, silky fur is characteristic feature; Persians and Angoras have been so interbred that they are now considered as one

ROYAL SIAMESE: *Felis catus*

Origin: Royal houses of Siam, now Thailand

Description: Body is fawn, bluish, or ivory, with chocolate brown legs, mask, and tail; eyes blue; fur short and close to body; tail not long, comparatively speaking; the most intelligent and companionable of all cat breeds

TABBY CAT: *Felis catus*

Origin: Developed in Europe through cross-breeding but originated in Egypt; came to America via European explorers and settlers

Description: Name is indiscriminately applied to all cats, but it is a distinct strain; ground color may be light or dark with spots, bars, or stripes of another shade, or color may be solid without markings

Since there is such a great variety of cat breeds, only general points of discussion as to care and feeding are considered. There are numerous books and pamphlets available on cats in general, and breeds, breeding, and care in particular. Many of these are excellent and are available at most pet shops.

KITTEN

HOUSING: At 6 or 7 weeks, may be taken from mother. Set aside some corner of house for it. Provide sleeping box or basket lined with soft, washable clean cloths. Change and wash bedding frequently to keep fleas from breeding. Keep basket out of drafts; cats and kittens can catch cold. Wise to keep sleeping basket after cat is full-grown; often keeps it from sleeping on beds and furniture where it is not wanted. *Housebreaking*—Fill a box with soft, clean soil, sand, or prepared mixture purchased at pet shops. When kitten is caught making mistake, speedily rush it to box; make it remain there for a moment. Never allow box to give off odor; replace contents daily if box is small, less often if it is large.

FOOD: When first taken from mother give warm milk in clean saucer 4–5 times daily. After a few days, add stale bread to warm milk. In week or so, give a little cooked cereal with milk. Occasionally give small amount of finely chopped, cooked meat; never give raw meat to a kitten. Place all food in containers used only for pet; wash containers daily; keep food containers separate from household's dishes and wash separately. *Water*—Essential; must be clean, fresh, and available at all times.

GROOMING

Cat fur is thick, soft, and constantly shed; cat keeps fur in good condition by licking it. Brushing each day is essential; especially necessary for long-haired cats. Otherwise, cat swallows too many hairs, and hairballs form in stomach. These can become dangerous.

FOOD

Give sufficient quantity at each feeding; cat will not overeat; will refuse food when its hunger is satisfied. When cat is running outside, it should have access to growing grass and catnip. Keep pet's food containers separate from household dishes; wash separately.

REQUIRES DAILY: *Cat food*—Twice daily; offer meat-gravy mixture, meat gravy mixed with potatoes and some cooked meat; prepared canned cat food may be used instead, contains all essentials. *Milk*—Fresh daily. *Vegetables*—Essential; must be cooked; give any pet likes. *Water*—Essential; must be clean, fresh, and available at all times.

REQUIRES OCCASIONALLY: *Fish*—May be raw or cooked; give any pet likes. *Meat*—Raw meat diet alone often causes form of indigestion commonly called "fits."

BIRDS

THERE are numerous varieties of birds which are suitable for cage life in either the school or the home. Many species become gentle and permit, even coax for, a certain amount of petting and handling. Some of the most attractive and interesting birds for cage life are the foreign birds, the greater number of which come from Africa and Australia, although equally interesting pets come from our domesticated birds and from our native wild birds.

American law prohibits the caging of a majority of native birds since they are the most important natural factor in keeping noxious weeds and insects under control. Most countries have regulations governing the capture and exportation of their native birds, so one may be sure that any attractive and interesting bird for sale in a licensed pet shop has found its way there legally.

Most dealers today handle only the hardier species of birds. The majority of them make excellent aviary inhabitants and as a rule breed well in captivity. Personal choice of a bird depends on whether it is to be bred or is to be trained as a pet.

NESTING AND REARING YOUNG: For breeding obtain cage-bred birds, since they adjust to new cages much more quickly. Naturally the outdoor aviary is the ideal situation for breeding birds, but there are many which will breed in smaller cages when provided with proper conditions.

Probably the most satisfactory birds for small-cage breeding are some of the foreign finches. Many of them breed throughout the year, while others have the seasons reversed and so breed through the winter months which gives school children an opportunity to watch this interesting activity.

Cages for a classroom should be fitted with rollers so they may be moved with little effort and a minimum of disturbance to the birds.

TRANSFER: Often birds that are transferred from an aviary to a cage, or from a larger to a smaller cage, require a certain amount of time to become adjusted to their new quarters. Some of the parrot-like birds often refuse to nest during the first year after the transfer.

TEMPERATURE: Care must be taken at all times to keep the cage in the proper position in the room. Tropical birds chill easily and often die from colds. The cage should be placed where morning sun may strike it each day, but in a spot free from drafts, and where, on the other hand, the sun and the heat are not too intense. Note that extended periods of direct sunlight can be fatal to a small bird, so shelter should be available.

BIRDS AS PETS: If a bird is to become a pet, obtain a very young bird. Young birds become gentle and respond to training much more quickly. Once a bird is given companionship with others of its kind, it loses all interest in humans.

TRAINING: Maintain the bird in a small cage, such as the usual type of canary cage.

Birds are exceedingly sensitive to sudden movements and to loud noises. They must be approached and handled with slow, even motions and spoken to in low tones. When a bird loses its fear of its trainer, the battle is won. After that, it is merely a matter of getting it to understand what one wishes it to do. Of course birds, like most higher animals, are individuals. Some species are more intelligent than others. Some may be tought to do simple tricks. Some become gentle but resist handling. Even among the same species one finds extremes in individual differences.

After the bird has become gentle and a real pet, it must be given more freedom. Allow it to play about the room for exercise and amusement. It is advisable to leave the cage door open so that it may stop for food during its play. Usually the pet goes into the cage of its own accord when it grows weary of its adventures. If one is lucky enough to have a spare room in the house which can be turned over to the pet, a potted shrub or a large branching limb set in one corner furnishes the pet with many hours of exercise and adventure. Many-branched limbs are essential as the different-sized twigs provide exercise for the feet of birds.

NOTE: Fresh water in clean containers is required daily for caged birds. This means that the container must be removed and thoroughly washed; otherwise a scum may form around its edges. If not removed, the scum may cause diarrhea as well as other serious ailments. Also, give fresh seed each day; wash container daily; dry thoroughly before refilling.

FOREIGN BIRDS

FINCH: Genus *Munia*

JAVA SPARROW: *Padda oryzivora*

Range: Originally native only to Java but has spread through Malay Archipelago to India, southern China, and Japan

Description: Top of head and neck black with exception of cheek and ear coverts which are pure white; bill red; back and breast gray, flanks washed with gray; wings soft brown; rump and tail black; abdomen white; length 5½ inches

Habitat: Throughout grass lands and especially where rice is grown; often occurs in small flocks

Voice: Male has tinkling song; female, a series of chirping notes only

Nest: In wild state makes globular nest of fine grasses, with small entrance hole at one side; usually placed in thorny bushes about 8 feet from ground

Eggs: 4–8 in a clutch; pure white

The Java sparrow is one of the most satisfactory of all birds for a pet either in a home or in a classroom. It is extremely hardy in captivity, is long-lived, learns quickly, and is easily tamed and trained. In its native countries it is a common household pet. It is also the bird used by the street fortune tellers so common in the Orient.

If a pet is desired, the bird should be maintained alone. If young are desired, one or more pairs may be placed in a large cage. As there is no obvious difference between the male and female, it is difficult to choose a mated pair. Since a Java sparrow is most decided in his choice of a mate, one must depend upon the pet shop or the breeder to isolate the mated pairs.

Two strains of colors have been developed from the wild bird—a pure white with a red bill was first created through selective breeding; then a mottled black and white was obtained by a cross of the wild bird with this pure white. Both these strains may usually be obtained at pet shops and from breeders.

SOCIETY FINCH: *Munia striata*

Domesticated: Available from aviaries or pet shops
Description: Colors: mottled brown and white; mottled fawn and white; and pure white; pure whites are weak strain, often born blind; length 2⅔ inches
Voice: Male sings small song inaudible to human ear; at same time spreads tail into wide fan and performs small dance for his mate
Nest: Rather untidy structure made of grasses placed in finch nesting box
Eggs: 4–6 in clutch; pure white

Society finches are entirely domesticated birds which originated somewhere in the Orient in the far distant past, so far that no one knows just how they were developed. They never existed in the wild state, are strictly "manmade," and have never known anything but cage life.

Society finches are excellent breeders. They are splendid to use in rearing young of other small birds. They accept eggs of other birds in exchange for their own with no concern. They are hardy, except for the pure white strain, and prefer to breed in cages rather than in an aviary.

FINCH: Genus *Taeniopygia*

ZEBRA FINCH: *Taeniopygia castanotis*

Range: Throughout continent of Australia
Description: General color above bluish gray; rump white; sides black; upper tail coverts black with broad bars of white; narrow black line at base of lower mandible followed by white bar margined with black; sides of face and ear coverts chestnut; throat and fore neck gray barred with black; band on lower fore neck black; abdomen and under tail coverts white; flanks chestnut spotted with white; bill red; eyes red; feet orange; length 4 inches; female lacks chestnut colorings and is much lighter than male

Habitat: In wild state congregates in small flocks and spends much time on ground where trees are thinly scattered and grass growth is abundant

Voice: Quaint, pleasing rhythmical song resembling toy music box

Nest: Untidy, bottle-shaped structure made of grasses and other plant materials; built on its side and lined with fine grasses and feathers

Eggs: 3–6 in a clutch; either pure white or creamy white

Zebra finches are hardy in captivity. They are short-lived but are prolific breeders. Several pairs naturally do well together provided their cage is sufficiently large. When overcrowded they fight over nest sites and sometimes males will fight over females.

When a female repeatedly lays sterile eggs, the pair is too old or the temperature is not sufficiently constant. These birds require warmth.

All these finches may be maintained the same way.

HOUSING

Use small animal cage for 1 pair, large bird cage if several pairs are to be housed (see Part IV). Cover cage bottom with 2–3 inches of bird gravel. Place branching limb in center of cage; arrange branches to leave ample flight space. *Warmth*—Avoid temperature extremes; roll cage into sun during early part of day; keep out of drafts; move away from windows at night; cover cage with heavy cloth at night during coldest part of winter; also protect from extremely high temperature; shift cage accordingly.

NESTING BIRDS

Provide birds with standard finch nesting box obtained at pet shops. Place box high up in cage on small top branches of limb. Place bunches of soft, dry, slender grasses in cage; birds select and construct to suit themselves. Many times birds reject artificial nest; will construct nest in crotch of branches; supply with plenty of nesting material.

INCUBATION PERIOD: Incubation does not begin until female has laid its full clutch of eggs. *Java sparrow*—Averages 13 days. *Society finch*—12–14 days. *Zebra finch*—18–20 days. *Warning*—When eggs of Java sparrow hatch, young are easily disturbed and frightened; nest must not be touched until young poke out their heads; young leave nest at 5–6 weeks.

FOOD: Nesting bird needs insect food; offer nestling mixture purchased at pet shops. Give health grit (see p. 254) weekly. After eggs hatch, parent birds feed soft food to young; add crumbled bits of stale sponge cake to adults' regular diet. Continue egg mixture and nestling food until young come off nest and begin to feed themselves.

REMOVAL OF YOUNG: When young can feed themselves, remove from parents and place in cage by themselves; continue feeding health grit to young 3–4 times weekly.

FOOD

SEEDS: *Java sparrow*—Native food is flowering grass seeds, cereals, and large quantities of rice; feed prepared parakeet mixture purchased at pet shops. *Zebra finch*—Native food is seed of wild grasses; feed prepared finch seed mixture purchased at pet shops. *Society finch*—Use prepared finch seed mixture.

OTHER FOODS REQUIRED DAILY: *Health grit*—Use prepared grit purchased at pet shops or make own (see Part III). *Green food*—Plant leftover seeds in container of soil kept in cage (see Part III) or buy ready-planted seed at pet shops. *Water*—Must be fresh and clean; use water bottle; clean daily.

CUTTLEBONE: Tie one piece to side of cage within easy reach of bird, another piece to limb of branch; give fresh pieces monthly.

BATH

Place about an inch of water in 8-inch flower pot saucer; wash container daily.

GRASS OR SHELL PARAKEET, BUDGERIGAR, OR BUDGIE: Genus *Melopsittacus*

PARAKEET: *Melopsittacus undulatus*

Range: Widely distributed throughout inland Australia
Description: All green; lower part of cheeks and throat yellow; small patch of dark blue on each cheek, below which are 3 black

spots; bare skin around nostril (cere) dark blue in male, *pale* blue in female; bill bluish lead color; lower back, rump, and upper tail coverts grass green, upper tail tinged with blue; central pair of tail feathers blue; tail long and graduated; length 7½ inches

Habitat: In flocks in areas with plenty of vegetation, both grass and trees

Voice: Full, voluble vocabulary of chattering noises, some musical and rhythmical; can be extremely noisy

Nest: Holes in trees

Eggs: 4–8 in a clutch; pure white

It was soon discovered by bird fanciers that this small bird could produce interesting variations in color phases. The first to be produced was an all-yellow; the second a turquoise or blue-green. Varying shades of blue have been developed from this turquoise, the rarest of all being a violet. But the two most exquisite colors are the snow-white and sky-blue. Most of these colors can be obtained in pet shops or from parakeet breeders.

Parakeets adjust readily to cage life. They are hardy in captivity, long-lived, and become interesting and affectionate pets. They are easily maintained when given proper food and care. But if one wishes to tame a bird, it must be a male and it must be kept alone. A parakeet no longer remains a pet if it has another of its own kind as a companion.

HOUSING

For single bird, use commercial canary cage. Give pet freedom of room; teach it to use cage for headquarters.

NESTING BIRDS

At least 6–8 pairs needed; single pair seldom breeds in captivity. House in small outdoor aviary; provide large, bare, branching limb, arranged to leave ample flight space. Provide standard parakeet nesting boxes with concave bottoms; buy at pet store. Place boxes high up and around aviary. Incubation begins as soon as first egg is laid; takes 21 days. Young are naked when hatched; feather out in 2 weeks. After a few days, babies lie upon their backs. At 4–5 weeks, young leave nest fully feathered and full grown. Do not disturb birds to watch feeding of young or to look into nest; open nesting box gently; avoid sudden, jerky movements.

FOOD: Male bird feeds female from moment first egg is laid. Put food for nesting birds in open seed dishes such as glazed flower pot saucers. Feed regular diet; add greens daily and milksop made with stale whole wheat bread (see Part III); change sop daily; never allow it to become sour or stale.

FOOD

In the wild, birds feed on grasses and herbaceous plants.

REQUIRES DAILY: *Seed*—Use prepared parakeet mixture; for a single bird, use cage seed cups; wash daily; dry thoroughly before refilling. *Health grit*—Especially important during nesting period; use prepared mixture bought at pet shops. *Water*—Must be fresh and clean; use water bottle; wash daily.

REQUIRES OCCASIONALLY: *Green food*—1 or 2 times weekly; give spinach, carrot tops, dandelion leaves, clover; sprouted bird seed grown in flower pot saucers (see Part III) or sproutings of ready-planted seed bought at pet store; greens must be fresh, clean, and dry. *Cuttlebone*—Tie pieces in several places in cage; replace with fresh pieces each month.

BATH

Parakeets do not bathe frequently. In the wild, may occasionally roll through tall grass heavy with dew. Cage pet likes to sit on owner's hand while water is sprayed over it from faucet. Use atomizer occasionally to spray bird lightly when it refuses to bathe.

TRAINING A PARAKEET TO TALK

Play and talk with it for a while each day, repeating the same sounds, words, and phrases. Some birds will learn more quickly than others, may develop large vocabulary. Parakeets that do not learn to speak are nevertheless interesting and entertaining.

COCKATEEL: Genus *Nymphicus*

COCKATEEL: *Nymphicus hollandicus*

Range: Widely distributed over interior of Australia and island of Tasmania

Description: Male: General color dusky gray; large white patch on each wing; fore part of head, sides of face, throat, and crest lemon-yellow; tip of crest feathers brown; ear coverts bright orange; sides of crown white; tail fairly long, central feathers projecting beyond rest; bill dark horn color; eyes brown; female: similar to male but wing patches smaller and less pure white; orange cheek patch present but lemon and white areas absent from head; length 13½ inches

Habitat: Feeds on ground in flocks; always perches on dead limbs of trees where difficult to see; will not perch on limbs with leaves

Voice: Male cockateel has lovely song which is rarely performed unless birds feel they are alone and all is quiet about them; other notes are the familiar screeching parrotlike calls

Nest: Holes in trees

Eggs: 4–7 in clutch; pure white

Cockateels are hardy in captivity, long-lived, and adapt themselves to cage life. Their size makes it necessary to give them plenty of room, as flight is important exercise for these beautiful birds. Because of their size and their chattering noises they are not successful as classroom pets but are highly recommended as house pets, especially if a very young bird is obtained and reared and trained alone. They are easily maintained when given proper conditions.

HOUSING

For single bird, use commercial parrot cage; give plenty of freedom in room; bird soon learns to use cage as headquarters only. Arrange branching, leafless limb so that it does not interfere with flight space. Provide a few limbs covered with lichens and loose bark; pets work at these and keep bills in condition; necessary.

NESTING BIRDS

Need large space; use small aviary or screened-in porch. In the wild, cockateels nest in hollow limbs, holes in trees, and in old stumps; usually select large holes in dead trees; eggs are laid on decaying wood at bottom of hole. Provide birds with small barrel, such as pickle or small nail keg; place high up and at back of cage. Place handful of sawdust-shavings mixture in barrel to simulate decaying wood. Incubation usually begins only after full clutch is laid; takes 18 days; hen broods during night, cock assists by day. Young almost as large as parents when they leave nest; do not disturb nest until young leave; parents often refuse to feed young when they are disturbed by humans.

Food for nesting birds: Add milksop food (see Part III) to regular diet.

FOOD

In the wild, cockateels feed on seeds of grasses and herbaceous plants.

Requires daily: *Seed*—Give prepared parakeet seed mixture obtained at pet shops plus sunflower seeds. *Health grit*—Prepared mix may be bought at pet shops or use home-made mix (see Part III). *Green food*—Fresh young sproutings of seed grown in flower pot saucers (see Part III) or sproutings of ready-planted seed purchased at pet shops. *Water*—Must be clean and fresh; use water bottle; wash daily.

Cuttlebone: Securely fasten several pieces in aviary; one piece sufficient in single cage; replace with fresh pieces monthly.

BATH

Habits are irregular; in wild, cockateels walk through grass heavy with dew. Use large container such as large flower pot saucer; fill container with water and place in cage at same time each day in early morning. Remove container after about an hour, whether or not birds have bathed.

LOVE BIRDS: Genus *Agapornis*

Fischer's Love Bird: *Agapornis fischeri*

Range: Northern Tanganyika
Description: Male and female similar; back, wings, and breast down to belly, green; neck all around and chest golden-yellow; throat and sides of face orange; crown of head olive-brown; forehead bright tomato-red; upper tail coverts cobalt-blue; tail with indistinct subterminal bar sky-blue; tips and base of inner webs of outer feathers brownish red; bill scarlet; length 5½ inches
Habitat: In or near baobab trees in open country
Voice: High-pitched twitter
Nest: Breeds in colonies; nest a rough pad made of any material available; also said to make or use an oval nest and to close entrance with thorns; nest placed in bases of fronds of palm trees or in baobab trees
Eggs: 5–6 in clutch; white

MASKED LOVE BIRD: *Agapornis personata*

Range: Northern Tanganyika
Description: Male and female alike; head blackish or blackish-brown merging into yellow on neck and upper breast; breast sometimes tinged with orange on throat; remainder of plumage green, paler on abdomen; lower rump tinged dull, dark blue; tail marked with black; bill red; large white circle around eye; length 5¾ inches
Habitat: Throughout wooded areas
Voice: Squeaking, chattering cries similar to other love birds but not as noisy
Nest: Made of fine twigs and strips of bark
Eggs: 4–6 in clutch; white

NYASALAND LOVE BIRD: *Agapornis lilianae*

Range: Nyasaland, Northern Rhodesia
Description: Male: Head and throat red, vermillion toward forehead; back of head and back of neck greenish-yellow; remainder of plumage bright grass-green; slightly paler and yellower on under parts; tail with blackish subterminal back and scarlet basal patch on all but central feathers; eye light brown; bill red; white circle around eye; legs and feet flesh color; female same as male but has paler head and throat; length 5 inches
Habitat: In flocks of 20 or more in undergrowth along banks of streams
Voice: Screeching, parrotlike calls
Nest: Made of twigs and vines placed in holes in trees
Eggs: 4–5 in clutch; pure white

PEACH-FACED LOVE BIRD: *Agapornis roseocollis*

Range: Angola south to the Orange River
Description: Male and female alike; dull green, paler on breast; forehead bright rose-red; cheeks and throat rosy-pink with grayish tinge at edges of cheeks; rump brilliant blue; tail short, blue-green with black and fiery pink markings; bill coral-red; length 6 inches
Habitat: In small flocks always close to water

Voice: Screeching, chattering cries similar to other members of group

Nest: Uses nests of other birds, especially weaver birds

Eggs: 4–5 in clutch; pure white

Those love birds that are bred primarily by aviculturists lend themselves readily to cage life when given plenty of space in which to exercise. Some will breed when given proper conditions. They are too noisy for a classroom but are suited for the home. The most satisfaction is obtained by taking a young bird as soon as it is able to feed itself and then training it as a pet. These birds are usually hardy in captivity, long-lived, and easily maintained.

HOUSING

For single birds use small commercial bird cage. Cover cage bottom with 2 inches of bird gravel. Place leafless branching limb in cage; arrange branches so that they do not interfere with flight space. Give pet freedom of room; train it to use cage as headquarters only; bird quickly learns this.

NESTING BIRDS

Use large bird cage (see Part IV) for a pair or place them in small outdoor aviary. Provide standard wooden nesting box for love birds; purchase at pet store. Place box high up at back of cage or aviary; leave in cage at all times as mated pair sleep in box at night. Provide 6–8-inch sections of honeysuckle or similar vines, bunches of long grasses, and pieces of green palm leaves as nesting material. Incubation takes 18 days. Female does most of incubating, although male spends much time on nest with her; male feeds female from time she begins to brood. Young leave nest before they are fully feathered; are then as large as parents. Great care must be taken not to disturb nest with young until they leave box.

FOOD

In the wild, Fischer's love birds feed on grass, millet, and acacia seeds; masked love birds feed on seeds of thorn trees; Nyasaland, on seeds, wild fruits, especially overripe millet; peach-faced, on large berries and berrylike seeds.

REQUIRES DAILY: *Seeds*—Give all species prepared parakeet seed mixture purchased at pet shops plus sunflower seed. *Health grit*—Give prepared grit purchased at pet shops, or as instructed on p. 254. *Water*—Must be fresh and clean; use water bottle; wash daily.

REQUIRES OCCASIONALLY: *Green foods*—2 or 3 times weekly; give spinach, fresh carrot tops, dandelion leaves; sproutings of seed grown in flower pot saucer (see Part III) or sproutings of ready-planted seeds bought at pet shops; greens must be fresh, clean, and dry. *Cuttlebone*—Tie several pieces in convenient places; replace with fresh pieces monthly.

BATH

Use 6-inch flower pot saucer. Place in cage at same time each day. If birds do not bathe, they may be lightly sprayed with atomizer.

DOMESTICATED BIRDS

DOMESTICATED FINCH: Genus *Serinus*

CANARY: *Serinus canaria*

Range: Native to Canary Islands; now found also on Madeira and Cape Verde Islands
Description: Male is all yellow bird streaked with dusky gray; Female much more greenish; bill thick and short like that of sparrow; length averages 4 inches
Habitat: In wooded or shrub areas, often close to habitations
Voice: Loud, clear, rolling song
Nest: Made of moss and plant fibers, placed in bush or tree, often near dwellings
Eggs: 4–5 in clutch; pale blue

From this wild bird, still found in its native habitat, has come the domestic canary so common today. Pairs of wild canaries were first taken to Europe early in the sixteenth century. Their lovely song and beautiful plumage soon made them great favorites everywhere. It was not long before bird lovers began to breed the wild birds selectively in order to improve the song and the color, with the result that there are now many and varied domestic canaries with exquisite songs and exotic colors.

Today those birds prized chiefly for their beauty are: Scotch fancy, which is a slender, graceful bird with high arched shoulders; the Manchester canary, noted for its large size; and the Norwich, which is crested. All of these are show birds first bred in England. Those prized chiefly for song are the ones that are trained in the Harz Mountains of Germany. Here older trained birds are used to instruct the young bird first as it begins to learn to sing. Usually it is the male birds that develop into beautiful singers.

The domestic canary is well adjusted to cage life and is easily maintained when kept clean and given proper food and plenty of water.

HOUSING

For single bird, use commercial canary cage. Cover bottom of cage with 2-inch layer of bird gravel. Place well-branched limb in cage; entertainment for bird.

NESTING BIRDS

For 1 pair of birds use large bird cage or small aviary. Provide with commercial nest. Provide nesting hair purchased at pet shops, bits of string and yarn, soft, dry grasses, and down feathers; do not use cotton, which becomes entangled in birds' claws; pets arrange nesting materials to suit themselves. Incubation averages 14 days; begins when full clutch is laid.

FOOD FOR NESTING BIRDS: Regular diet until eggs hatch. After eggs hatch, give parent birds nestling food purchased at pet shops in addition to regular diet. As nestlings grow, decrease amount of nestling food; give small amount of crushed hemp or poppy seed; give whole-wheat bread soaked in milk at intervals. Baby can feed itself at 4-5 weeks; at 8 weeks, best to remove young to another cage or to outdoor aviary.

FOOD

In the wild, canaries feed on seeds of many plants, tender plant shoots, and fruits; especially fond of figs.

REQUIRES DAILY: *Seeds*—Give prepared canary seed mixture purchased at pet shops; regular canary cups may be used, but feeding more interesting to watch when seeds are placed in open dishes, such as flower pot saucers. *Health grit*—Give prepared grit purchased at pet shops or make your own (see Part III). *Green foods*—Best choice is sproutings of bird seed planted in flower pot saucers (see Part III); otherwise, use ready-planted seed bought at pet shops; fresh, green, crisp lettuce may be given; when available, give fresh apple, wild chickweed, or fresh young weed growth; all green food must be clean, fresh, and dry.

CUTTLEBONE: Fasten several pieces in convenient places; replace with fresh pieces monthly.

BATH

Use flower pot saucer or other small dish; place in cage at same time each morning; remove after bath.

DOVES AND PIGEONS

The terms dove and pigeon are interchangeable and loosely used, but mean practically the same thing. For the most part "dove" refers to the smaller species; "pigeon" to the larger. All belong to the same family.

Doves and pigeons are probably among the oldest domesticated birds. The earliest records are from Egypt about 3000 B.C., where birds were raised for food. The wild bird from which the domestic one was developed was the rock dove of Europe, still found today along the rocky coasts of Europe.

Much later, the domestic pigeon began to be developed as a pet and for a show bird. It makes an excellent pet as it is intelligent, develops interesting relations with its owner, and is easily trained. It is a long-lived bird also; a record of sixteen years exists, but just how long a pigeon could live is not yet known because fanciers are constantly exchanging birds in attempts to improve stock. When a pet dove or pigeon is given a mate and sets up housekeeping, it no longer reacts as a pet but is interested only in its own business.

ROCK DOVE: Genus *Columba*

DOMESTIC PIGEON: *Columba livia*

> *Range:* Worldwide in tropical and temperate regions
> *Description:* Typical wild birds gray with whitish rump, 2 black

bars on secondary wing coverts; broad black band on tail; feet red; domestic birds gray, tan, black, white, and mixtures of varieties; length 13 inches
Habitat: In cities, about farms, along cliffs
Voice: Soft gurgling coo
Nest: Roughly made of twigs and sticks; placed on ledges of buildings; on cliffs in the wild
Eggs: 2 in clutch; pure white

Pigeons are not satisfactory for a school room unless they can be given freedom of the entire building. When a pet is allowed such freedom it will spend most of its time with the children, going in the yard to play with them, returning with them to the classrooms. In other words, the school building is home to the pet pigeon, and pigeons possess strong homing instincts.

TURTLE DOVE: Genus *Streptopelia*

RINGED TURTLE DOVE: *Streptopelia risoria*

Range: Most commonly found in southwest United States along coast; widely domesticated
Description: All pale, creamy-colored bird, narrow black ring on hind neck; tail moderately long, rounded, white at corners; primary wing feathers much darker than body color; length 12 inches
Habitat: City parks
Voice: Purrlike coo which rises then drops in pitch
Nest: Frail, platformlike; made of sticks, placed on limb of tree
Eggs: 2 in clutch; pure white

The ring-necked dove is equally as excellent for a pet as the pigeon. It is also intelligent, very gentle, affectionate, and altogether delightful. It is easily maintained when properly housed and fed, and given freedom in the room. At home a small aviary or screened-in porch is ideal.

HOUSING

As domestic pigeon requires cage large enough to be headquarters, use small animal cage for single bird (see Part IV). Pigeons prefer to stand on flat surfaces; place 18" × 12" shelf along back of cage; fasten half-inch molding along front for raised edge. Ringed turtle dove needs more space than pigeon; use large animal cage (see Part IV). Doves prefer to rest on limbs; provide bare, branching limb; add shelf for nesting doves. Cover bottom of either type cage with 2 inches of bird gravel.

NESTING BIRDS

Both doves and pigeons will place nest on shelf. Provide birds with coarse, *clean* straw or hay cut into 4–6-inch pieces; birds arrange materials to suit themselves; both birds share in nest-making. First egg laid 8–12 days after mating; incubation 18 days; incubation begins when full clutch is laid. Hen usually broods from late afternoon until morning; cock broods rest of time; interesting ceremony of formal bowings and affectionate billings and cooings accompanies exchange of places.

NESTLINGS: Soon after hatching, young are fed "milk," a cheesy liquid formed in stomach of both parent birds 1 or 2 days before eggs hatch. When young are 3–4 days old, parents begin giving them small grains in addition to "milk." At 1 week, young are fed entirely on grain; feed themselves at 6 weeks. Young grow rapidly; pin feathers appear at 5–6 days; at 4–5 weeks, young are fully feathered and as large as parents.

FOOD

In the wild, doves and pigeons feed on seeds, waste grain, fruits, and insects.

REQUIRE DAILY: *Seeds*—Prepared food sold as "pigeon mix" or "dove mix" may be used; otherwise, feed wheat, kafir, buckwheat, Canada and maple peas, hulled oats, and millet; all grain must be old, perfectly dry, and free from weevils; damp food causes "sour crop" which is fatal. Feed barley and cracked corn only if bird runs free; too fattening for caged birds. *Green food*—Once daily; give lettuce, onion tops, clover, and sprouted oats; must be fresh, clean, and dry. *Health grit*—Use prepared grit purchased at pet shops or make your own (see Part III). *Water*—Must be fresh and clean; use water bottle; pigeons and doves have throat muscles which enable them to suck up water like a horse.

REQUIRE OCCASIONALLY: *Canary seed*—Use as treat. *Salt brick*—

Place piece near food dishes; moisten occasionally; now and then, replace with fresh piece.

BATH

Place bath water in large, flat, relatively shallow container; birds show by their behavior whether the container is large enough and the water deep enough. Offer bath only 2 or 3 times weekly.

BARNYARD FOWL

Some of our most common domesticated birds are the barnyard fowl, the best known of which are chickens, ducks, and geese. Present day breeds of chickens have descended from the wild red jungle fowl of India which still exists today in its native habitat. As a result of domestication and selective breeding, there are now numerous breeds of chickens which vary widely in color, size, and commercial use. Many are bred to produce eggs only; others for food.

The Bantams, a pygmy breed, are used for brooding eggs of game birds, and for pets. It is generally agreed that the original Bantam was a wee bird carried from China or Japan to the city of Bantam in Java. From Bantam it was probably carried to Europe and finally to America. The interesting fact is that the original breed of Bantam has been entirely lost. The breeds of today are merely pygmies of their larger barnyard prototypes.

The majority of domestic ducks have been developed from certain strains of wild ducks through crossing and selective breeding. The mallard, which is a common game bird and one that tames and domesticates easily, is definitely one of the ancestors of many of our present-day domestic breeds.

The derogatory term "goose" is incorrect as the goose is an exceedingly intelligent bird. A pet goose becomes quite devoted to its master or mistress, obeys calls and commands, and in many ways proves itself an individual of no small character.

Geese have been domesticated for many centuries, probably long before ducks were. They are found depicted on monuments of ancient Egypt, and they were sacred to the Romans. There is an old legend that tells how Rome was saved from a night attack by Gauls in 390 B.C. by the alarm given by cackling geese. And Julius Caesar wrote that he found the Britons using a kind of wild goose for pets— not for food! This was the graylag goose which still lives and thrives in its natural habitat, and which is the direct ancestor of our domesticated geese of today.

It should be noted that many cities prohibit keeping any barnyard fowl.

JUNGLE FOWL: Genus *Gallus*

RED JUNGLE FOWL: *Gallus gallus*

Range: Northwestern Himalayas, east through Burma and Indo-China, then China and Java

Description: Cock: Bright red wattles on head; head, neck, and upper breast red-yellow; bright red over wing shoulders; blue across mid-wing; tips of wings yellowish red; long, narrow, yellow-red feathers fall away from back on each side; white rump patch; tail feathers long and metallic green-blue; breast and belly deep blue; length 26–28 inches including 11–13-inch tail. Hen: Head dull red; no wattles; back and breast marked dark and light brown; breast pale brown; tail dark brown; length 17 inches overall

Habitat: In teak forests; in deep forests during rainy period, near villages during cold weather; roosts in scrub, jungle surrounding paddy fields; often feeds in flocks in early morning and late afternoon

Voice: Calls of both cock and hen like those of domestic fowl; cock's crow is shorter, last note abruptly cut off

Nest: Made of few leaves at base of bamboo clump or of bush; breeds throughout year

Eggs: Vary in number; resemble small hen's eggs

Since all chickens have descended from the above wild species, any breed may be chosen to train as a pet for the home or the classroom, but the nicest of all is the Bantam. Probably nothing more thrilling can happen in a room of first- or second-graders than to have a Bantam hen produce a brood of chicks. Bantams may be purchased at pet shops.

HOUSING

Use small animal cage for headquarters and also as protection at night if chicken is maintained in classroom. Cover bottom of cage with 3 inches of coarse sand or bird gravel. Cover sand with thin layer of clean straw. Place perch across middle of cage about half way up; perches must not be round; use flat strip of wood with smoothed edges, and narrow enough for birds to grasp comfortably with feet.

NESTING BIRDS

Bantam hen preferred because of its small size, but large hen may be used if Bantam is not available. Bantam usually ready to nest by February or March. Provide square wooden box, 4–6 inches deep and large enough for hen to set in comfortably. Fill box with clean, soft hay. Place box in one corner of cage away from sides so that droppings can be easily removed without disturbing nest; prevent straw on cage bottom from becoming damp. Cage must not be in draft, too close to heating unit, or in too much direct sunlight. Incubation averages 21 days; begins when full clutch is laid. Number in clutch varies. Chicks hatch by pipping and pushing out of shell.

FOOD FOR NESTLINGS: For first 24 hours, chicks take no food. On second day, give stale bread or biscuit crumbs mixed with minced boiled egg (boil egg at least 30 minutes). As chicks become active quickly and need room to exercise, advisable to keep them in cage with mother 2–3 days only after they begin feeding; then return all to farmyard or supplier. Otherwise, at 2–3 weeks, give "pheasant meal"; also give hardboiled egg and green food, such as chickweed, lettuce, grass cuttings, and so on. At 5–6 weeks give chicks adult diet.

FOOD

In the wild, feed on grains, young plants, and insects. Containers not needed; birds prefer to pick food from sand and straw.

REQUIRES DAILY: *Seeds*—Give prepared "scratch feed," a mixture of wheat, buckwheat, and kafir; buy at feed store. *Green food*—Give grass cuttings, clover, cabbage leaves, lettuce, watercress, and chickweed. *Grit*—Essential; buy at feed store. *Water*—Must be fresh, clean, and available at all times; use water bottle.

REQUIRES OCCASIONALLY: Give finely ground fresh bone or meat scraps 3 times weekly.

BATH

Chickens bathe by rolling in clean, fine dust. Provide 18″ × 16″ × 6″ box filled with fine dust or clean wood ashes. Place papers or old canvas under box to catch material thrown out by dusting birds. Keep box in same corner of room all the time. Pet confined in classroom needs freedom for dusting; then allow it to be free in room several hours daily.

DUCKS: Genus *Anas*

MALLARD DUCK: *Anas platyrhynchos*

Range: Northern parts of Northern Hemisphere, Mexico, North Africa, and India

Description: Male has glossy green head; narrow white collar; body grayish, with chestnut breast; tail white with upcurled, black, central feathers; bill yellowish; feet orange; wing speculum purple-blue; Female is mottled brown with whitish tail, bill dark, patched with orange; feet orange. Wing speculum violet-blue, bordered with white when in flight; length 20½–28 inches

Habitat: Fresh water marshes, irrigated lands, grainfields, ponds, rivers, lakes, and bays

Voice: Male makes a quiet *yeeb*; female makes a raucous *quack, quack-quack*

Nest: Down-lined hollow placed among reeds or in grass

Eggs: 8–10 in clutch; greenish-buff

Ducks lack the intelligence of geese and are more difficult to care for in the open because they are untidy and need water. An adult duck may be kept in a cage for 2 or 3 days without great discomfort. Feed it grains moistened with water or milk. By the second day it will require a bath, a process worth watching. If there is a sink in a classroom, fill it with water. Use a large dishpan if a sink is not available. Place duck near the water and watch what follows.

A couple of ducklings may be maintained for a few weeks in a classroom and create a great deal of interest, especially for small children.

GEESE: Genus *Anser*

GRAYLAG GOOSE: *Anser anser*

Range: Throughout northern Europe and part of northern Asia

Description: Head and neck light brown; upper parts grayish brown, darkest on wings; shoulders and lower back and rump bluish-gray; tail ash gray, tipped and bordered with white; upper and lower tail coverts pure white; breast suffused with brown; belly dull white with few dark blotches or bars; both gander and goose marked alike; gander always larger than goose, but great variation in size among them; average length 30–34 inches; wingspread 36 inches

Habitat: On and at edges of lakes, bays, marshes, beaches along shore, over cultivated fields, and tundra

Voice: In flight, a loud, sharp, and deep, sonorous *ackh*, very like domestic goose. When settles down in a flock, a *clonking* clamor

Nest: Little or no lining; made in thick heather, grass, or rushes

Eggs: 4–6 in clutch; yellowish-white; once clutch complete, goose constantly adds down until all are covered

Geese make wonderful pets when one has plenty of yard space for them to live in. Naturally the adult bird is too large for a school pet, but a couple of goslings are suitable and create a great deal of interest, especially for small children.

Ducklings and goslings may be established and maintained as follows:

HOUSING

Make open pen out of large wooden box 8–12 inches deep (see Part IV). Cover bottom with several inches of clean sand of any kind. Cover sand with thin layer of clean hay or straw. Nesting box is necessary; use inverted cardboard box or carton with hole cut in one side for entrance. Place soft hay in box for warmth at night.

FOOD

Place all food in glazed flower pot saucers, which are easily cleaned. Both ducklings and goslings must have fresh, clean water available at all times; use widemouthed water bottle.

If goslings are but a few days old when brought in, they must be fed carefully; give stale bread crumbs mixed with small amount of corn meal and bran and moistened sufficiently to make crumbly. Ducklings that are but a few days old may be given finely chopped greens, such as clover, alfalfa, rye, and corn. Also give ducklings wheat, bran, corn meal, and hulled ground oats mixed with animal meal and just moistened with milk; add 1 part grit to 5 parts of this mixture. Grit and other foods can be bought at pet and feed stores.

At 8 days, give birds animal meal mixed with corn meal. At 4–5 weeks, give adult food consisting of cooked vegetables mixed with bran middling bought at feed store. At this point goslings should be returned to farm or supplier. Note that goslings should not be allowed to swim until all down is replaced by complete coat of feathers; otherwise, they may be chilled.

NATIVE WILD BIRDS

Among the native wild birds of the United States there are three fascinating rascals not protected by law which make intriguing pets. They are crows, jays, and magpies.

Wherever these birds occur in any numbers, they soon acquire the reputation of marauders and disturbers of the peace. Farmers and cattlemen seldom have a good word for them, and sometimes an ornithologist uses an invective or two toward these opportunists of the bird world. In no place in the United States do these birds receive any protection.* In some localities they are persecuted and indiscriminately shot. In many instances deliberate drives are made against them. Yet, in spite of all this, they seem to hold their own, thrive, and go on multiplying in increasing numbers. At the same time, they consume carrion and destroy innumerable injurious insects and their larvae, many destructive rodents, spiders, frogs, crayfish—and sad but true they also destroy native birds and their eggs, young chicks, and much young grain.

All three birds are cunning, mischievous, and intelligent, the crow and the magpie being the most intelligent of the three. The crow and the magpie are much more imitative, though the jay is clever at reproducing other bird noises. The crow is excellent at imitating the human voice, though the magpie surpasses it. The magpie learns to repeat words and whole sentences. It learns this by itself simply by hearing the words constantly repeated in the conversation which goes on around it. No *splitting of the tongue* is necessary to enhance its imitative powers. This is not only useless, but also it is *cruel*. Like so many other old wives' tales, this notion has been handed down

* The somewhat rare yellow-billed magpie is protected in California.

through the ages, and the average person, forgetting he has any reasoning power, accepts it, without thought, as a fact. The tongue of a bird primarily assists it in acquiring and manipulating food, while the structures in the throat have to do with the voice. Hence any splitting of the tongue cannot enhance the bird's imitative powers which, after all, depend upon the ability of the bird.

To rear these birds successfully as pets, they must be taken from the nest while they are fledglings. This means that they must be handfed, but the returns are so great in pleasure and entertainment that the effort is well worth it. It makes no difference to these babies that they are removed from the nest so long as their appetites are appeased. In a few days they lose all fear and are quickly responsive to the hand that feeds them.

CROWS: Genus *Corvus*

COMMON CROW: *Corvus brachyrhynchos*

Range: Throughout Canada south to southern United States

Description: Large, chunky bird; totally black; in strong sunlight shows purplish gloss; bill and feet strong and black; gregarious; length 17–21 inches

Habitat: Woodlands, farmlands, groves along rivers, and along shores

Voice: Loud, raucous *caw*; a little-known fact is that the crow does sing a musical, warbling song indulged in only when bird is far away from all outside intrusions and quiet surrounds it

Nest: Well-made bowl of sticks placed high up in trees

Eggs: 4–6 in clutch; greenish spotted with brown and gray

A pet crow which has been reared by hand will remain about its home until it learns to fly well. In order to keep it close after it is full-grown, it may be necessary to clip one wing. However, this deprives it of its natural way of life. It seems wiser to allow it to leave and take its place in nature. Often such a pet returns from time to time of its own free will.

A pet crow maintained in a school need not have the wing clipped unless children wish to play with it out-of-doors.

JAYS: Genus *Cyanocitta*

EASTERN BLUE JAY: *Cyanocitta cristata*

Range: From Gulf of St. Lawrence and northern Manitoba to southern Florida and Gulf of Mexico

Description: Large bird; bright blue above; head with crest; white bar on each wing; secondary wing feathers tipped with white; outer tail feathers tipped with white; white around eyes extending around throat; narrow black band outlining white throat

Habitat: In woodlands, groves of trees, and especially about habitations

Voice: Harsh, raucous slurring *jay*; also some musical notes

Nest: Bowl-shaped structure made of twigs lined with rootlets; placed in large bushes or trees

Eggs: 3–5 in clutch; color varies but always spotted

JAYS: Genus *Aphelocoma*

SCRUB JAY: *Aphelocoma coerulescens*

Range: From southwestern Washington, western and southern Oregon, extreme southern Idaho, southern Wyoming, south locally throughout western United States, west of Plains

Description: Head, wings, and tail blue; back light brownish; white line over eye; sides of head blackish; throat and upper breast white with dusky streaks; sides of breast blue; underparts dusky gray; length 11–13 inches

Habitat: In foothills where oaks and chaparral abound; in brush covers along rivers, in piñon and juniper forests, and about habitations

Voice: Harsh, rasping notes, some repeated in rapid succession

Nest: Twigs lined with rootlets; placed in bushes or low trees

Eggs: 3–5 in clutch; greenish, spotted with darker green or brown

Fledgling jays are hardy in captivity and develop rapidly when given proper quarters, food, and care. This means giving them plenty of freedom and things with which to play. Mature pets usually remain about the home and yard without the necessity of clipping a wing. They require close watching, however, while at liberty in the garden, as they have no fear. They must be protected from possible injuries and especially from cats.

MAGPIES: Genus *Pica*

BLACK-BILLED MAGPIE: *Pica pica*

Range: From southwestern Alaska, Saskatchewan (east of Cascade-Sierra Divide), central and southern California, south central Nevada, southeastern Utah, northern New Mexico, western Kansas, northern Arizona, and western Texas

Description: In flight, black and white bird with long tail; large patches of white on shoulder and in outspread wing; belly white, sharply cut off from black breast; middle tail feathers *very* long, each outer pair shorter; bill and feet black; length 17½–22 inches; tail 9½–12 inches

Habitat: In foothills, valleys; on ranches, in sagebrush country, along river thickets, in shelter belts, and prairie brush; in Alaska along the coast; often gather in groups.

Voice: Series of rapidly repeated short, harsh calls plus querulous nasal sound

Nest: Bulky structure made of mass of twigs, in center of which is placed deep cup of mud or cow dung, lined with wattles, pine needles, dry grass, and shreds of bark; two holes made, one on each side of nest, one for exit and one for entrance; usually returns to same locality to nest year after year; often builds on top of old nest

Eggs: 6–9 in clutch; gray-green, speckled and streaked with brown

YELLOW-BILLED MAGPIE: *Pica nuttalli*

Range: Only in great central valleys of California and adjacent foothills; also valleys of coast range from San Francisco to Santa Barbara County

Description: Same as black-billed magpie but has yellow bill, spot of bare yellow skin behind eye; length of body 16–18 inches; tail 9½–10¼ inches

Habitat: In groves of trees along streams, scattered oak groves, about ranches and farms, as well as about habitations at edges of towns; always in groups

Voice: Common note in series—short *eeck, eeck, eeck,* and a much lower *charr*

Nest: Bulky structure made of mass of twigs, in center of which is placed deep cup of mud or cow dung, lined with wattles, pine needles, dry grass, and shreds of bark; two holes made, one on each side of nest, one for exit and one for entrance; usually returns to same locality to nest year after year; often builds on top of old nest

Eggs: 5–8 in clutch; olive, spotted with brown or buff

Magpies are hardy in captivity when captured as nestling birds and carefully tamed, trained, and maintained. Time spent with them often results in a most interesting talking bird. But they require a great deal of freedom, as they are large and need exercise. They usually remain about the premises where they were reared and fed.

The above crows, jays, and magpies may be maintained as follows:

FLEDGLINGS

HOUSING: Use small, sturdy cardboard box filled with soft, warm cloths. Protect baby from chilling at night.

FOOD: In the wild, fledglings are fed only insects. Feed nestling food purchased at pet shops; also give finely chopped hardboiled eggs. Feed every hour at first; gradually lengthen to every 2 hours. Increase interval again when bird attempts to feed itself; at this point, add a few meal worms to the daily diet (see Part III).

HOUSING

Transfer fledgling to cage when it becomes active. Use commercial canary cage for young jay; large bird cage for crow and magpie (see Part IV). Cover cage bottom with thick layer of bird gravel. Place limb with sturdy branches in cage as perch. Train pet to use cage for headquarters by keeping food and water there. Birds are attracted by any small object that glitters, makes a little noise, or can be carried about and hidden; provide pets with bright trinkets such as buttons, big pins, colored glass, pieces of metal, and beads; when pet is at large, remove from room any bright object that can be broken, hidden, or lost.

Pets need much exercise; must be given freedom in room as well as in garden about premises. Hand-reared birds must be watched when they are outside to prevent casualties, as they lack the fear wild birds possess.

FOOD

In the wild, crows eat quantities of injurious insects, snakes, toads, frogs, many rodents, nestlings of other birds, wild berries, sprouting grain, and carrion. Jays feed on nuts, insects, grains, birds' eggs, nestling birds, and mice. Magpies are omnivorous; eat rats, mice, sometimes snakes, other birds and their eggs, grains, seeds, berries and other fruits, and carrion. Diet in captivity same for all three.

REQUIRE DAILY: *Animal food*—Give chopped raw meat, any available insects, meal worms, and raw or cooked eggs. *Green food*—Important; give fresh vegetables in season, such as green peas, fresh corn, fresh spinach; give those pet seems to like best. *Nuts*—For jays; in winter; give in shell; jays can crack them. *Corn*—For crows; give fresh green corn in season; at other times, soak dry corn in water to soften. *Fruits*—Give any pet likes, in season, especially melons. *Water*—Must be fresh, clean, always available; use water bottle; wash daily.

REQUIRE OCCASIONALLY: *Fresh beef bone*—Weekly; remove all fat and most of meat; birds enjoy working over bone. *Cuttlebone*—Necessary; keep in cage at all times; replace with fresh pieces monthly.

BATH

Use large, flat pan with 2 inches of water.

AMPHIBIANS

AMPHIBIANS make up a small and rather inconspicuous group among the large number of vertebrate animals, but the members of this group are almost the easiest of all vertebrates to obtain and to watch. Their activities, their habits, and their development from egg to adult are quite easily observed in the open as well as in captivity. Most are adapted for life in the water when young, and at least partly for land when adult. Because of this characteristic these animals have been given the name amphibian from the Greek word *amphibios*, which means leading a double life.

Many amphibians are small creatures, secretive in their habits and in some areas active for only short periods during the year. Others are sedentary or move about only short distances in their lifetime. Most of them commonly require water in which to breed, and all must live where moisture is sufficient for development of their eggs and to prevent excessive evaporation from their skins.

Amphibians may be characterized generally as follows:

1. Are vertebrate animals.
2. Are cold-blooded, hence are directly affected by temperature of the surrounding atmosphere.
3. Are found most commonly in temperate or warm climates.
4. Are usually aquatic in young stage and breathe through gills.
5. Are aquatic, semi-aquatic, or terrestrial as adults, and usually breathe through lungs; a few species breathe through the skin.
6. Usually lay eggs in water; if not in water, where there is sufficient moisture.
7. Eggs are covered by a protective albuminous jelly.
8. Skin is usually smooth, moist, and scaleless.

The class Amphibia is divided into three groups of animals, all of

82

which are related. The groups are: salamanders and newts, frogs and toads, and the caecelians, which are tailless, legless, blind creatures found only in the tropics. Since the latter are rare and seldom seen, they are not discussed here.

SALAMANDERS AND NEWTS

Salamanders and newts make up the one group of amphibians that retain their tails throughout their lives. The terms salamander and newt are used interchangeably, though there is a distinction between the two animals. Salamanders spend much of their time on land, while newts are much more aquatic. Some species of newts seldom, if ever, come out on land, and retain gills throughout their lives. Both salamanders and newts are indiscriminately called "water dogs," especially by children. In this discussion the word "salamander" is used to refer to all tailed amphibians.

There are many species of salamanders found throughout the United States and Canada with varying habitats. Many are entirely aquatic; others partially; and all these are found in ponds, rivers, streams, swamps, and ditches. Others may be wholly or partially terrestrial, and are found in forests and fields, burrowing in the ground, and living in trees. Regardless of the habitat, all must have moisture in which to hatch their eggs and to develop the larval or tadpole stage.

Newts belong to that group of salamanders that are generally considered as pond dwellers. They appear to prefer ponds that are not too deep and that have an abundance of aquatic vegetation. Newts seem to be restricted in their distribution also, as the greater number of species are found in the eastern half of the United States.

BODY CHARACTERISTICS: Salamanders may remind some people of lizards, as they appear to be built on a similar plan. However, the skin of the salamander is smooth; the legs are quite small; and the toes are without claws. In addition, the tail is quite long and is not round, and many of them are slow-moving creatures.

Eyes: Eyes, when present, are usually prominent on the head. When closed they protrude into the roof of the mouth, but they may or may not have movable eyelids. There is no nictitating membrane.

Ears: Salamanders have no ears, as such, but in some species the front legs, or the lower jaw, are adapted to transmit vibrations from the ground.

Teeth: Small teeth are present on the jaws. In some species they are also present in the roof of the mouth. Teeth are used for holding prey.

Tongue: The tongue is broadly attached to the floor of the mouth, or it is attached to the front and can be thrust out.

Legs: Most salamanders have four small legs of equal size, usually with four toes on the front pair and five toes on the hind pair.

Tail: The tail is long, seldom round, but flat on each side, and used for swimming. As it propels the salamander through the water, the small legs are held back against the body.

VOICE: Most salamanders are mute.

SHEDDING: The skin is shed periodically during the growth of the animal. It comes off in definite patches and usually floats away on the water. Sometimes it is swallowed as soon as it is shed.

REGENERATION: Salamanders have the ability to regenerate injured or lost tails or toes.

HIBERNATION: Some species of salamanders hibernate during winter months in damp, protected spots under cover or in the ground. During intense summer heat some estivate; that is, they retreat into some cool, damp spot where they remain until the temperature lowers.

FOOD: Salamanders are completely carnivorous. They feed on insects of all kinds, worms, sometimes other small salamanders. Large species may even take small frogs.

REPRODUCTION: *Courting:* During the breeding season male and female salamanders are attracted to each other by their sense of smell. It is apparent that the skin of the females possesses definite odors which attract the males, while the males have scent glands located at the base of the tail and on the under side of the head to attract the females. Once a pair has located each other, a rather unique courting process takes place which varies in its phases according to the species of salamanders. It may consist of the male rubbing his chin against the head of the female; or he may caress her by rubbing her with his tail. Sometimes he may carry the female on his back, or they may circle about each other in a sort of "dance." The entire process is in preparation for mating.

Mating: The mating process is unique among most salamanders. When the proper moment is reached after the courting maneuvers, the male deposits, either in the water or on the ground, a small, irregularly shaped bundle of jelly which contains his sperm cells. The female then picks this up with the lips of her cloaca where it rests in a small chamber and remains to fertilize the eggs as they leave her body. There are two exceptions to this procedure. The hellbenders, which are wholly aquatic, fertilize the eggs outside the body. That is, the male spreads his sperm over the eggs as the female deposits them. The sirens, which are also completely aquatic, are thought to fertilize the eggs in the same manner.

Eggs: Eggs of all salamanders are protected by a covering of albuminous jelly. Depending on the species, they may be deposited singly attached to water plants, strung along rosarylike, attached to pond plants or debris in a firm ball of jelly, or deposited singly or in bunches in some protected moist or muddy spot on land.

CARE IN CAPTIVITY: Many salamanders are excellent inhabitants for a woodland terrarium (see Part II), provided no more than one or two are kept at a time. Some will learn to take food from one's fingers, but they never respond in the same manner as toads and some frogs.

EASTERN NEWT: Genus *Diemictylus*

RED SPOTTED NEWT: *Diemictylus viridescens viridescens*

Range: Eastern North America, from St. Lawrence Basin in Quebec and southern Ontario to New Brunswick to Great Lakes and south to Georgia and Alabama

Habitat: Ponds, especially those which contain an abundance of plant life

Description of adult: Body drab-olive, but may vary from yellowish-brown to dark greenish-brown; row of black-ringed, red spots on each side of backbone; belly yellow with black spots; reaches length of 3 inches from snout to vent

Food: Consists largely of insects of all kinds; worms, leeches, tiny mollusks; and crustaceans, young amphibians, and frogs' eggs

Eggs: So small that they are difficult to find; deposited singly; fastened to water plants; female often uses hind legs to fold leaf of plant over egg to protect it; eggs hatch in about 1 month

Larva: Greenish-yellow with gray line on each side of center back; tail and body crest extend almost to head; buds of forelegs visible, also small gills; gills soon become large and bushy; aquatic larval period lasts 1, 2, or 3 months at which time larva loses gills, body and tail crests, develops legs, and a granular skin plus brilliant color; crawls from water onto land and becomes an eft

Red eft: Brilliant light red above; row of black-bordered round spots on each side of back; under parts yellow; stage may last 1 to 3 years, although in some locations it may be omitted entirely; at end of this period, eft returns to water and becomes aquatic adult; eft lives in moist situations in woods and is more often seen abroad than most other salamanders; it hides under stones, old bark, moss, and so on

WESTERN NEWT: Genus *Taricha*

CALIFORNIA NEWT: *Taricha torosa*

Range: Coast ranges of California from Mendocino County to vicinity of San Diego, and Sierra Nevada

Habitat: In and near streams and ponds

Description: Tan to reddish-brown above; under parts pale yellow to orange; light color of upper jaw extends onto lower eyelid; eyes of medium size, color greenish or yellowish with horizontal black bar across pupil; reaches length of 2¾–3½ inches from snout to vent

Food: Live insects, worms, and possibly smaller amphibians

Eggs: Deposited from December to May, depending upon location; laid in spherical masses of jelly attached to sticks, leaves, plant stems in ponds, streams, lakes, and reservoirs, often quite near surface; hatch in 5–10 weeks

Larva: Has well-developed gills, soon develops 4 legs; greenish-yellow and almost transparent; eyes prominent. Transformation may take a year at which time usually leaves water; remains terrestrial until maturity at end of third year when it returns to water to breed

MOLE SALAMANDERS: Genus *Ambystoma*

SPOTTED SALAMANDER: *Ambystoma maculatum*

Range: Nova Scotia and Gaspé Peninsula to central Ontario; south to Georgia and eastern Texas

Habitat: Common in woods, often hiding under old logs and rocks and in ground; more abundant in ponds during breeding period

Description: Large, stout body; black with row of black, yellow, or orange spots on each side; reaches length of 7 inches from snout to vent

Food: Live insects, worms, and other small amphibians

Eggs: Breeds in March or April; eggs deposited several days after fertilization; may be in single mass or several small masses; attached to submerged plants; protective jelly clear or milky; hatch in 1–2 months

Larva: Sandy or greenish-yellow, with darker spots scattered over back; buds of forelegs visible; dorsal fin high—extends to forelegs; metamorphosis completed in 2–4 months

Mole salamanders are so called because they spend the greater part of their lives underground. During breeding season, however, they gather in large numbers near bodies of water to court, mate, and deposit eggs. This is usually completed in a few nights.

EASTERN TIGER SALAMANDER: *Ambystoma tigrinum tigrinum*

Range: Long Island to northern Florida; Ohio to Minnesota and south to Gulf; absent from most of Appalachian uplands

Habitat: Under rocks, old bark, stumps near lakes, ponds, and slow-moving streams; during dry weather found in burrows of ground animals, such as ground squirrels, marmots, in crevices, or in rotted stumps and logs

Description: Color varies in different geographical areas, but most commonly blackish or sooty with spots, bars, or blotches of yellow, cream, or ash-white; under parts grayish fading into flesh color with indistinct yellowish markings; reaches length of 2–6 inches from snout to vent

Food: Live insects, worms, and other larval salamanders as well as its own

Eggs: Breeds December–February, March–April, or July and August, depending upon geographic location; eggs deposited singly or in clusters; attached to twigs, plants, weeds, and so on, usually in shallow water, quiet ponds, lakes, and reservoirs

Larva: Greenish-olive with sooty spots and blotches; undersurface

unmarked; gills and 4 legs well developed; in some locations larval
period requires 2 years; some larvae never attain adult form

WOODLAND SALAMANDERS: Genus *Plethodon*

RED-BACKED SALAMANDER: *Plethodon cinereus cinereus*

Range: South Labrador and Maritime Provinces to Minnesota;
south to North Carolina and southeast Missouri

Habitat: Vicinity of coniferous forests

Description: Red phase: broad band of red or orange from head
to base of tail; sides black; belly bluish-black or charcoal speckled
with whitish flecks; lead phase: back uniform dark gray or black;
belly same as for red phase; reaches length of 2½–3½ inches from
snout to vent

Food: Large variety of small invertebrates, including earthworms,
insects, etc.

Eggs: Breeds on land September–November; eggs not deposited
until following June–July; placed in cavities, in and under rotted
logs; fastened in small groups by common stem from roof of cavity;
female usually guards eggs; hatch in 1–2 months

Larva or juvenile: Hatches with short, flat, leaflike gills which disappear in 2 or 3 days; larva is now adult but has not yet attained
full growth; since it is terrestrial creature, has no need of gills or tail
and back fins; reaches full growth and maturity in 2–3 years

Woodland salamanders are widespread and abundant throughout
the forests of the eastern United States. They prowl only at night
and hide during the day. There is no aquatic tadpole stage as the
eggs hatch into a form that is like the adult but is small in size and
must grow to maturity.

WESTERN RED-BACKED SALAMANDER: *Plethodon vehiculum*

Range: Southwestern British Columbia and Vancouver Island;
western Washington, and northwestern Oregon

Habitat: Humid woods with damp and water-soaked soil; hides
under old logs, rocks, bark, leaves, moss, in crevices of fallen as well
as standing trees, and under other forest floor litter

Description: Well-defined stripe along back usually extending to tip of tail; stripe may be reddish-brown, tan, yellowish-tan; some without stripe; sides black or dark brown suffused with white flecks; undersurface sooty with bluish cast, yellowish or orange flecks and fine specklings of whitish; reaches length of 2–2¼ inches from snout to vent

Food: Live insects, worms, young stages of salamanders

Eggs: Deposited in spring and early summer; placed in damp places under stones, old logs, or bark, in rotten logs, or cavities in ground; hatch in early fall or winter

Juvenile: No gills; resembles adult with more distinctive stripe and less flecking with black; thought to require 3 to 4 months to reach adulthood

FROGS AND TOADS

Frogs and toads make up the group of amphibians that have no tails in the adult stage. Their bodies are squat and short. The front legs tend to be short, while the hind ones are large and long and enable the animal to hop, jump, or walk. The toes on the hind legs are webbed and enable the animal to swim. Frogs and toads tend to be small, with the frogs usually the smaller of the two.

These amphibians are found all over the world with the exception of the Arctic regions but are more numerous in tropical areas.

Frogs and toads too often are mistaken for one another, but there is a distinctive difference in appearance which can be observed easily by anyone. These differences are as follows:

Frog	*Toad*
1. Skin relatively smooth and moist	1. Skin usually dry and covered with warts
2. Moves on land by leaps or jumps	2. Moves on land by hops or a crawl-like walk
3. Body tends to be more slender, sometimes with a definite waist	3. Body squat and pudgy
4. Head tends to be narrow and long	4. Head tends to be short and broad
5. Must live in or close to water at all times	5. Obtains moisture when required by sitting in a puddle for a few moments; found in ponds only at mating time

6. Lives in ponds, pools, and streams, in damp cellars, holes in trees where water collects, and in and on vegetation at edges of pools or streams.

6. Lives in cool, damp, and shady spots during daylight hours and searches for food at night.

On close examination of the frog, it will be seen that there are numerous, indistinct, granular glands under the skin. These are mucous glands which help to keep the skin moist and extremely slick. Thus a frog is able to escape an enemy rather quickly.

Contrary to superstition, a toad's warts cannot be transferred to the skin of human hands. These warts have two important functions: The smaller ones, and by far the most numerous, are heavily thickened patches of skin that help to prevent excessive dryness. The larger granular glands, such as the large parotid situated behind the eye, serve as protection. These glands secrete a thick, sticky, milky substance which acts as a poison. They function only under pressure or injury to the toad. If the poison gets into the eyes, in open wounds, or is taken internally, it can cause severe irritation and possibly death. This has happened to young and inexperienced dogs that have captured toads.

To distinguish one species of toad from another is quite impossible for the layman. It requires the knowledge and experience of a person who has made a study of these friendly creatures. For the layman, it is enough to recognize that a toad is a very important creature in any garden. It is most effective in helping one to control insect pests. There should be comfortable hiding places in a garden for these friendly helpers, as many species have a habit termed "homing instinct." They choose a particular spot in some garden or park, which may be in damp soil under dried or decaying vegetation, under moss about edges of a pool, or inside drain pipes leading into pools or ponds. They wander from these spots during the night, often great distances, in search of food, but early morning hours find them back in their chosen homes.

BODY CHARACTERISTICS: *Eyes:* Eyes are prominent on the head; in fact they bulge. When closed they protrude into the roof of the mouth and thus assist in forcing food into the throat. Notice that when a frog or toad swallows, the eyes always close. A well-developed nictitating membrane is present in both frogs and toads.

Ears: Frogs and toads are able to hear very well indeed. The so-called eardrum, or tympanum, is a conspicuous circular membrane located just below and back of the eye. The dorsolateral fold runs above it on the frog, while the large parotid gland is above and back of it on the toad.

Teeth: Toads have no teeth, but some species of frogs have teeth in the roof of the mouth.

Tongue: The tongue is attached at the front edge of the lower jaw. The free end lies at the back of the mouth toward the throat. The tip of the tongue is covered with a sticky substance which holds the prey as it is caught and places it in the throat when the tongue springs back into the mouth.

Voice: The males of both frogs and toads have a well-developed voice. Many species of female frogs also have a voice, which is softer and less resonant than that of males.

SHEDDING: The skin is usually shed periodically during growth, then regularly after maturity. It is shed all in one piece. As it loosens it is pulled into the corners of the mouth and finally swallowed. The whole process takes but a few short moments.

REGENERATION: Frogs and toads are not able to regenerate lost or damaged toes.

HIBERNATION: During winter months frogs bury themselves deep in the mud of ponds and streams or deep in soil. Toads back deeply into their burrows, which may become covered with leaves and often with snow; there they remain throughout the winter months.

REPRODUCTION: *Courting:* Courtship among frogs and toads consists chiefly in the croakings or calls of the males which draw the females to them. This takes place very close to the water where mating and egg-laying will take place, and always occurs at night.

Mating: Once a mate is found the male grasps the female firmly, usually just back of her arms. The pair may remain in this position for several days before the female produces the eggs. As the female lays the eggs the male sprays his sperm over them. As soon as all the eggs are laid the female is no longer the plump creature she was, so the male releases her and they go their separate ways. It is thought that but one male fertilizes the eggs of but one female per season, but this is a question. However, a female that has found no mate does not extrude her eggs but absorbs them in her body.

Eggs: Depending on the species, eggs of frogs and toads may be deposited in masses on the surface of water; attached to water plants in small clusters; attached to plants singly; or wound about plants in long, beadlike strings. Eggs are always in a protective, albuminous, jellylike covering.

LARVA OR TADPOLE: The egg hatches into a very tiny creature which at first is flat and which spends most of its time for the first few days holding on to plants or other objects in the water. Small suckers on the head of the tadpole give off a sticky substance which enables it to cling to objects.

As the tadpole grows it appears to be made up of a round head-body and a long tail. Soon gills are visible on each side of the head. In a few days the gills disappear; they have become covered by a fold of skin called the operculum. The tadpole breathes by taking water into the mouth, passing it over the gills and out through an opening on the side of the body called a spiracle. This is usually located on the left side of the body.

As growth continues, the hind legs appear. They are very small when they first break through the skin but shortly take on the form of legs. Soon they, along with the tail, aid the tadpole in swimming.

Next the forelegs appear. They have been developing inside the gill chamber. Usually the left leg comes through the spiracle first. The right leg comes through the operculum.

It is now time for the head to begin showing the shape of the adult, and the tail begins to be absorbed. At this time the creature is unable to eat because of the changes taking place in the head, but the absorption of the tail supplies the necessary nourishment.

The gills are also beginning to disappear as the lungs develop. This is noticeable as the tadpole frequently comes to the surface of the water to gulp air.

During the tadpole stage, food has consisted primarily of plant life. Now it suddenly changes to that of small animal life. The tail is completely absorbed; the entire creature seems fully formed. In fact, it is a miniature frog or toad and is ready to shift for itself.

CARE IN CAPTIVITY: Adult frogs and toads make excellent inhabitants for a woodland terrarium (see Part II). Toads become gentle very soon and are most entertaining when capturing their food. Some of the larger frogs will become gentle also, but none responds quite as readily as do toads.

TREE FROGS: Genus *Hyla*

SPRING PEEPER: *Hyla crucifer*

Range: Maritime Provinces to northern Florida; west to eastern Manitoba and eastern Texas

Habitat: Marshes, swamps, ditches, ponds, and pools in wooded areas, especially where there is brushy second growth; seldom seen except during breeding season

Description: Skin smooth; color varies through shades of brown, gray, or olive; dark X-like cross on back, often imperfect; toes end in discs; small; reaches 1¼ inches

Voice: Single clear note repeated rapidly like high, piping whistle; large chorus of peepers heard from distance may sound like sleigh bells; male has throat pouch that looks like balloon when inflated as he peeps

Food: Terrestrial insects, largely winged, such as true bugs, flies, beetles, and so on

Eggs: Breeds April–June; eggs deposited singly, submerged among fine grasses or matted vegetation; usually near bottom of pond

Tadpoles: Require 90–100 days to complete metamorphosis

PACIFIC TREE FROG: *Hyla regilla*

Range: Pacific coastal region, Cascades, and Sierra Nevada; northern Rocky Mountains in Idaho; south into northern Lower California

Habitat: Ponds, springs, streams, irrigation canals, and vegetation about them; damp cellars, culverts; nooks and crevices in old buildings; often quite some distance from water

Description: Color varies greatly; may be green, shades of brown, gray or almost black; conspicuous blackish stripe from nostril to some distance behind eye; usually dark Y-shaped mark on head; several long, broken, dark stripes become bars, spots, or blotches; undersurface usually plain, pale yellow or whitish; yellow may become more pronounced toward tail and especially on undersurface of legs; usually reaches length less than 2 inches from snout to vent

Voice: Out of all proportion to size of creature; individual call a

2-syllable sound uttered in rapid succession; an entire chorus drowns out any other sound in area; croaking occurs during night hours; vocal sac swells out under chin like a balloon

Food: Terrestrial insects, largely winged, such as true bugs, flies, beetles, and so on

Eggs: Breeds January–May; eggs deposited in masses, close together, or separated an inch or so; attached to vegetation, such as sticks, leaves, stems of plants, and so on; always placed in quiet water to depth of about 4 inches

Tadpole: Blackish, dark brown, or dark olive, heavily spotted with black or dark brown; underpart whitish with bronze tinges; tail mottled with blackish

The most striking feature of the tree frogs is their ability to change color with their surroundings. An all-green frog when placed in a different environment may change to pale green, gray, or brown, and may even show patterns. These changes depend upon conditions of light, moisture, temperature, and general activity. It is fascinating to children to place these small frogs in a variety of conditions, such as a jar with moist, brown leaves, or bright green grass, or a mixture of both, and watch the color changes take place.

TRUE FROGS: Genus Rana

Bull Frog: Rana catesbeiana

Range: Every state with the exception of Alaska; has been introduced into western states

Habitat: Aquatic; prefers larger bodies of water, such as lakes, ponds, bogs, and sluggish streams

Description: Large, smooth-skinned; plain or nearly plain green above or with gray or brown markings on green background; underparts whitish often mottled with gray; yellowish wash on throat of males; largest frog grows 3½–6 inches from snout to vent—a record exists of 8 inches

Voice: Deep vibrating series of bass notes that sound like *jug-o-rum;* vocal sac internal, merely an enlargement of throat which makes flattened pouch when inflated

Food: Carnivorous; includes great variety of insects, small birds, small frogs, and young of turtles

Eggs: Breeds May–July; in southern range February–October; eggs laid on surface of water in large mass that may cover 3–5 square feet; usually hatch in 4–5 days

Tadpole: Requires 2 years to complete metamorphosis

LEOPARD FROG: *Rana pipiens*

Range: Throughout United States and Canada, but only along eastern borders of California, Oregon, and Washington

Habitat: Clear or murky water, shallow or deep ponds, or pools, cattail swamps, marshy areas, grassy overflows, in irrigation ditches

Description: Slender, smooth-skinned; ground color of black, brown, green, or tan; dorsolateral folds light in color; between these folds white-bordered, round spots irregularly placed; sides of body spotted same glistening white, occasionally light yellow; in Arizona *only* may be orange; reaches length of 2–4 inches from snout to vent

Voice: Both male and female vocal but female thought to be silent during breeding season; vocal sacs on either side between angle of mouth and shoulder; call resembles woodpecker tapping dead tree, followed by series of deep croaks

Hibernation: Burrows in sediment at bottom of ponds for winter months

Food: Carnivorous; includes great variety of insects, small birds, small frogs, and young of turtles

Eggs: Breeds February–December, depending upon geographical range; eggs laid in masses attached to aquatic vegetation; hatch in 2–4 weeks

Tadpole: Brownish with translucent tail crests; finely speckled with black; belly cream; intestines show through skin, reaches full growth in 2–2½ months

The true frogs are the typical frogs. That is, they are generally narrow-waisted, have smooth, moist skins, and long legs. The toes of their hind feet are webbed, but the fingers extend beyond the webs and are free. Some species have raised folds of glandular tissue along the back; some do not. The females of some species are also vocal.

True frogs are found all over the world but only the various species of one genus—*Rana*—are represented in North America.

The bull frogs, along with leopard frogs, green frogs, and the pig frog—all members of the genus *Rana*—are the creatures that give their lives so that restaurants may serve what was once only a Continental dish but is now also American—frogs' legs. It now begins to look as though this may be a matter for conservationists in the not too distant future, as these frogs are also used in experimental science laboratories.

TOADS: Genus *Bufo*

COMMON AMERICAN TOAD: *Bufo terrestris*

Range: Eastern North America
Habitat: Plowed fields and gardens
Description: Body short, broad; shades of browns, reddish, dark olive, or gray; patches of dark spots, with 1 or 2 *large* warts in each spot; belly dirty white with scattered dark spots; parotid gland kidney-shaped; reaches length of 2–4 inches from snout to vent
Voice: High, musical trill, of great sweetness; vocal sac expands into large bubble, flecked with charcoal-gray; may trill from middle of day to far into night
Food: Great variety of insects, both in adult and larval stages
Eggs: Emerges from hibernation in March, April, or May depending upon weather conditions; does not breed until rain pools available in which to deposit eggs; eggs laid in strings; wound about and through whatever vegetation may be at bottom of puddle; hatch in 3–12 days
Tadpole: Velvety black; tail crest translucent and milky-white; tail short with rounded tip; tadpoles group together; require about 2 months to complete metamorphosis

GREAT PLAINS TOAD: *Bufo cognatus*

Range: Great Plains from Canada to Texas, Utah, and extreme southeastern Nevada and California, and south into Mexico
Habitat: Grazing or farm lands; along irrigation ditches; flood plains; and overflow bottom lands
Description: Body broad; brown, gray or greenish; light middorsal stripe along back; back marked with spots; green spots on legs;

oblique row of green spots extending backward from parotid glands; underparts light in color; hands and feet light with dark tips; reaches length of 1⅞ inches from snout to vent

Voice: Harsh, vibrating trill, somewhat shrill. Vocal sac extends to enormous, sausage-shaped pouch which projects upward and in front of head

Food: Great variety of insects, both in adult and larval forms

Eggs: Breeds April–September, always after warm rains; eggs deposited in springs, small streams, flooded fields, and edges of large, temporary pools; in clear, shallow water; laid in strings

Tadpole: Black in early stages; becomes lighter and develops some patterns with growth; tail fin high arched with fine line of dark color; little color in lower fin

WESTERN TOAD: *Bufo boreas*

Range: Western North America from southern Alaska to Lower California

Habitat: Near large water courses, in tules about lake shores, along streams, and in mountain meadows and valleys

Description: Brown, gray, or green; light streak down back, sometimes broken; warts light colored, set in black blotches; undersurface whitish or buff with some dark spotting; female larger, stouter, and heavier than male; reaches length of 2½–5 inches from snout to vent

Voice: Low, tremulous notes, somewhat birdlike; calls uttered for second then repeated at short intervals; colony of toads at breeding time makes continuous chorus; notes on one pitch; no resonating vocal pouch present; tame toad held in hand often gives series of small, birdlike twitters pleasing in tone

Food: Great variety of insects, both in adult and larval stages

Eggs: Breeds January–July; eggs usually deposited in shallow water in strings entwined about vegetation

Tadpole: Black; tail tip rounded; tail fins translucent; with growth body and tail become stippled with gold which gives an olive-green color

The above frogs and toads are excellent inhabitants for a woodland terrarium (see Part II) when but one or two of a kind at a time are maintained. Toads become gentle much more quickly and are much more responsive than frogs, but some of the larger frogs will also become gentle to a degree.

All the adult amphibians discussed above are similarly maintained.

HOUSING OF ADULT AMPHIBIANS

As adults require space to move about as well as places under which to hide, set up regular woodland habitat in large terrarium (see Part II). Terrarium pool must be large enough and properly established, since moisture is essential at all times.

EGGS, LARVAE, AND TADPOLES

EGGS: Use medium-sized, flat-bottomed dish, enamel pan, old aquarium, or low aquarium jar. One egg mass in container sufficient, since eggs need room in which to hatch. Water should be cool; protect from freezing and overheating. Eggs must be well covered by water, except eggs laid on surface, such as those of bull frog, which must be placed in shallow water. Pond water is best; otherwise, use tap water if free of chlorine and other chemicals. Let container of tap water stand overnight to reach room temperature and evaporate chemicals. Change water every 2–3 days or add to it to make up for evaporation loss.

SALAMANDER LARVAE: Must be housed alone or with same size of own kind; even then may feed on each other. Use aquarium or aquarium jar. Provide sediment scraped from bottom of pond plus algae and pond weeds. These contain minute plant and animal life which serve as food and also as protection for larvae as they work through it. Place 2–3 flat rocks on sediment; one rock must extend above surface of water. Fill container with about 4 inches pond water; allow sediment to settle; when water has cleared, transfer larvae into it. *Food*—In the wild, larvae feed on small aquatic animals such as water fleas, fairy shrimp, daphnia, mosquito wigglers, and other salamander larvae; many of these can be bought at tropical fish shops. When hind legs develop, add bits of scraped raw liver to natural food; remove all particles of liver soon after larvae feed, as even slight water pollution kills very suddenly. Keep larvae supplied with pond weeds, since compact roots and stems contain much small animal life.

FROG AND TOAD TADPOLES: House as salamander larvae. Tadpoles may be housed together, but do not overcrowd; 6–8 tadpoles at a time in one habitat sufficient. *Food*—Native food, with few exceptions, consists of plant life; keep habitat plentifully supplied with aquatic plant life.

FOOD FOR ADULT AMPHIBIANS

All adult amphibians are carnivorous; in the wild, eat only live food. In captivity, give as much natural food as possible.

SALAMANDERS AND NEWTS: Feed on insects, worms, leeches, tiny mollusks and crustaceans, young amphibians, and frogs' eggs. *Mole salamanders*—Feed live earthworms; in addition, offer small strips of raw meat moved about as though alive. *Newts*—Give small pieces of meat; crumbs of canned dog food. *Efts*—Give live insects. *Woodland salamanders*—Give tubifex worms purchased at tropical fish shop.

FROGS: Feed on wide variety of insects and worms; largest frogs also eat small fish, small birds, and the smaller amphibians. *Note*— Frogs maintained in outdoor pools often leave pool, will even negotiate house steps, to get at screen door so as to capture night-flying insects drawn to door by light left on in room. This is fascinating to watch.

TOADS: Eat all kinds of insects—both adults and larvae—worms, and smooth-skinned caterpillars.

REPTILES

IN the large and varied group of reptiles are found some of the most grotesque creatures in nature, some of the most graceful, and some of the most beautiful in color and design. The word reptile implies to the average person something repulsive. This attitude is due to false fears and lack of knowledge. An interesting reptile maintained under proper conditions soon changes the observer's reactions and attitudes. Since the majority of reptiles of the United States are harmless creatures and excellent friends to man, it is worthwhile becoming acquainted with a few representatives.

Children have no natural fear of reptiles, least of all snakes. Fear of them is acquired through observing and imitating the thoughtless and uncontrolled exhibitions given by some adults. Children who have had this feeling of repulsion shocked into them can be taught to overcome it, or at least to reduce it greatly. Reptile pets are valuable in a school for this reason above all others. Experience has been that the reptile pets of a school room usually stand in the highest favor, and a snake is often the most popular of all.

The class of reptiles is divided into four groups called orders. The first order is made up of members now extinct with the exception of a single living species, the tuatara of New Zealand, which is lizard-like in form but differs from all other living reptiles in its anatomy. The other three orders are the lizards and snakes, turtles and tortoises, crocodiles and alligators (Crocodilians).

LIZARDS AND SNAKES

Lizards

Lizards are commonly distributed through the tropical and semi-tropical areas of the world with limited numbers occurring in the temperate zones.

Lizards and snakes belong to the same large order, and, though they possess many characteristics in common, each belongs to a distinct suborder. The layman is inclined to describe a lizard as a snakelike animal with four legs, eyelids, external ear openings, and a detachable tail. There are, however, many species of lizards which possess none of these characteristics; in fact, there are some that can scarcely be distinguished from snakes. The fundamental difference lies in the skeleton.

Of the large number of lizards existing in the world there are but two that are venomous. These are closely related, and both occur in the New World. The Gila monster (pronounced *hee*-la), *Heloderma suspectum*, occurs in the desert regions of southern Utah and Nevada, Arizona, western New Mexico, and Sonora, Mexico; while the Mexican beaded lizard, *Heloderma horridum*, is found only in Mexico. These two sluggish lizards do not strike as do snakes. They make a snapping bite at the enemy, get a "bulldog" grip with the jaws, and literally chew the poison into the wound. The teeth in the back of the lower jaw of these lizards are grooved, and when the venom is excreted from the poison glands, it is carried along the grooves of the lower teeth. In order to enter the wound, the poison must be worked into it by a chewing motion of the jaws.

These two lizards are not recommended for pets in the home or classroom, but can be maintained under careful adult supervision.

HIBERNATION: Many lizards hibernate during the winter while others remain active throughout the year. Hibernating locations are under rocks and stones, under the bark of trees, and in the ground. Early warm days of spring bring lizards out of hibernation, but a cold snap sends them back again.

CAPTURE: Food-getting is of paramount importance with lizards; hence, their attention is quickly caught by objects in motion. This makes many of them rather easy to capture. A green oat straw with a slipnoose in one end is a means of capturing such species as the fence lizards. The lizard becomes so intent upon watching the straw that it may be snared before it runs away.

Many lizards may be captured by quickly covering the entire body of the animal with the hand. In capturing any lizard, it is necessary to be quiet and quick, and to remember that the animal should not be grasped by the tail because some lizards detach from their tail when caught by it.

LIBERATION: No lizard, in fact no captive animal, should ever be set at liberty unless it is possible to set it free very near the spot where it was captured. When it is turned loose outside its own range, it is faced with unnatural conditions and often meets with a sudden, tragic end, and it may interfere seriously with accurate range records if found in localities where it does not naturally occur.

PARASITES AND DISEASES: Lizards and snakes are subject to certain species of parasites and to various diseases. The reptiles of a given locality naturally develop a reasonable amount of immunity to these difficulties, but specimens brought in from other localities transmit their parasites and diseases which generally prove fatal to the local reptiles. Specimens from zoos, circuses, and private collections should be carefully inspected before they are placed in cages with local pets.

Once parasites become established in a reptile vivarium, it is difficult to eradicate them. The wisest thing to do is to dispose of the pets, burn the cages, and make a new start.

BODY CHARACTERISTICS: The body of a lizard is covered with scales, but the scales are not covered by a delicate skin as they are in the snake. This gives many lizards a rough, spiny, or prickly feeling to the touch. The colors in the scales combine to form definite patterns or markings on the body of lizards. Lizards are cold-blooded creatures, hence feel cold to the touch.

Eyes: The majority of lizards in the United States have functional eyes with movable eyelids. The two exceptions are the geckos, which are night wanderers, and the rather rare xantusias or night lizards.

Ears: In contrast to snakes, most lizards have external ear openings as well as the tympanum or ear drum, which is nearly on a level with the skin.

Tongue: There is great variation in the tongue of lizards. In some species it is sticky, being used to capture insects in the same manner as does the toad or frog. In others it is forked, and colored, and functions as do those of snakes. Still others possess a flat, fleshy tongue which assists in pulling food into the mouth and acts as a sense organ as well.

Teeth: All lizards possess teeth, but no fangs such as are found in some snakes. The size of the teeth varies with the size of the lizard. Among those lizards which make suitable pets, none possesses teeth large enough to cause much of a wound, though they may just break the skin when they bite.

Tail: The tail is an important structure with many lizards. Some of the larger species use it as a means of defense by dealing blows with it. With some the tail is the appendage which saves the life of the animal, as it may be detached from the body, thus providing escape. The tail does not become disjointed, as is usually thought. The break never occurs at a joint but through one of the tail bones. The portion of the tail "dropped" wiggles and twists vigorously for some time after it has been detached. The tissue surrounding the area where the break occurs produces a rod of cartilage and connective tissue which forms a new tail, but it never grows to the graceful proportions of the original one.

Food: The majority of lizards are insect feeders. A few are cannibalistic, and some are nearly or wholly vegetarian, feeding on the blossoms and buds of plants.

Shedding: Lizards, like snakes, shed the skin as they feed and grow. As a rule it is shed in patches though some species, such as the alligator lizard, shed it all in one piece as does a snake. Many times the dry air of a schoolroom makes shedding difficult. No lizard is comfortable until all the old skin is completely shed. If the animal is having difficulty, try placing a moist cloth over it for a few minutes. This usually softens the dry patches of skin so that they may be removed readily.

Sex: Scientists as well as laymen have difficulty distinguishing between the sexes in lizards. There are too many small structural differences which vary with the species but are not obvious. However, in those species which possess gular sacs or throat fans as does the anole, the difference is obvious, as only the male possesses this structure.

Reproduction: Lizards may be oviparous, that is, egg-laying; viviparous, that is, bearing the young alive; or ovoviviparous, that is, hatching the eggs within the body so that the young emerge alive. Eggs of oviparous lizards are usually oval, soft, and tough-shelled, and are placed in some protected spot where they hatch by the warmth of the sun. The period of incubation varies according to location and temperature. It usually averages 8–10 weeks.

Size: Whenever the length of a specimen is given, it includes both the body and the tail.

Care in captivity: *Housing:* A great many lizards make interesting pets which become very tame and soon learn to take food from one's fingers. Most lizards are easily maintained in the woodland or desert habitat of the terrarium. As a rule several kinds of lizards may be placed in the habitat together. However, some species are cannibalistic and must be housed alone.

Temperature: Temperature is a most important matter with animals that are housed in all glass or partial glass cages. Not many people realize how intense the heat can become in such a habitat. The effect becomes that of a hot house. Sunlight may seem mild in the room and the temperature extremely comfortable, but under glass the temperature can and does rise rapidly. In such a situation the result can be the death of all the reptiles in the cage in a very short time. Great care must be exercised in the placement of reptile cages with relation to the amount of sun they may receive.

Feeding: Lizards feed largely on insects. However, there are many species which feed not only on insects but also on spiders and their relatives, on plants, and on small lizards, small snails, and even small snakes. It is necessary to know what the food requirement is for each pet.

ARTIFICIAL HATCHING: As a rule lizard eggs that are deposited in captivity seldom hatch because of the excessive dryness of the soil in the cage. Also, the eggs are small and are usually deposited in the debris of the cage so that they are not discovered until too late to save them.

Artificial hatching may be tried; when it is successful the thrill is worth the effort. Use a small box in which is placed a layer of damp sphagnum moss or damp, coarse sawdust. Place the eggs on this layer. Then cover them lightly but completely with the same damp mixture. The box should be placed where the contents may be kept at room temperature. The moss must never be too wet or too dry; excessive moisture as well as excessive dryness kills the embryos.

ALLIGATOR LIZARDS: Genus *Gerrhonotus*

ALLIGATOR LIZARDS: *Numerous species*

Range: Pacific Coast from British Columbia to Lower California, southern Texas, New Mexico, and Arizona.

Description: Olive-brown; body slender, covered with large square scales; deep fold running along each side of body; head distinct from neck; snout pointed; legs small; tail very long; reaches an average length of 15 inches

Habitat: In debris of underbrush; among groves of trees; under pieces of old bark; under dead logs; in oak and chaparral areas in foothills and valleys; in open grassy places; often along creek banks; among stones and loose debris such as bark and old leaves; in ruins of old buildings

Reproduction: May be either oviparous, ovoviviparous, or viviparous; number of eggs or young varies with size and species of female

In some species the resemblance to an alligator is striking; in others it is slight.

All are similar in habits and in their reactions to captivity. When alligator lizards are first captured, some have a tendency to bite; in fact some may be belligerent and put up a good fight. They are quick to bite, often jumping at the finger or hand with the mouth open. If teased, these lizards retain an irritable disposition. Because of this characteristic it is advisable for an adult to handle these animals for a time before children are permitted to play with them.

Alligator lizards tame readily and soon cease to bite anyone who handles them gently. It is well to remember to grasp the entire body of the lizard gently when picking it up, and to avoid catching it by the tail.

These lizards like to conceal themselves under moss, bits of wood, or in deep grass. These things should be provided for them in their artificial habitat. They are hardy in captivity, do not hibernate as a rule, and so make excellent winter pets for a classroom.

HOUSING

Provide woodland habitat of terrarium (see Part IV); keep it somewhat dry. As retreat, provide decayed stumps and small logs under which pet may crawl.

FOOD

In the wild, alligator lizards feed primarily on insects, though some species are cannibalistic. Feed live insects such as grubs, beetles, slow-moving bugs; other small lizards; meal worms in all stages of development. Place meal worms in shallow dish from which they cannot escape (see Part III). *Water*—Essential at all times; place in flat, open dish.

ANOLES: Genus *Anolis*

CAROLINA ANOLE: *Anolis carolinensis carolinensis*

Range: Atlantic and Gulf coastal plains from North Carolina to Florida and westward to eastern Texas; northward in the Mississippi valley to Arkansas and Tennessee

Description: Changes color readily; from dark brown to bright green with intermediate shades which may include light brown, yellowish-green, yellow, and bright green; gular sac or throat fan in male is bright red; female lacks gular sac but sometimes has faint spot of color in middle of throat; climbing habits are due to peculiar pads on feet which enable lizard to hang on to fairly smooth surfaces; when mature reaches length of 8 inches. Because of ability to change color, anoles are popularly but inaccurately called "chameleons."

Habitat: In trees, shrubs, vines, low vegetation, on fences, sometimes in old wooden buildings; requires shade and some protection; in dry areas seeks out moist spots

Reproduction: Oviparous; eggs deposited June–July; usually 2, buried few inches under loose, slightly moist debris; soft-shelled; hatch in 6–7 weeks

KEY WEST ANOLE: *Anolis sagrei stejnegeri*

Range: Key West and adjacent keys, Monroe County, Florida

Description: Changes color readily; throat faintly streaked with dark green; gular sac carmine at base, becoming maroon forward; when sac at rest, a wide, white streak present; reaches length of 6 inches

Habitat: In trees, shrubs, walls of buildings, and particularly on trunks of coco palms

Reproduction: Oviparous; eggs deposited June–July; usually 2, buried few inches under loose, slightly moist debris; soft-shelled; hatch in 6–7 weeks

Anoles are excellent inhabitants for a woodland terrarium. They make gentle pets and soon learn to take food from one's fingers.

They never eat bananas as the circus crier claims when he sells these pretty creatures. They lap the banana in a desperate effort to obtain the moisture which is so essential to their existence. However, the banana does furnish an excellent medium in which to breed fruit flies, a favorite food of anoles (see Part III).

Both anoles are similarly maintained.

HOUSING

Provide woodland habitat of terrarium (see Part II); plant or place broadly branching hardy shrub in habitat. In summer give pet run of screened porch, as it needs plenty of space in which to move about. Needs sleeping box during winter and cool summer nights of northern climates; fill any small pasteboard box with loose, soft kapok. *Warmth*—Anoles must be kept warm when removed from natural range; place cage in warmest corner of room during winter.

FOOD

In the wild, anoles feed on large variety of insects. Give flies, meal worms, cockroaches, young grasshoppers, small moths, fruit flies, and any other available insects pet takes (see Part III). *Water*—Essential; lightly sprinkle plant growth of cage daily during warmest time of day; anole laps drops from leaves of plants.

CHUCKWALLA: Genus *Sauromalus*

WESTERN CHUCKWALLA: *Sauromalus obesus obesus*

Range: Southeastern California, southern Nevada, and western Arizona, south to Yuma, Pima, and Pinal counties

Description: Young chuckwallas have several brown, broad cross-bands on body and tail; as young grow, bands break up and disappear; tail bands do not change much; general appearance of adult chuckwalla one of dull browns and reds, but great variation among individuals in intensity of these 2 colors; can change color in response to changes in temperature, motion, and especially to light

Habitat: Restricted to desert areas which abound in large rocks and boulders, and in ancient lava beds; hides in cracks and crevices of rocks, where it protects itself from capture by inflating lungs

Reproduction: Oviparous; 6–8 eggs deposited July–August in sandy soil or under some rock and left to hatch many weeks later; when pet maintained under proper conditions, eggs may be deposited in captivity

The chuckwalla is not hardy in captivity when removed from its natural range as it is almost impossible to keep it sufficiently warm. When a "chuck" lies sluggishly in its cage and refuses food, it is a definite indication that the pet is too cold. Unless the temperature can be maintained at 65–70 degrees F. during the day and dropped to 60–55 degrees F. during the night, the lizard soon starves to death. Because of this difficulty, it is not advisable to try to maintain chucks as pets out of their natural range. When properly maintained in captivity in their natural range, these lizards make attractive pets as they soon become gentle and accustomed to handling.

HOUSING

As pet needs much room, use large reptile cage (see Part IV). Cover cage bottom with 4–6 inches of building sand or fine gravel. Place cage where it receives greatest amount of direct sunlight throughout day. *Retreat*—Necessary; construct rock pile at one end of cage; place rocks so that lizard may squeeze in between them as well as bask on top.

FOOD

In the wild, chuckwallas feed entirely on tenderest plant leaves, flowers, and fruits. Give young, tender grass, cantaloupes, watermelon, bananas, lettuce, and some vegetable greens such as radish tops. *Water*—Obtains moisture from plants it eats; sprinkle greens lightly twice a week.

COLLARED LIZARDS: Genus *Crotaphytus*

EASTERN COLLARED LIZARD: *Crotaphytus collaris collaris*

Range: Missouri, south of Missouri River, westward and southward to southern California, northward in the Great Basin to Idaho; northern states of Mexico along border

Description: Body short, stout; head large and distinct from neck; hind legs long and powerful; tail long; color variable from yellow, pale gray or bright green, double black collar behind head, separated by yellowish space; when full grown, reaches length of 12 inches or more

Habitat: In desert areas strewn with rock piles which afford quick escape spots for these nonclimbing lizards

Reproduction: Oviparous; 4–24 eggs; deposited July–August, buried in sand under some rock, and left to hatch many weeks later

WESTERN COLLARED LIZARD: *Crotaphytus collaris baileyi*

Range: Southern and western Texas, westward to southwestern California, and northward through Great Basin to Idaho and Oregon

Description: Similar to *C. collaris collaris* but head narrower and snout longer

Habitat: In desert areas strewn with rock piles which afford quick escape spots for these nonclimbing lizards

Reproduction: Oviparous; 4–24 eggs; deposited July–August, buried in sand under some rock, and left to hatch many weeks later

Collared lizards may become gentle in captivity and may tolerate a certain amount of gentle handling. However, they are usually considered unpredictable as they often bite. They are among the most beautiful and interesting of lizard pets, and make a handsome addition to the lizard cage or the desert terrarium. They must be maintained alone, however, or with others of their kind.

Collared lizards are especially hardy in captivity when maintained within their natural range. They must be kept warm at all times, especially in winter, when maintained outside their natural range.

HOUSING

As pet needs much room, use large reptile cage (see Part IV). Place flattish rocks about for retreats and as basking surfaces. Place cage where it receives some direct sunlight during part of each day. Do not allow pet to become overheated or chilled.

FOOD

In the wild, collared lizard feeds on insects, small lizards, and snakes; blossoms, leaves, and buds of desert plants. Give meal worms, flies, beetles, grasshoppers, crickets, and, when possible, small lizards and snakes; blossoms of dandelions and clover (see Part III). *Water*— Essential; sprinkle plant growth in cage daily; lizard laps drops of water from leaves of plants.

GLASS LIZARDS: Genus *Ophisaurus*

WESTERN SLENDER GLASS LIZARD: *Ophisaurus attenuatus attenuatus*

Range: Mississippi basin, north to Chicago region, west to Nebraska and south to Louisiana, west through central and southern Texas

Description: Ground color of back buff with light stripe along middle; 3 dark lateral stripes on each side; lateral fold on each side; legless; reaches length of 14 inches

Habitat: Common in pine, flat woods, mesic hammock, borders of low hammock, and damp, grassy locations generally; apparently crepuscular

Reproduction: Oviparous; 8–17 eggs deposited June–July in loose debris; incubation period 56–61 days

EASTERN SLENDER GLASS LIZARD: *Ophisaurus attenuatus longicaudus*

Range: South of Ohio River and east of the Mississippi to the Atlantic and Gulf coasts; northward in the east to Virginia

Description: Pattern of cross bars on back; ground color dark brown; back of head spotted with dark brown and white; usually 3 dark stripes separated by white along sides of body; nearly continuous row of dark brown spots below lateral folds; ear opening roundish-oval, larger than nostril; legless; reaches length of 18 inches

Habitat: Common in pine, flat woods, mesic hammock, borders of low hammock, and damp grassy locations generally; apparently crepuscular

Reproduction: Oviparous; 8–17 eggs deposited June–July in loose debris; incubation period 56–61 days

COASTAL GLASS LIZARD: *Ophisaurus compressus*

Range: Coastal area and offshore islands of South Carolina, Georgia, and Florida, and sand pine scrub and adjacent flat woods areas of peninsular Florida

Description: Forward part of body heavily marked with irregular white spots; back uniformly yellowish-tan; 2 dark brown lateral stripes along sides of body; sides of head heavily marked with brown, yellow and white; legless; reaches length of 12 inches

Habitat: Common in pine, flat woods, medium dry, slightly elevated areas, borders of low hammock, and damp grassy locations generally; apparently crepuscular

Reproduction: Oviparous; 8–17 eggs deposited June–July in loose debris; incubation period 56–61 days

EASTERN GLASS LIZARD: *Ophisaurus ventralis*

Range: Atlantic and Gulf coastal plains from central Virginia through South Carolina, North Carolina, Georgia, and Florida, through eastern Louisiana, extensions along river valleys as far as southeastern Oklahoma, east central Missouri, and the Piedmont of Georgia

Description: Lateral folds on each side of body; also 3 narrowly separated black lateral stripes; back light brown; mature lizard appears to be green which is optical illusion; ear opening oval, larger than nostril; legless; reaches length of 14 inches

Habitat: Common in pine, flat woods, medium dry hillocks, borders of low hammock, and damp grassy locations generally; apparently crepuscular

Reproduction: Oviparous; 8–17 eggs deposited June–July in loose debris; incubation period 56–61 days

The glass lizards should be handled gently and with the greatest care upon capture, as the slightest roughness or injury causes them quickly to break their tails into several pieces. Since the tail is two-thirds of the body length, very little lizard is left.

The glass lizards are hardy in captivity when maintained under proper conditions.

HOUSING

Use woodland habitat of terrarium (see Part II). House alone; glass lizards are cannibalistic.

FOOD

In the wild, glass lizards feed on insects and their larvae, variety of spiders and other arthropods, small snails, small snakes, and small lizards. Give any available insects, meal worms in all stages of development, bits of raw meat dipped in well-beaten egg, raw eggs, earthworms, spiders and their relatives, slugs. *Water*—Essential; sprinkle leaves of plants daily; lizard laps drops from foliage.

HORNED LIZARDS: Genus *Phrynosoma*

HORNED LIZARDS: *Numerous species*

Range: Washington, Oregon, California, Nevada, Utah, Idaho, Arizona, New Mexico, Texas, Colorado, Arkansas, Kansas, North Dakota, and Wyoming

Description: Variations in sizes but all roundish, flat-bodied creatures, with fairly short but sharp-pointed tails; characteristic patterns in markings; colors in markings vary from light yellowish-brown to dark browns, deep reddish-browns, and tans; skin itself a pale yellowish-tan

Habitat: Found in almost any type of flat, dry land, in warm areas of their ranges, with scanty vegetation and sandy, loamy, or even rocky soil; strictly diurnal

Reproduction: Both ovoviviparous and oviparous; young of ovoviviparous species born fully formed, encased in thin, transparent membrane through which they break soon after birth; 6–12 young; oviparous forms deposit eggs in slanting burrow several inches deep, cover with soil, and leave to hatch several weeks later; young of both forms able to fend for themselves at once

Probably no lizards are more interesting or attractive to children than the so-called horned "toad." In every respect this little animal is a lizard and should be called horned lizard, but so long as children and adults use the other name it will probably remain. The characteristic feature is the presence of stiff, erect spines on the back of the head, though there are some members of the group which possess only rudimentary spines or mere tubercles or swellings in place of the spines. The skin is also covered with small spinelike protuberances.

Some species of horned lizards have the unusual ability to squirt blood to a distance of several feet from the eyes, which become swollen with blood when this occurs. A very complicated mechanism for increasing blood pressure in the head, plus a very thin nictitating membrane (third eyelid), make this possible.

Horned lizards are hardy in captivity when properly maintained. The secret is to keep a temperature of 68–70 degrees F. during the day. The cage should be placed where it receives some direct sunlight. When the temperature of the room drops below 70 degrees F., the lizards become sluggish and refuse food. Horned lizards also hibernate during the winter months; hence their cages should be set away in some cold anteroom or basement during this time, or the pets should be liberated in their own locality before this time. A pet lizard does not often survive the winter months in a schoolroom that is warm during the week and cold during the week ends. This variation in temperature causes hibernation to be intermittent which is detrimental to the pet.

HOUSING

Use small reptile cage (see Part IV). Cover bottom with 5 or 6 inches of ordinary building sand. Arrange growing plants characteristic of locality from which pets came. Arrange a few small, flat, irregularly shaped rocks to form shady retreat from sun. Place cage where it receives some direct sunlight. Lizard requires warmth to maintain activity, but care must be taken not to allow strong sunlight to pass through glass onto it; concentrated heat quickly kills almost any animal.

FOOD

In the wild, horned lizards feed on insects, especially ants. There is evidence that some species eat berries. Feed small insects such as crickets, small grasshoppers, cockroaches, beetles, insect larvae, meal worms, flies, and ants (see Part III). Food must be alive; give during middle of day when lizards are warmest and most active. Do not feed too many meal worms or beetles at one time or as steady diet;

hard covering of these insects eventually causes fatal intestinal diffi-culties. *Water*—Needed occasionally; lightly sprinkle plants once weekly, more often during extremely warm weather; lizard laps drops from foliage.

SPINY LIZARDS: Genus *Sceloporus*

NORTHWESTERN FENCE LIZARD: *Sceloporus occidentalis occidentalis*

Range: British Columbia, southward through western Washington and Oregon to southern California

Description: Gray, sometimes greenish; 2 series of distinct wavy bars across back; chin and sides of abdomen of male blue; scales keeled; reaches length of 6–7 inches

Habitat: About fences, piles of wood, sometimes stones, old brush heaps, roadside banks with dry vegetation, and old gopher holes

Reproduction: Oviparous; number of eggs deposited varies, placed in depression made in semimoist soil; eggs laid readily in captivity, but hatch only when soil moisture precisely right (see Artificial Hatching at beginning of this chapter)

SAN JOAQUIN FENCE LIZARD: *Sceloporus occidentalis biseriatus*

Range: Eastern Oregon and southwestern Idaho, through Nevada and western Utah, extending through central California to the coast, thence southward into northwestern Lower California

Description: Back brown, olive, or gray-buff marked with blotches or cross bands of dark brown; top of head same color with lines of dark brown; blue gular patch on throat; tail same color as back but with dark brown rings; belly grayish or near white; large patch of deep blue along each side of belly; females may have 2 lateral patches of blue; reaches length of 6–7 inches

Habitat: In rocky areas, on trunks and limbs of trees, on fences, and old buildings; not ground-loving but forages for food on ground; hastily climbs and hides for protection

Reproduction: Oviparous; 1–7 eggs deposited in depression made in semimoist soil; eggs laid readily in captivity, but hatch only when soil moisture precisely right (see Artificial Hatching at beginning of this chapter)

FLORIDA SCRUB LIZARD: *Sceloporus woodi*

Range: Peninsular Florida

Description: One of smallest of genus; brownish or olive-gray; seal-brown band on each side; male with iridescent blue throat patch enclosed by black band; scales keeled; reaches length of 5–6 inches

Habitat: Closely associated with rosemary bushes growing in open sandy areas

Reproduction: Oviparous; number of eggs deposited varies; placed in depression made in semimoist soil; eggs laid readily in captivity, but hatch only when soil moisture precisely right (see Artificial Hatching at beginning of chapter)

SOUTHERN FENCE LIZARD: *Sceloporus undulatus undulatus*

Range: Atlantic coastal plain from southeastern South Carolina to central Florida and westward in the Gulf coastal plain through southeastern Louisiana

Description: Gray, brown or greenish; narrow, wavy black cross bands on back; males with dark blotches under chin enclosing bluish color; 2 large bluish patches on abdomen; female with little or no blue; scales keeled; reaches length of 5–6 inches

Habitat: Common among old logs, stumps, and other timber of sandy pine areas; also frequents old fences and piles of wood

All these spiny lizards make excellent pets. They readily accustom themselves to handling and often learn to take food from one's fingers.

HOUSING

Use handmade glass vivarium box for 1 pair of lizards; small reptile cage for more than 1 pair (see Part IV). Cover bottom with 2–3 inches of sandy soil. Arrange bits of bark, dead and decaying small log, and a few flat rocks on sand to provide basking surfaces. For climbing, place heavily branching twig, strong enough to support weight of lizards, across one corner of cage; plant small boxwood or privet in another corner. *Temperature*—Advisable to move pets into cold anteroom where they may hibernate when winter comes.

FOOD

In the wild these lizards feed entirely on insects. Give flies, beetles, meal worms, other insect larvae, and any other available insects. *Water*—Essential; sprinkle foliage of plants daily, preferably during warmest part of day, so long as pets are active; lizards lap drops of water from foliage.

STRIPED SKINKS: Genus *Eumeces*

FIVE-LINED SKINK: *Eumeces fasciatus*

Range: Eastern United States and southern Ontario, northward to east central New York, upper Michigan, and Massachusetts, westward to central Texas, eastern Oklahoma, and eastern Kansas; northwestward along the Missouri bottomlands in Nebraska and South Dakota; absent from Florida

Description: Young are black with vivid yellow lines running down back and sides; tail brilliant blue; adult is dull olive-brown with bright red head; female has indistinct stripes

Habitat: Usually found on ground in moist areas under stones, in piles of leaves, in rotten logs, under old slabs of bark

Reproduction: Oviparous; 2–18 eggs deposited in clutches, number depending on size of female; female lies with body coiled about eggs until they hatch in several weeks

WESTERN SKINK: *Eumeces skiltonianus*

Range: South central British Columbia and Vancouver Island, southward in eastern Washington, Idaho, and western Montana, Oregon, and northern California, southward along the coast of California, into northern Lower California, southward in the Great Basin in eastern Nevada and western Utah into northwestern Arizona.

Description: Young are olive with 2 whitish lines running along each side of body, embracing a dark band; adult is olive with same stripes but much fainter; reaches average length of 6–8 inches

Habitat: In most of its range found among forests and low woods but also in grassy meadows strewn with loose rock

Reproduction: Oviparous; 2–5 eggs deposited in clutch under some protecting object such as rocks or piles of bark; covered with loose soil and left to hatch in few weeks

Young skinks are usually brightly colored, with 3–5 narrow stripes; the adults lose these bright colors and become dull olive or brown. Because of their brilliant colors the young are intensely interesting inhabitants of a woodland terrarium. Skinks are extremely agile and secretive in their habits.

The five-lined and western skinks are shyer than most captive lizards, but they will overcome their fear if those handling them are gentle, patient, and slow in their movements.

HOUSING

Provide woodland habitat of terrarium (see Part II). Pile flat rocks, slabs of bark, old limb or two over each other as retreat. Prevent habitat from becoming too moist. *Temperature*—Advisable to move habitat to a cool room so that pets may hibernate in winter.

FOOD

In the wild, skinks feed on insects, eggs of ground-nesting birds, newborn wood mice nesting in fallen, decayed trees. Give any available insects, meal worms, beaten raw egg, newborn mice when available (see Part III); occasionally give bits of raw meat dipped in beaten raw egg. *Water*—Essential; lightly sprinkle foliage and sides of cage daily; skinks lap water drops from foliage.

Snakes

Snakes and lizards belong to the same large order, and though they possess many characteristics in common, each belongs to a distinct suborder. The fundamental difference lies in the skeleton.

Snakes are highly specialized animals and beautifully adapted to their habits of living. Zoologists tell us that they once had legs and were lizards.

At present, there are 2,600 kinds of snakes in the world. Approximately one-eighth of these possess well-developed poison fangs; of these, little more than half are dangerous to man. In the United States there are only four types of dangerously poisonous snakes: the copperhead of the eastern and southeastern states, the water moccasin of the southeastern states, the coral snakes of the southern states, and the widely distributed rattlesnakes. All other snakes are harmless, and among them are many species which adapt themselves readily to captivity and handling. However, nearly all will attempt to bite when first captured.

HIBERNATION: Most snakes hibernate during the cold months of the year. At some time in the fall, depending upon the range, snakes begin to seek out hibernating locations. These locations may be holes under rocks, rock fissures, deep holes in the ground, natural fissures or crevices in the ground, used and abandoned ant tunnels, old rodent holes, and in the case of water snakes the mud in the bottom of wells. These locations are called "dens." Some snakes burrow into the soil while others merely crawl and squeeze into the openings they find. Snakes commonly hibernate in large groups. However, the individuals of a species are nearly always found together in their own group within the "den."

Many snakes that hibernate in their natural wild state do so for short intervals or not at all when maintained in a warm room throughout the winter. As long as the snake is warm and active, it must have food.

CAPTURE: All of the harmless snakes which provide good pet material can be caught by hand, but it requires stealth coupled with agility. One method is to sneak up from behind and quickly grasp the snake close behind the head. This prevents it from biting or struggling as it is lifted from the ground, and gives the captor the advantage in handling it while he puts it in a sack.

LIBERATION: No snake, in fact no captive animal, should ever be set at liberty unless it is possible to set it free very near the spot where it was captured. When it is turned loose outside its own range, it is faced with unnatural conditions and often meets with a sudden, tragic end, and it may interfere seriously with accurate range records if found in localities where it does not naturally occur.

PARASITES AND DISEASES: Snakes and lizards are subject to certain species of parasites and to various diseases. The reptiles of a given locality naturally develop a reasonable amount of immunity to these difficulties, but specimens brought in from other localities transmit their parasites and diseases which generally prove fatal to the local reptiles. Purchasing specimens from zoos, circuses, snake shows, and commercial snake dealers is very inadvisable because inspection will not disclose mites and diseases.

Once parasites become established in a reptile vivarium, it is difficult to eradicate them. The wisest thing to do is to dispose of the pets, burn the cages, and make a new start.

BODY CHARACTERISTICS: The body of the snake is covered with scales over which is a delicate skin. The colors in these scales combine to form definite patterns. A snake that is healthy and in good condition is glossy and shiny, but never slimy. It is cool to the touch because it is a cold-blooded animal.

Eyes: A snake does not have movable eyelids. There is an eye covering, however, which is a continuation of the skin and looks like a glass cap.

Ears: The snake has no external ears. Even the internal ear structure is rudimentary and is thought to function but slightly. The snake does not hear; it responds to vibrations picked up by the body from the substratum. Until recently it was thought that the tongue also caught vibrations of sound, but experiments have definitely proved that the forked tongue of the snake has little or nothing to do with hearing.

Tongue: The tongue is a most important structure. It is usually black, though it may be yellow, red, or green; and it is forked at the tip. When not in use it lies in a pocket on the floor of the mouth. It has nothing to do with poison, even in a venomous snake. It could not possibly pierce the skin as it is composed largely of delicate nerve tissue. Its function in detecting odors is to transfer minute particles from its tip to a structure called Jacobson's organ where "smell" takes place. The tongue does not detect odors by itself.

Teeth: Most snakes have teeth. Some have long fangs in the upper jaw which are connected with poison glands. Most have long, recurving, solid teeth, on both the upper and lower jaw, used for holding food.

Whether or not snakes are immune to their own poison has long been a moot question. No definitive experiments have been made, but many herpetologists have made observations upon specimens in their collections bitten by themselves and others when fighting. Sometimes the snake bitten died several or many hours later, but more often it showed no ill effects whatever. The consensus among herpetologists is that poisonous snakes are more or less immune to their own poison. However, before it can be stated as a fact, laboratory-controlled experiments must be performed.

FOOD: The food of a great number of snakes is made up largely of destructive rodents such as rats, mice, and gophers. This makes snakes highly valuable to agriculture. This is true of the poisonous as well as the non-poisonous snakes.

Capturing of Prey: Snakes hunt for and capture their prey in several ways. Some, such as the bull snakes and rat snakes, strike with the mouth open, driving their backward-curving teeth into the prey. These teeth help to hold the animal while the body of the snake coils about it, killing almost immediately. This type of attack is called constriction; it does not crush the bones of the prey but merely squeezes the heart and cuts off respiration, causing a quick death.

Other snakes, such as the garters and hog-nosed, capture the prey, such as toads and frogs, by grasping it with the mouth; they then begin to swallow it while it is still alive.

Another group of snakes, such as the rattlers, strikes the prey, driving hypodermiclike fangs into the body, at the same time ejecting poison from glands at the base of the fangs. This action takes place too quickly for the human eye to follow. When the prey is lifeless and all body movements cease, the snake proceeds to swallow its food.

Swallowing: A snake is able to swallow an animal many times larger than the diameter of its throat due to the unusual construction of the bones of the head. The lower jaw is not a single bone but two nearly straight bones joined at the front by an elastic ligament. In addition, the upper and lower jaw bones are so hinged that the lower may become detached or unhinged from the upper, allowing a maximum amount of stretching.

When a snake begins to swallow its food, it usually grasps it by the head. The upper jaw bone and the corresponding lower jaw bone reach over the prey, close down on its body, and grasp it with the backward curving teeth. This holds the body of the prey while the opposite sides of the jaws move forward, pulling the animal part way into the mouth. This is repeated, each side of the jaw working in alternation, until the food reaches the throat, which is elastic and stretches. At the same time the muscles of the neck move in a sinuous manner so that the food is literally held and pulled inward. This action assists the jaws. When the lower jaw becomes so distended that it is nothing more than a tight band, the upper jaw and the muscles of the neck continue to pull the food into the throat. If the prey is so large that it takes some time for it to be swallowed, the snake rests at intervals, during which it forces out, between the animal and the floor of the mouth, a tubelike structure through which it obtains a breath of air. Then it takes up the task again. When the food is finally swallowed the head resumes its normal shape, only a lump in the snake's body indicating what has become of the prey. After feeding, a snake is sluggish and usually conceals itself in some well-secluded spot until the process of digestion is well under way.

SHEDDING: Rapidity of growth depends upon the amount of food a snake obtains each season. During the process of growth the skin is shed many times. When it is time for a snake to shed, the old skin becomes dull in color and the eyes take on a milky appearance which is caused by the old glassy eyecap being pushed away from the new cap and the space between the two being filled by an oily fluid which creates opaqueness. This affects the vision of the snake with the result that it becomes more wary and more prone to strike during this period. The old skin is loosened by an oily substance which makes shedding possible.

The old skin breaks loose around the jaws at the line of the lips. The snake helps to peel the skin back by crawling among objects and rubbing against them. In this manner the skin is rubbed back over the head and the body while the snake crawls out of it in the same way as a glove is pulled off a finger. Snakes maintained under proper conditions in captivity shed perfect skins. There are times when the air of a room becomes so dry that the snake has difficulty in shedding. It is advisable to put a small pan of water in the cage if the pet shows signs of difficulty in loosening the old skin. When it refuses to crawl into the pan of water, the pet may be wrapped in a wet, soft cloth to help loosen the old skin. It may be necessary to wrap the creature a second time, though one application of the wet cloth is usually sufficient to soften the old skin so that it may be shed.

SEX: Since the sex of snakes is much less obvious in some species than in others, it is not always easy to determine this feature. In a male snake the tail tends to be a smooth continuation of the body, while in the female the tail tends to be narrower than the body. In other words, the tails of males are longer and thicker while with females there tends to be a constriction where the tail begins.

REPRODUCTION: Snakes, like lizards, are oviparous, ovoviviparous, or viviparous.

Oviparous snakes lay eggs which are deposited in some secluded spot where conditions of heat and moisture are just right to incubate the eggs.

Ovoviviparous snakes produce the young fully formed but tightly coiled in a thin, transparent membrane. Sometimes this membrane bursts during the process of birth and the young appear to crawl from the mother's body. Usually the membrane is broken by the use of the temporary egg tooth when the young snake struggles to straighten out.

When the young are born alive, the snake is said to be viviparous.

CARE IN CAPTIVITY: *Housing:* Many of the harmless snakes make interesting and excellent pets. A few species can be made comfortable in the woodland habitat of a terrarium, but the remainder should be established in special snake cages (see Part IV).

Temperature: Temperature is a most important matter with animals that are housed in all-glass or part-glass cages. Not many people realize how intense the heat can become in such a habitat. The effect becomes that of a hothouse. Sunlight may seem mild in the room and the temperature extremely comfortable, but under glass the temperature rises rapidly. In such a situation the result can be the death of all the reptiles in the cage in a very short time. Great care must be exercised in the placement of reptile cages with relation to the amount of sun they receive.

Feeding: Sometimes snakes refuse to eat when several are housed together. When this occurs, the one refusing food should be placed by itself and fed alone. Even then it may still persistently refuse food, in which case it should be liberated. No snake, when first captured, will feed with an audience standing about the cage. After a snake becomes gentle, and used to handling and seeing people about, it feeds naturally without being disturbed by the presence of observers. Until this stage is reached, food should be placed in the cage when the room is quiet. No snake should be handled just after feeding. Snakes are sensitive to sudden, jerky movements and respond with lightning rapidity. The person placing food in the snake's cage should be slow and deliberate in his movements.

Many captive snakes will feed on live white mice and rats. Sometimes a snake refuses to take the pure white strains but feeds readily on the colored ones. The rule is to feed small snakes about once a week, the large ones every ten days. However, a pet may go for a longer period before it feeds, and a few feed more often. Snakes usually indicate their desire for food by nervously moving about the cage.

It must be remembered, however, that some snakes feed on other snakes, some feed on frogs, and some small ground varieties feed on insects, slugs, and lizards.

Many captive snakes often accept freshly killed food when it is dropped in their cages. There is an advantage to this type of feeding as it prevents any large rodent from biting the snake if the rodent is not killed at once by the snake. It also prevents the snake from bruising its nose in case it should miss the rodent and strike the side of the cage. Many excellent specimens have been injured seriously by such action.

When a pet snake refuses to take freshly killed food, it is advisable to place only one small rat in the cage at a time. If the snake is not hungry and refuses to attack the rat in a short time, the rat should be removed from the cage. Never leave a live rat in a cage with a snake overnight for the rat will often kill the snake, even a rattlesnake.

ARTIFICIAL HATCHING: Snake eggs deposited in captivity seldom hatch because of the excessive dryness of the soil of the cage. They will hatch, however, if removed from the cage and placed in a container with the exact amount of moisture and the proper temperature. This is a great gamble but always worth trying, for a hatching snake is one of the most fascinating of sights.

Artificial hatching may be tried out in two ways. One is to place the eggs in a box filled with damp sphagnum moss. The eggs must be placed in such a way as to leave a thick layer of damp moss both below and above them. The moss (and here, apparently, lies the secret of success) must not be too wet nor must it become too dry. Excessive moisture or dryness kills the embryo. The box should be placed where the contents may be kept at a constant room temperature.

The second method is to place very damp paper toweling in the bottom of a glass dish. The eggs should be placed on this moist paper and the dish covered. The dish must be put where the room temperature will be constant. Incubation takes several weeks. If conditions are right, this will be indicated by the changing shape of the egg as the embryo develops.

BULL SNAKES: Genus *Pituophis*

PACIFIC GOPHER SNAKE: *Pituophis catenifer catenifer*

Range: British Columbia, Washington and Oregon, west of the Cascades, and California west of the Sierra Nevada, southward to the northern boundary of Santa Barbara County
Description: Yellowish ground color; blotches along back and sides vary from black to reddish brown; attains average length of 4 feet
Habitat: Entirely terrestrial; prefers areas with thick, protective covering of vegetation
Reproduction: Oviparous; 10–20 eggs deposited May–July; sometimes female coils about eggs until they hatch

The Pacific gopher snake is hardy in captivity, long-lived, and becomes gentle in a short time. It has a tendency to grow fat, lazy, and pampered, but is much beloved by children because of the complacency with which it allows itself to be handled.

This snake can be given more exercise by hanging a branching limb out of the edge of the cage or placing a good-sized, heavy branch in one corner of the room and allowing the pet to move about in it during the day.

BULL SNAKE: *Pituophis catenifer sayi*

Range: Southern Alberta and Saskatchewan, southward through the Great Plains and Prairie states, east of the Rockies, into northeastern Mexico, eastward through southern North Dakota into southwestern Minnesota, and southwestern Wisconsin, parts of Illinois, and adjacent Indiana, throughout Missouri, except extreme southeastern area, northwestern Arkansas
Description: Ground color greenish, orange, reddish, or orangeyellow; square reddish-brown or black blotches down back; smaller and lighter blotches along sides; belly yellow with dark blotches; bull snake may be distinguished from the other harmless blotched

snakes in its range by its keeled scales and single anal plate; attains average length of 5 feet, maximum of 8

Habitat: Meadows, grass lands, cultivated agricultural areas, vacant farm buildings, trees, and areas where rodents abound

Reproduction: Oviparous; 5–20 eggs; rough-skinned, leathery, adhere to each other; deposited July–August; hatch August–October

The bull snake ranks high in the economic scale because its food consists primarily of those rodents that are destructive to farm crops. It is fairly hardy in captivity but frequently refuses to eat.

PINE SNAKE: *Pituophis melanoleucus*

Range: Eastern United States

Description: Ground color dull white; row of large black blotches not sharply defined along back, far apart on latter portion of body; row of smaller blotches on each side; tail ends in hard spine; belly white; head small; snout pointed; good field characteristic for identification of pine snake is its habit of hissing loudly and sharply when alarmed; attains average length of 5 feet, maximum of 7½

Habitat: Pine forests along coast with sandy soil

Reproduction: Oviparous; 7–24 eggs deposited May–July in small burrows in sand; adhere to each other in cluster

As a rule, pine snakes are ill-tempered in captivity. Only occasionally does one become gentle enough not to resent handling; hence, they are not good pet material. When such a specimen is brought in, it should be kept for a few days for observation only and then released in the locality from which it was captured.

The pine snake ranks high in the economic scale because its food consists primarily of those rodents that are destructive to farm crops.

HOUSING

Use large reptile cage (see Part IV), as bull snakes need room. Cover bottom of cage with thick layer of pea gravel. Pile a few broad, flat rocks and pieces of old rotted logs at one end of cage as retreat. Provide sturdy, branching limb across back of cage for climbing. Place cage where it receives some sunshine daily; protect from overheating and chilling.

FOOD

Feed native food listed below. As bull snakes are constrictors, they may take freshly killed food dropped in cage (see Feeding, above). All species need water; use small flat, container; place in center of cage.

NATIVE FOOD: *Pacific gopher and bull snakes*—Rodents, birds, nestlings, birds' eggs. *Pine snake*—Young rabbits, squirrels, other rodents, birds and their eggs.

GARTER SNAKES: Genus *Thamnophis*

MOUNTAIN GARTER SNAKE: *Thamnophis elegans elegans*

Range: Southern Oregon, between Coast Range and Cascades from southern end of Willamette Valley southward; northern California, southward on the coast to Napa County; southward east of the Sacramento Valley in the Sierra Nevada (in California and Nevada) to Fresno County, with an isolated population in the San Bernardino Mountains

Description: Black above with broad ocher middorsal stripe; lateral greenish-white stripe along each side; underside grayish-drab; reaches length of 32 inches

Habitat: Near mountain streams and ponds and in open pine and oak woods

Reproduction: Viviparous; 4–27 young dropped at a time, depending on size of snake; able to fend for themselves at once

EASTERN RIBBON SNAKE: *Thamnophis sauritus sauritus*

Range: Michigan and Ontario to Maine, southward to Mississippi, Alabama, and Georgia

Description: Glossy black with wide yellow middorsal stripe; narrower stripe of same color along each side; chin and throat white; belly pale greenish-yellow; tail fully half length of body; reaches length of 36 inches

Habitat: In vicinity of streams, ponds, lakes; in swamps and marshes; damp meadows and woodlands

Reproduction: Viviparous; 3–20 young dropped at a time, depending on size of snake; able to fend for themselves at once

WESTERN RIBBON SNAKE: *Thamnophis sauritus proximus*

Range: In central United States, eastern Louisiana west of Mississippi River to southern Illinois, east of Wabash Valley to southwestern Michigan; southern Wisconsin across Iowa, eastern Nebraska, Kansas to eastern New Mexico; thence southeast to Mexico; also in Arkansas, Colorado, Iowa, Illinois, Indiana, Kansas, Louisiana, Minnesota, Mississippi, Missouri, Nebraska, New Mexico, Oklahoma, South Dakota, Texas, and Wisconsin

Description: Upper part black or very dark brown; middorsal stripe yellowish; 2 lateral stripes yellowish; throat and lower part of neck white; belly greenish-white. Tail less than one-third length of body; reaches length of 50 inches

Habitat: In plant growth along borders and edges of bodies of water; in creek bottoms, lowlands, and overflow lands

Reproduction: Viviparous; 4–11 young dropped at a time, depending on size of snake; able to fend for themselves at once.

Garter snakes are the most abundant of all North American serpents. They are found all over the continent where snakes of any kind occur. There are many species and subspecies of which the foregoing are merely selected examples.

Garter snakes are hardy in captivity and make good pet material. They often become so gentle that they take food from one's fingers. They discharge a malodorous substance from the glands at the base of the tail when first captured, but this does not occur often after the snake loses its fear.

HOUSING

Garters need ample room; use woodland habitat of terrarium (see Part II). Cover bottom with layer of charcoal topped by thick layer of humus mixed with leaf mold. Cover soil at one end of cage with sod that has heavy growth of grasses, reeds, or weeds brought from area where pet was captured; as garters like to crawl and hunt through moist areas, keep sod damp at all times. At other end of cage, place large section of old bark and piece of old log. Also provide heavy branching limb, strong enough to support weight of snake, along side of cage, as garters sometimes climb. Place habitat where it receives some sunlight each morning; protect it from overheating.

FOOD

In the wild, garters feed on slugs, toads, frogs, lizards, mice, earthworms, salamanders, shrews, fish, spiders, and insects; food is grasped by mouth and held down by part of body while it is swallowed live. Give native food plus meal worms; some garters learn to eat bits of meat rubbed with flesh of fish. *Water*—Necessary; use large, flat container; place in center of terrarium close to green area.

GREEN SNAKES: Genus *Opheodrys*

EASTERN ROUGH GREEN SNAKE: *Opheodrys aestivus aestivus*

Range: From southwestern Connecticut in Coastal plain and the Piedmont to Florida; west to Mexico; northwest to southeast New Mexico; northeast across Texas and Oklahoma, to southeastern Kansas; across Missouri, southeastern Iowa, and Illinois, Indiana, and Ohio to Allegheny Mountains
Description: Primarily green; underside of head white; belly pale yellow-green; reaches length of 47 inches
Habitat: Arboreal; always found climbing about in low shrubbery
Reproduction: Oviparous; 4–11 eggs, depending on size of snake, deposited July–August; hatch August–September

EASTERN SMOOTH GREEN SNAKE: *Opheodrys vernalis vernalis*

Range: Glaciated and mountainous areas of northeastern North America east of prairie-forest border, southward to Madison County, North Carolina
Description: Small, smooth-skinned; all green; tail long; underside of head light; reaches length of 26 inches
Habitat: In grass-covered fields, meadows, low bush areas, and sphagnum moss bogs
Reproduction: Oviparous; 3–12 eggs, depending on size of snake, deposited July–August; hatch August–September

WESTERN SMOOTH GREEN SNAKE: *Opheodrys vernalis blanchardi*

Range: Northern Great Plains and prairie region, westward to Black Hills, and in Rocky Mountains, in Colorado and New Mexico

Description: Similar to eastern smooth green but underside of head, neck, and chin white; underside of tail sulphur-yellow; reaches length of 24 inches

Habitat: In low bush country, upland prairies, and such places as supply basking surfaces with retreats close by

Reproduction: Oviparous; 6–12 eggs, depending on size of snake, deposited July–August; hatch August–September

HOUSING

Green snakes are hardier when given plenty of room; use large reptile cage (see Part IV). Cover bottom with thick layer of pea gravel topped by 2–3 inches leaf mold. Provide several potted shrubs and large, well-branched limb for climbing. Construct retreat of low, flat rocks, piled casually over each other and leaning against flower pot. Place large piece of sod planted with tall grass on top of leaf mold at one end of cage. Place cage where it receives some direct sunlight daily; protect it from overheating and chilling.

FOOD

Green snakes are not constrictors. In the wild, they feed on insects, smooth-skinned caterpillars, spiders, snails, slugs, centipedes, and frogs. Give grasshoppers, crickets, spiders, meal worms—try as many varieties of food as available; also try frogs, snails, slugs (see Part III). Sometimes a smooth green snake will take only smooth-skinned caterpillars; advisable to liberate it when its natural food is no longer available; set it free in area where it was captured. *Water*—Use flat, open container; place in center of cage.

HOGNOSE SNAKES: Genus *Heterodon*

PLAINS HOGNOSE SNAKE: *Heterodon nasicus nasicus*

Range: Second tier of states west of the Mississippi to the Rocky Mountains, with an isolated colony in the sand region near Havana, Illinois, southward to New Mexico and adjacent northeastern Mexico

Description: Identified at once by presence of black area covering central portion of abdomen; reaches length of 25 inches

Habitat: Always found in sandy areas regardless of whether it is plain, hill, river, or grassy meadow land

Reproduction: Oviparous; 5–24 eggs, depending on size of snake, deposited July–August

Mexican Hognose Snake: *Heterodon nasicus kennerlyi*

Range: Tres-Pecos, Texas, and southern New Mexico; southward into Mexico
Description: Differs from others in number of scales of head; undersurface black and white spotted; probably attains average length of 20 inches
Habitat: Sandy areas
Reproduction: Oviparous; average of 7 eggs; deposited in June

Eastern Hognose Snake: *Heterodon platyrhinos platyrhinos*

Range: Eastern United States, southward from New Hampshire to central Florida; westward through Ontario to Minnesota, and present in all the first tier of states west of the Mississippi
Description: Body brown, red, or yellow with large patches of dark brown or black from neck to base of tail; patches become half rings on tail; alternating small blotches run along each side; sides of abdomen spotted with black; abdomen yellowish or greenish; great variation in color and pattern from dark gray to slaty black with no patterns at all; reaches length of 42 inches
Habitat: Thickly wooded, dry, sandy areas, preferably on hillsides or so-called uplands
Reproduction: Oviparous; 6–42 eggs, depending on size of female, deposited June–August

South Florida Hognose Snake: *Heterodon platyrhinos browni*

Range: Eastern Dade County, Florida
Description: Back with 17 black saddles on body, 8 on tail, with small, round, alternating spots along sides; light area below spots; reaches length of 30 inches
Habitat: Palmetto and limestone flat woods; in hothouses, and in truck crop fields
Reproduction: Oviparous

Southern Hognose Snake: *Heterodon simus*

Range: North Carolina southward to central Florida; northwestward to Indiana

Description: Stout; pale, brownish-gray to yellow; blackish-brown patches along back; alternating small spots along side; abdominal surface mostly light, unspotted; reaches length of 24 inches
Habitat: Sandy country
Reproduction: Oviparous

This snake is called hognose because of its peculiar upturned, shovellike snout which looks like a hog's nose.

All hognose snakes are prize bluffers. They are unique in their attempts to save themselves from danger. When frightened, they flatten the head and neck in such a way as to resemble those of a cobra, and hiss loudly. If the danger does not remove itself, the snake flops over on its back and simulates death.

A hognose snake seldom attempts to bite. All become extremely gentle in captivity, make excellent pets, and tolerate much handling.

HOUSING

Requires ample room; use large reptile cage (see Part IV). Cover cage bottom with thick layer of pea gravel topped by 2–3 inches of coarse sand and sandy soil. Pile several broad, flat rocks over each other casually to form retreat; do not place rocks against long sides of cage as hognoses like to stretch full length along sides. Place cage where it receives partial sunshine during part of day; protect from drafts, overheating, and chilling.

FOOD

Hognoses are not constrictors; food is grasped by mouth and held down by part of body while it is swallowed live. In the wild, hognoses feed on toads, frogs, rats, mice, chipmunks, small birds, insects, worms, salamanders, small snakes, lizards. Give native food. *Water—* Use large flat container; place in center of cage.

INDIGO SNAKES: Genus *Drymarchon*

EASTERN INDIGO SNAKE: *Drymarchon corais couperi*

Range: South Carolina to Florida and west to Louisiana, in the Atlantic and Gulf coastal plains
Description: Entire body shiny bluish-black, including belly, with

exception of chin and sides of head which may be reddish or orange-brown; scales smooth; reaches length of 8½ feet

Habitat: Sandy palmetto-covered hills, along roadsides of pine barrens, on sandy oak ridges, or in moist localities

Reproduction: Oviparous; 5 or more eggs

Texas Indigo Snake: *Drymarchon corais erebennus*

Range: Central southern Texas; southward into adjacent Mexico

Description: Mixed brown and black; blue-black toward tail; top of head reddish-brown; underchin white or pale buff; forward half of belly salmon-colored; rear half gray; averages 7 feet

Habitat: Cane fields, savannas, woods, thickets about shores of ponds and streams; chiefly a ground snake but sometimes climbs on top of low bushes to bask in sun

Reproduction: Oviparous

The indigo snakes are the most delightful of all snake pets and are great favorites with children. They are good fighters when cornered. Some species flatten the neck vertically, hiss, and rapidly vibrate the tail, which produces a rattling sound. But once captured, they seldom attempt to bite, become tame quickly, and are generally hardy in captivity. Some appear to like being handled, while others may be restless when held.

HOUSING

Indigo snakes need much room; must be housed alone. Need large reptile cage (see Part IV), freedom of room, and provision for crawling. Cover cage bottom with thick layer of pea gravel. Provide good-sized, heavy, branching limb in cage. In room, provide very large, heavily branched limb, which may be set in tub of gravel or sand. *Warmth*—Essential; place cage where it receives much sunlight but is protected from drafts. During winter, if pet is out of its natural range, place cage near heating unit; provide pen lined with soft, warm cloths in which it can coil.

FOOD

Indigo snakes are not constrictors; food is grasped by mouth and held down by part of body while it is swallowed live. In the wild, indigos feed on mice, rats, frogs, fish, lizards, other snakes including rattlers, and turtles' eggs. Give native food. Sometimes pet takes baby rabbits, baby guinea pigs, and gophers. If pet takes nothing but other snakes, return it to its native habitat; feeding in captivity too difficult. *Water*—Use large, flat container; place in center of cage.

KING AND MILK SNAKES: Genus *Lampropeltis*

SCARLET KING SNAKE: *Lampropeltis doliata doliata*

Range: Eastern Kentucky and Tennessee, and North Carolina to Florida, Gulf states as far west as southeastern Louisiana

Description: Small, brilliantly marked with red, black, and yellow rings; red rings do not cross belly; head small and pointed; snout red; back of head black. These are smallest of king snakes, attaining average length of 15 inches. (This snake closely resembles the dangerously poisonous coral snake. To distinguish between the two, remember that snout of the scarlet king snake is red; in the coral snake it is black. In the scarlet king snake the red band always lies next to the black; in the coral snake there is a yellow or light band separating the red from the black. Remember it this way: Red and black; no attack.)

Habitat: In fields, under bark of dead pines, under old logs, and in holes in ground; partially nocturnal

Reproduction: Oviparous; 3 or more eggs deposited in piles of sawdust, manure, rubbish heaps, under logs, boards, in loose soil, and in sand; sometimes adhere in a cluster

LOUISIANA MILK SNAKE: *Lampropeltis doliata amaura*

Range: Lower Mississippi Valley, eastward to Meridian, Mississippi, and westward into eastern Texas as far as Dallas; through Arkansas to extreme southeastern Oklahoma

Description: Russet red saddles along back, bordered in front and back with black rings; between black rings is sulphur yellow ring; neck sulphur yellow edged with black; front of head rufous with black spots; snout yellowish; grows to length of 25 inches

Habitat: Sandy soils, cotton fields, corn fields of bayou bottoms, edges of cypress swamps, and in old logs

Reproduction: Oviparous; eggs deposited in piles of sawdust, manure, rubbish heaps, under logs, boards, in loose soil, and in sand; sometimes adhere in a cluster

WESTERN MILK SNAKE: *Lampropeltis doliata gentilis*

Range: Found in second tier of states west of Mississippi, Montana, Colorado and Utah, New Mexico and Arizona
Description: Bands on back red or scarlet edged with black or brown; spaces between white or sulphur yellow; head black, or black with flecks of red or white; sulphur-yellow band back of head; underside of head white or pale yellow; grows to length of 36 inches
Habitat: Roadside holes, banks of river bluffs, treeless prairie, and flat rock hillsides
Reproduction: Oviparous; 8–12 eggs deposited June–August in piles of sawdust, manure, rubbish heaps, under logs, boards, in loose soil, and in sand; eggs sometimes adhere in a cluster

RED MILK SNAKE: *Lampropeltis doliata syspila*

Range: Iowa through Missouri and northern Arkansas, eastern Kansas and Oklahoma, eastward through southern Illinois and Indiana, central Tennessee
Description: Row of saddles along back vary from russet, rufous, to red-brown, bordered with black; space between saddles very light, sometimes white; top of head light; light half-collar behind head; grows to length of 42 inches
Habitat: Open country, wooded hills, open fields, dense woods, copperhead snake dens, decaying logs, under loose bark, flat rocks, boards, and so on
Reproduction: Oviparous; 6–12 eggs deposited June–July in piles of sawdust, manure, rubbish heaps, under logs, boards, in loose soil, and in sand; sometimes adhere in a cluster

COASTAL PLAIN MILK SNAKE: *Lampropeltis doliata temporalis*

Range: Southern New Jersey, Delaware, and Maryland, through Virginia to North Carolina
Description: Back marked with saddles of brick-red outlined with

black; saddles separated by pale gray; black-edged, dull collar back of head; nose and face gray, flecked with black; edges dark blood-red; grows to length of 30 inches

Habitat: Coastal plains with bogs and pine barrens of loose, sandy soil; probably burrows in soil

Reproduction: Oviparous; eggs deposited in piles of sawdust, manure, rubbish heaps, under logs, boards, in loose soil, and in sand; sometimes adhere in a cluster

EASTERN MILK SNAKE: *Lampropeltis doliata triangulum*

Range: Southern Maine through New England, New York, and northern New Jersey, southward in the Appalachians into North Carolina and Tennessee, westward through Quebec, Ontario, Michigan, and Wisconsin to eastern Minnesota, southward through northern Illinois, Indiana, and Ohio

Description: Brown saddle spots along back edged with black or chestnut brown; spaces between saddles pale fawn or buff; light buff spot edged with black on top of neck; heart-shaped, cream-colored spot on rear of head, edged with black or brown; throat and chin white; attains length of 54 inches

Habitat: Widespread; found about dwellings in search of rats and mice; also in bogs, hills and open country; secretes itself in and under old logs, stumps, rock piles, and rubbish

Reproduction: Oviparous; 6–24 eggs deposited June–August in piles of sawdust, manure, rubbish heaps, under logs, boards, in loose soil, and in sand; sometimes eggs adhere in a cluster

Milk snakes are usually not hardy in captivity. The majority of them refuse to take food and are also secretive in habit. They should not be killed as they are of great economic value. It is advisable to keep a specimen for no more than a week, then liberate it in the area where it was captured. Maintenance for this short period is the same as for the king snakes.

EASTERN KING SNAKE: *Lampropeltis getulus getulus*

Range: Southern New Jersey to northern Florida and westward to southeastern Alabama

Description: Black with narrow yellow or white cross bands, forked on sides and connected in chainlike fashion; abdomen black with white or yellow blotches; as a rule specimen from northern part of its range has black ground color with white markings; those from the southern part usually have brown ground color with yellow markings; attains average length of 3½ feet, maximum of 6

Habitat: Moist woods, brush plains, under tree trunks, along roadsides, borders of creeks, in pastures, meadows, and about farm buildings

Reproduction: Oviparous; 5–24 eggs, depending on size of snake, deposited July–August; hatch September–October

CALIFORNIA KING SNAKE: *Lampropeltis getulus californiae*

Range: Southern Oregon, through California and southern Nevada, southwestern Utah and western Arizona; adjacent northern Lower California

Description: Black or brown with white or pale yellow cross bands which continue as blotches on abdomen and appear as rings; snout and lip plates yellow; reaches length of almost 4 feet

Habitat: Along streams with brush and trees, in grassy lands among rocks, in dense thickets, along roadsides, in foothills, and upland regions; slow-moving but quick to take cover

Reproduction: Oviparous

SPECKLED KING SNAKE: *Lampropeltis getulus holbrooki*

Range: Southern Nebraska and Iowa and southwestern Illinois, through Kansas and Missouri, Arkansas, and most of Oklahoma; eastern Texas, Louisiana, Mississippi, and western Alabama

Description: Black with pale green or white spots in center of each scale; abdomen yellow with large black blotches; attains length of 5 feet

Habitat: In open pine woods and along edges of swamps; hides under old logs, bark of fallen trees, rock, and so on

Reproduction: Oviparous; 6–14 eggs, depending on size of snake, usually deposited June–August; hatch September–October

These three species of king snakes are the ones most common to their locales. They are hardy in captivity, long-lived, and make excellent pets.

HOUSING

King and milk snakes need room; must be housed alone or with others of their own kind. Use large reptile cage (see Part IV). Cover bottom of cage with thick layer of pea gravel. As retreat, pile numerous flat rocks at one end of cage. Near them, pile large pieces of old bark and portions of old, decaying stumps with plenty of rotted wood and leaves. It is wise also to place a large piece of sod with fairly tall grass near retreats. Provide sturdy, branching limb along one side of cage for snake to crawl on; or place limb outside of cage and give pet freedom of the room. Place cage where it receives some sun each day, but protect it from overheating.

FOOD

In the wild, milk and king snakes feed on mice and other small rodents, birds, lizards, and other snakes. Scarlet king snakes also feed on insects and fish. Give native food to scarlet king (see Part III). Give other milk and king snakes native food; also give earthworms; in addition, they may take freshly killed rats and mice dropped in cage. *Water*—Use small, flat container; place in center of cage.

RACERS: Genus *Coluber*

NORTHERN BLACK RACER: *Colubur constrictor constrictor*

Range: Eastern North America from southern Maine southward to northern Florida and westward, mainly south of Ohio River, to the Mississippi

Description: Adult is uniformly slate-back above and beneath; chin and throat white; moderately slender; tail long; young are pale gray above; large brownish blotches on back; black spots on sides; during second summer, pattern becomes obscure; third summer become color of adult; grow to length of 6 feet

Habitat: Almost any type of terrain—forests, plains, lowlands, uplands, swamps, marshes, roadsides, sandy areas, and even sparsely settled areas

Reproduction: Oviparous; 3–40 eggs deposited June–July; hatch August–September; unique in appearance as they are snow-white, tough, leathery-shelled, and look as though covered with coarse grains of sand

WESTERN YELLOW-BELLIED RACER: *Colubur constrictor mormon*

Range: Southern British Columbia, through the Great Basin to southern Arizona, and throughout Washington, Oregon, and California

Description: Adult is olive-green or brownish, often with bluish tint along sides; abdomen plain yellow; young are light, with blotched markings on back and sides; grow to length of 2½ feet

Habitat: Widespread and common; found in almost any type of terrain, such as valleys, mountains, grassy and bushy areas, plains, ditch banks, cultivated fields, irrigation ditches, sagebrush country, orchards, and vineyards

Reproduction: Oviparous; 3–6 eggs deposited June–July; unique in appearance as they are snow-white, tough, leathery-shelled, and look as though covered with coarse grains of sand

The majority of racers are quick, nervous, highly strung snakes. Few of them are hardy enough in captivity to make good pets. It is advisable to keep a specimen for no more than one week, for observation, then liberate it in the area where it was captured. Racers are of great economic value and should not be killed, since they feed on numerous destructive rodents.

HOUSING

Racers need plenty of room and must be housed alone. Use large reptile cage (see Part IV). Cover cage bottom with a thick layer of pea gravel. Place large section of sod with growth of fairly tall weeds or wild grass across one end of cage as grass cover. Place branching limb across one corner of cage, preferably over grass, for crawling. Limb must be strong enough to hold weight of snake. Place cage where it receives some sunlight each day, but protect it from overheating.

FOOD

In the wild, racers feed on rats, mice, and other small rodents, young birds, tree frogs, lizards, insects, and young of other snakes. They are not constrictors; their scientific name is misleading; they grasp their food by their mouth and hold it down by part of their body while they swallow it live. In captivity, give young rats, mice, tree frogs, insects, meal worms, and, when available, lizards and small snakes (see Part III). *Water*—Essential; use large, flat enamel pan; place in center of cage.

RAT SNAKES: Genus *Elaphe*

CORN SNAKE: *Elaphe guttata guttata*

Range: New Jersey to Florida in the Atlantic coastal plain, mountains of Virginia and Tennessee, westward to Louisiana, and northward in the Mississippi Valley to Kentucky and Missouri

Description: Ground color pale red, reddish-brown, or yellow-brown; large crimson saddles narrowly bordered with black on back; smaller blotches along each side, with still smaller blotches below these; abdomen white with large black squares; wedge-shaped marking between eyes; red stripe across forehead; red stripe from behind eye to angle of mouth; attains average length of 4 feet, extremely gentle in captivity and an attractive pet

Habitat: In cornfields, along roadsides, about barns and outbuildings of rural settlements; in pine woods, fields, open areas, and wooded hills; hides in rotting logs, under old bark, in holes in ground, in piles of trash, hay, and manure; in pine woods often found climbing up rough bark of trunk

Reproduction: Oviparous; 12–24 eggs deposited in hollow logs, rotted stumps, sawdust and trash piles, June–July; hatch August–September

BLACK RAT SNAKE: *Elaphe obsoleta obsoleta*

Range: Eastern North America, from southern New England (Rutland County, Vermont) to northern Georgia, westward through New York and Ontario to southeastern Minnesota, eastern Kansas, and Oklahoma, and to northeastern Texas; absent in the Mississippi embayment area

Description: Adult is shiny black, brown, or brownish-black with white spots on edges of scales; scales keeled; head broad and square; belly yellowish, mottled with dark spots. Young have many brown blotches down middle of back; 2 alternating series of smaller blotches along sides; ground color gray; may reach average length of 4 feet, some have been recorded at 8 feet

Habitat: Largely arboreal; found in wooded areas, barns, granaries, old buildings; in attics; on ground under rocks, decaying logs, in and on hollow logs, in moist woodlands, and scrubhill country

Reproduction: Oviparous; 6–12 eggs placed in hollow logs, rotted stumps, sawdust and trash piles; deposited May–June

This snake is hardy in captivity but is erratic in temperament. Some become excellent pets while others never do. Take great care in handling it (wear gloves); do not allow children to handle it until its temperament has been well determined.

Yellow Rat Snake: *Elaphe obsoleta quadrivittata*

Range: Vicinity of Point Lookout, North Carolina, southward along coast through all of peninsular Florida

Description: Adult is bright yellow, pale brown, or olive; 2 black or brown stripes on back and 1 on each side; young are pale gray with dark brown blotches; develop adult coloring about 3rd year; grow to length of 5 feet

Habitat: Chiefly about and in barns, old buildings, deserted houses and cabins, schoolhouses, in trees, in caves, and poultry yards of farms; common in upland woods and rat-infested buildings

Reproduction: Oviparous; 8–41 eggs placed in hollow logs, rotted stumps, sawdust and trash piles; deposited June–August

Western Fox Snake: *Elaphe vulpina vulpina*

Range: Upper peninsula of Michigan through Wisconsin, southeastern Minnesota and northern Illinois; northwestern Indiana southward to the Wabash River; westward through Iowa to eastern Nebraska and South Dakota

Description: Head reddish or reddish-brown; pattern a series of large chocolate or black blotches flanked on each side of body by rows of smaller blotches; ground color above yellowish or light brown; belly yellow checked with black. Reaches length of 63 inches

Habitat: Essentially ground dweller; found in open country, about outbuildings, in briar patches; in rolling hill country, near marshes and small bodies of water

Reproduction: Oviparous; 7–29 eggs placed in hollow logs, rotted stumps, sawdust, and trash piles; deposited in July

The name "fox" comes because of the odor, resembling that of wild foxes, from a substance discharged by glands at the base of the tail when the snake is first captured. It soon becomes gentle in captivity and after that no longer uses this defense.

HOUSING

Rat snakes need plenty of room; must be placed alone or with others of their kind. Use large reptile cage (see Part IV). Cover cage bottom with thick layer of pea gravel. As retreat, pile numerous flat rocks at one end of cage. Near them pile large pieces of old bark, portions of old, decaying stumps with plenty of rotted wood and leaves. It is also wise to place a large piece of sod with fairly tall grass near retreat. Place sturdy, branching limb along one side of cage for crawling; in addition, place limb outside of cage and give pet freedom in room. Place cage where it receives some sun each day, but protect it from overheating.

FOOD

In the wild, rat snakes feed on rats, mice, and other small rodents, nesting birds, young gophers and rabbits, young chicks, chicken eggs; sometimes on tree frogs, insects, and other snakes; are constrictors. Give rats, mice, baby chicks; young of rabbits when possible; as much other native food as possible. *Water*—Use flat container; place in center of cage.

ROSY BOAS: Genus *Lichanura*

COASTAL ROSY BOA: *Lichanura roseofusca roseofusca*

Range: Coast and desert foothills, Los Angeles and San Bernardino counties, California, south to northern Lower California, Mexico

Description: Medium-sized; pale olive-gray above; deep gray below; median dorsal stripe cinnamon brown, with lateral fawn-colored, zigzag bands; grows to length of 42 inches

Note: Quiet, extremely gentle snake, but does not feed well in captivity; advise liberation after few days of observation

Habitat: Frequents shady places which are sometimes damp; rocky canyons, rocky hillsides; appears to be most active during cloudy and rainy weather

Reproduction: Viviparous; 6–10 young

DESERT ROSY BOA: *Lichanura roseofusca gracia*

Range: Desert regions of southeastern California and southwestern Arizona; adjacent parts of Lower California and Sonora, Mexico

Description: Light gray, light pinkish, or even white above; pale greenish-blue or gray on sides; pinkish-buff beneath; middorsal and lateral stripes reddish-brown, distinct, and more or less even; reaches length of 44 inches

Habitat: Desert areas, barren mountains with rocky slopes

Reproduction: Viviparous

RUBBER BOAS: Genus Charina

PACIFIC RUBBER BOA: *Charina bottae bottae*

Range: Coast Range of California, northward from Monterey County into Oregon. The Sierra Nevada from Tulare County northward to Placer County, California, Douglas County, Nevada; coastal British Columbia and Washington, including Vancouver Island, west of the Cascades

Description: Small, thick, burrowing snake; skin smooth; tail blunt and short; uniform brownish-green; sides olive-brown; belly orange-yellow; grows to length of 24 inches

Note: When first captured rolls into curious ball with head hidden and tail held up as though it were the head, which it resembles

Habitat: Found in forested mountain areas and in mountain meadows, especially moist, shady areas; slow-moving, extremely gentle

Reproduction: Viviparous; 3 or more young

ROCKY MOUNTAIN RUBBER BOA: *Charina bottae utahensis*

Range: Montana and forested areas in north central Utah, central Nevada, western Wyoming, Idaho, western Montana, eastern Washington and Oregon, and northeastern California, southeastern British Columbia

Description: Small snake, brown, smooth-skinned with lovely sheen; belly deep yellow to orange; tail short and blunt; slow-moving, extremely gentle; crepuscular; reaches length of 27 inches

Habitat: Most often found in forested areas of mountains, or wooded areas, and in mountain meadows

Reproduction: Viviparous; 2–8 young born in fall or following spring

HOUSING

Use large reptile cage (see Part IV); be sure larger specimens have enough room. Cover cage bottom with thick layer of pea gravel topped by 2–3 inches of humus or good sandy soil. Place grassy sod and large sections of moss over soil at one end of cage. As retreat, pile small, rather flat rocks close to green area; add sections of old, rotted logs and pieces of stumps. For climbing species, provide branching limb across one end of cage. Place cage where it receives some direct sunlight each day but is out of drafts. Protect cage from overheating; snakes maintained outside their range must also be protected from chilling.

FOOD

In the wild, boas feed on young rats, mice, birds and their young, insects, and lizards. Boas are constrictors; however, they sometimes grasp prey with mouth and swallow it without using constriction. In captivity, give young rats, mice, and baby chicks. If snake kills prey but does not proceed to swallow it, prey is probably too large; offer smaller mouse or rat. If snake does not feed readily, first be sure that pet is thoroughly warm and active; then place small colored rat or mouse in cage. A snake that continually refuses food should be liberated in the area where it was captured. *Water*—Use flat enamel pan; place in center of cage.

WHIPSNAKES: Genus *Masticophis*

SONORA WHIPSNAKE: *Masticophis bilineatus bilineatus*

Range: Southeastern Arizona and southwestern New Mexico; southward in Mexico to Oaxaca

Description: Large, elongate; blue-gray, with 2 lateral white or yellow stripes *not* extending as far as tail; underside of head white, chin dotted with black; row of indistinct dark dots down middle of belly; light yellow toward head; pinkish under tail; reaches length of 67 inches

Habitat: Arboreal; found in trees, bushes, on limbs, in bushy ground, in region of mountains

Reproduction: Oviparous; 7 or more eggs deposited in June

EASTERN COACHWHIP SNAKE: *Masticophis flagellum flagellum*

Range: Southeastern United States from North Carolina to peninsula of Florida and westward along the Gulf Coast to Louisiana, an apparently isolated population ranging from southern Illinois and Missouri through northwestern Alabama and eastern Oklahoma into western Louisiana and eastern Texas

Description: Large, very quick-moving; drab toward head, becoming lighter toward tail; underparts chiefly white. Reaches length of 8½ feet

Habitat: Dry, high, pine forests and cut-over pine lands, sand hills and dry wooded ridges, grass lands and rocky hillsides

Reproduction: Oviparous; 8–24 eggs deposited July–August

The coachwhip snake is hardier in captivity than other whipsnakes, but it never becomes accustomed to handling. It constantly maintains a defensive attitude, hence, is not recommended as a pet for children. Its bite is harmless, but it can frighten a child. It should be handled by an adult, maintained for a few days only, then liberated in its native area.

DESERT STRIPED WHIPSNAKE: *Masticophis taeniatus taeniatus*

Range: Great Basin and bordering areas from Idaho through eastern Oregon, Utah, and Nevada, eastern California, Arizona, and southwestern New Mexico

Description: Color down middle of back olive-brown; becomes drab on tail; deep olive on top of head; 2 prominent light stripes along sides of body; underside of chin white; midbelly light yellow; underside of tail solid coral or flesh-pink; reaches length of 61 inches

Habitat: Varies from sagebrush country, dry desert areas to foothills with rocky slopes; climbs easily in brush and shrubbery
Reproduction: Oviparous; 4–8 eggs deposited May–June

HOUSING

Whipsnakes need plenty of room, but may be housed with others of their kind. Use large reptile cage (see Part IV). Cover cage bottom with thick layer of pea gravel. If snake is to be kept longer than two weeks, place a thick layer of sand over the gravel at one end of cage. Place large section of grassy sod on sand in one corner. Scatter large rocks over each other on remainder of sand. For climbing species, provide large, heavy, branching limb along one side of cage and across corner. Warmth is essential when snake is maintained outside its natural range, but guard against too much direct sunlight.

FOOD

In the wild, whipsnakes feed on mice, rats, and other small rodents, young of birds, lizards, and other snakes. Whipsnakes are not constrictors; food is grasped by mouth and held down by part of body while it is swallowed live. Give rats, mice, small birds, baby chicks, and young of other snakes when possible. *Water*—Use enamel pan; place in center of cage.

TURTLES AND TORTOISES

Turtles

This group is commonly made up of the turtles and terrapins, both of which are called turtles and are aquatic or semiaquatic; tortoises, which are strictly terrestrial; and certain turtles which are marine. As good pet material does not come from the marine turtles, they are not discussed here.

HIBERNATION: Most turtles hibernate during the winter. Some species drop to the bottom of a stream, lake, or pond where they dig down into the mud and lie dormant until the spring temperature is sufficiently warm to bring them out. Other species burrow into the soil under dead and decaying vegetation or tunnel into banks where they remain through the coldest months of the year.

CAPTURE: Turtles found on land are not difficult to capture. Those that are more or less aquatic are difficult to capture even with the use of a net. However, if one comes upon them on land, and they are far enough away from water, they can usually be picked up by hand. The most interesting turtles are the small, colored creatures which are the young of a variety of species and are usually obtained from pet shops.

LIBERATION: Some of the larger specimens of turtles, such as the box and western pond turtle, should be liberated during the summer if they have been pets in a school room. It is advisable to return them to the area from which they were obtained. If one has become a great pet, as often happens, then the creature should be given to someone who has a fairly large garden where it may roam and still have contact with humans in order to obtain the additional food to which it has been accustomed.

PARASITES AND DISEASES: In the wild state some turtles suffer from leeches and other parasites which attach themselves to the soft parts of the skin, but all are very susceptible to countless internal parasites. If the young in captivity do not receive a sufficient amount of direct sunlight and do not have damp soil in which to burrow, they develop soft shells and a disease of the eyes. When this occurs, the creatures do not live long.

BODY CHARACTERISTICS: *Shell:* The characteristic feature of turtles is the shell or horny body covering. The upper part of the shell is properly termed the carapace, while the lower part is termed the plastron. The carapace and plastron are connected on each side of the body by a bony bridge. The head, legs, and tail may be drawn into the shell.

Both the carapace and the plastron are formed of platelike sections fused together and covered with a horny exterior. These plates are called shields.

The shell of most turtles is marked with interesting colors and gay patterns. In some species the color and pattern may occur also on the head and neck of the animal. With the exception of a few species, the young of turtles are much more brightly marked than the adults. There is extreme variation in the markings of young turtles, even among the same species, and few of them resemble the adults.

Painting the carapace of young turtles not only causes the shell to soften but interferes with its growth as well. This reduces the vitality of the pet and shortens its life. A painted specimen should have the paint removed immediately. It can be flaked off by using a sharp, thin blade such as a razor blade, which must be used cautiously to avoid cutting the shell.

Eyes: Turtles have well-developed eyes with movable eyelids. Their sight is extremely keen. Their ability to distinguish colors approximates that of man.

Ears: Turtles possess well-developed middle and inner ears, but it has been determined that they do not hear in the ordinary sense of the term. However, they do pick up vibrations which are transmitted through their shells.

Teeth: Turtles do not possess teeth. Their horny beaks have sharp cutting edges which make it possible for them to bite or pull their food into small pieces.

Tail: The tail of most turtles is short, rather stout at the base, and tapers to a fine point. It is easily tucked under the edge of the carapace, as are the legs and the head when the creature is frightened.

Feet: The feet of turtles have claws of varying lengths, and the toes of many species are webbed for swimming.

AGE: Turtles are reputed to live to a great age, but this is probably an exaggeration. Of North American species kept in captivity, the record for longevity is shared by an alligator snapping turtle and a wood turtle, each of which reached a known age of 58 years. Some species, such as the giant Galapagos tortoises, are believed to live well over a century, but this is naturally difficult to prove.

In those species that hibernate at regular intervals, growth takes place during the active period of the animal, and is indicated by rings built up at the edges of each shield. These growth rings give some idea of the age of the animal, but the system fails with older specimens, in which the earlier rings become worn down.

In other species the shields are shed regularly or sporadically so that no growth rings show. With such a specimen, age cannot be determined.

It is thought that the turtles of the United States probably reach maturity at the age of five to seven years, but that they continue to grow for several years after that, in some cases indefinitely.

FOOD: Turtles may feed on both animal and vegetable matter,

which will be listed for the various species discussed. Many turtles feed under water, hence it is necessary to know which do and which do not.

Capturing of prey: Food is usually grasped by the horny beak and bitten off as desired. Often the food is held down by one or the other of the front feet so that the bite may be more easily torn off.

Swallowing: There is no peculiarity among turtles in the manner of swallowing their prey.

Sex: Differences between the sexes of turtles are only occasionally obvious to the layman. The male eastern box turtle usually has a red eye, the female a dark eye. In spotted turtles, on the other hand, the female usually has a bright orange eye, whereas that of the male is dark. Other color differences occur in other species, but generalization is impossible.

Reproduction: Turtles are oviparous. After mating, the female chooses the proper location where soil, moisture, and temperature will be right for incubation of the eggs. She digs a hole in the soil several inches deep with her hind legs, lays the eggs in it, covers them with soil, packs it down with her hind legs, then leaves the nest, never to return to it again.

The eggs are laid in early spring and late summer. They may hatch from August through October. The young often remain in the nest until the following February or March, and they take no food during this time.

Care in captivity: Children often house the young of various turtles in old fish bowls or dishes of water. Frequently the pets are in diseased and weakened conditions from lack of proper food and care.

They should never be maintained in fish bowls or dishes of water. Turtles require long hours out of the water. They require soil in which to dig in order to be healthy in captivity. The majority of young turtles are hardy in captivity and grow fairly rapidly when maintained under proper conditions.

Housing: The most comfortable habitat for young turtles, and the one which most nearly resembles the native one, is the woodland terrarium. One or two young turtles may be equally comfortable in the woodland habitat of a handmade vivarium box (see Part II).

Feeding: Young turtles sold in pet shops and markets in the fall of the year have been dug out of the soil of their nests with the result that they may appear sluggish and refuse food. They should be allowed to bury themselves in the soil of the terrarium to complete hibernation, and they should not be disturbed until the following spring. They will emerge from the soil voluntarily in the spring and will be ready for food.

Offer them small, live earthworms, bits of *green* fresh lettuce placed on the surface of the water in the habitat. Many feed under water.

ARTIFICIAL HATCHING: If it is possible to reproduce the conditions that exist in a nest of turtle eggs, success may follow. The essential factors are moisture, temperature, and light. A heavy wooden box, is the best container, since it does not change temperature as quickly as one of metal or glass. Fill the box with debris from the nest. Place the eggs in a depression in the center of the debris. Cover the eggs with a thick layer of debris. Cover the container with a piece of glass that can be shifted so that moisture and heat may be controlled to some extent. Too much moisture or too little moisture will kill the embryos. The same is true of heat.

BOX TURTLES: Genus *Terrapene*

EASTERN BOX TURTLE: *Terrapene carolina carolina*

Range: Eastern Maine to Georgia, west to Michigan, Illinois, and Tennessee

Description: Shell high and domelike; carapace may be yellow, orange, or olive on black or brown; same colors on plastron; either dark or light colors may predominate; reaches shell length of 4–6 inches

Habitat: Commonly found in open woodlands, near brooks or ponds; also in water and lush foilage of stream banks and streams; during hot, dry summers found in large bogs, mudholes, and swamps where it soaks for hours; in extreme heat burrows under logs and rotting vegetation but brisk summer showers bring it out again; in northern part of range hibernates in burrows during winter

Reproduction: Oviparous; 2–7 eggs deposited June–July

FLORIDA BOX TURTLE: *Terrapene carolina bauri*

Range: Peninsular Florida and the lower keys

Description: Shell narrow, elongate, higher posteriorly, with rear margin flared; 2 stripes on each side of head from rear edge of eyes;

carapace marked with narrow yellow lines; usually 3 toes on hind feet; reaches shell length of 5–6½ inches

Habitat: Flatwoods, upland hammocks, and limestone flatwoods; does not hibernate for any length of time; only partially buried during coldest days

Reproduction: Oviparous; 1–9 eggs deposited mid-April–June

GULF COAST BOX TURTLE: *Terrapene carolina major*

Range: Panhandle of Florida (western) and southern Georgia, along Gulf Coast to eastern Texas

Description: Shell relatively long with median keel; rear edge flaring; carapace dark brown or black with or without pattern, scattered spots or lines; plastron nearly solid black; head and soft parts of body dark brown to deep black, either spotted or plain; 4 toes on hind feet; largest of American box turtles; shell length at least 7 inches

Habitat: Pine flatwoods and upland hammocks; often in ponds or shallow lakes

Reproduction: Oviparous; number of eggs unknown; deposited in loose soil and decaying wood April–May

THREE-TOED BOX TURTLE: *Terrapene carolina triunguis*

Range: Southern South Carolina throughout Atlantic and coastal plains to eastern Texas, exclusive of Florida; northward in Mississippi Basin through Oklahoma and Arkansas to eastern Kansas and Missouri, Tennessee Kentucky and southern Illinois

Description: Shell narrow, keeled above, flaring at posterior margin; carapace usually olive or dull brown without pattern; plastron plain yellow or gray; head and forelegs usually spotted with orange or yellow; usually 3 toes on hind feet but sometimes 4; reaches shell length of 4½–5 inches

Habitat: In woodlands, meadows, often in and near streams

Reproduction: Oviparous

ORNATE BOX TURTLE: *Terrapene ornata ornata*

Range: Southern Wisconsin, northern Iowa, southern South Dakota, southward to Gulf Coast of Texas; westward reaches southeastern Wyoming and eastern Colorado; from Texas extends across northern Mexico and southern New Mexico to southern Arizona

Description: Shell oval and broad, rather high but flattened on top; carapace low and short; chocolate to reddish-brown; light lines radiate from upper hind corners with broken central light line; plastron as long as or longer than carapace; definite pattern of light lines which extend in all directions over dark background; head and legs spotted with yellow, especially above; reaches shell length of 5–6 inches

Habitat: Prairie lands, savannas, woodlands, sand hills, and swamps; takes refuge under ground during middle of day in dry weather

Reproduction: Oviparous; 3–5 eggs deposited in June

Box turtles spend all or the greater part of their lives on land. They make excellent pets. They are usually found in the mature or half-grown state, when they are too large to house in a terrarium for any length of time. However, they make wonderful pets for a home garden.

Box turtles differ from other turtles by having a hinged plastron. This makes it possible for the creature completely to enclose its head, feet, and tail so that it looks like an oval box.

Man's ruthlessness and carelessness have reduced the number of box turtles to the point where they are now rare. Some states have enacted laws which prohibit the possession of these turtles. Check state laws before seeking a specimen for a pet.

HOUSING

As box turtle needs plenty of room and freedom, it is best maintained as a house and garden pet. If it is to be observed at school, place it in woodland habitat of a large terrarium (see Part II); keep it for a few days and then return it to freedom of home and garden.

In home garden in natural range, provide area in garden where pet can bury itself for hibernation during winter. Outside its natural range, maintain pet in a room where temperature is kept constant; provide box of soil at least 12 inches deep to permit possible hibernation. Few specimens survive cold northern winters.

FOOD

YOUNG TURTLES: In the wild, feed largely on insects and their larvae, slugs, earthworms, snails, plus a small amount of plant matter. Give as much native food as possible; supplement with meal worms (see Part III) and bits of hamburger. *Water*—Essential; use large, flat, enamel pan.

ADULT TURTLES: In the wild, feed largely on plants—quantities of fungi, wild berries, various fruits—plus some animal matter. Give fungi, melon rinds, tomatoes, apples, berries and other fruits in season, fresh, green lettuce, meal worms, and hamburger. *Water*—Essential; use large, flat, enamel pan.

COOTERS AND SLIDERS: Genus *Pseudemys*

FLORIDA COOTER: *Pseudemys floridana floridana*

Range: Northern Florida and adjacent Atlantic coastal plain
Description: Shell high, highest in middle, wide behind; carapace light to dark brown; plastron light yellow; head and legs light brown with yellow stripes. Feet webbed; 4 lower nails on front feet; 5 nails on hind feet; reaches shell length of 8–15 inches
Habitat: Rivers, lakes, ponds, swamps, especially in bodies of water with an abundance of vegetation
Reproduction: Oviparous; 12–20 eggs deposited May–June

REDBELLIED TURTLE: *Pseudemys rubriventris*

Range: Atlantic coastal plain from Massachusetts to south central Virginia
Description: Shell elongated-oval, flattened; carapace brownish-gray with crisscross marks; plastron orange or red; head dark brown with light stripes; upper jaw deeply notched and cusped; toes webbed, 4 longer nails on forefeet, 5 on hind feet; reaches shell length of 11–12 inches
Habitat: Ponds, lakes, streams, both in clear, rapid currents and in slow, heavily silted areas; also in brackish water
Reproduction: Oviparous; 6–12 eggs deposited June–July

YELLOW-BELLIED TURTLE: *Pseudemys scripta scripta*

Range: Northern Florida to Princess Anne County, Virginia
Description: Shell relatively short and broad, oval; carapace more or less keeled with rear edge sharply notched; dark brown to black with pattern of transverse light bars; plastron yellow with deep

black, smudges on lateral edges; head and legs brown to almost black with yellow stripes; large yellow patch on head behind eyes; reaches shell length of 5–7 inches.

Note: This turtle is often found in pet shops along with the red-eared turtle

Habitat: Most frequently in ponds, especially small, deep ones, and in small streams and sloughs and at edges of lakes; in northern part of range, hibernates in mud and among aquatic plants at edges of lakes

Reproduction: Oviparous; 10–12 eggs deposited May–July

RED-EARED TURTLE: *Pseudemys scripta elegans*

Range: Mississippi Basin, westward into Texas, northward to Kansas, Iowa, Illinois, Indiana, and southeastern Ohio

Description: Carapace not keeled, about as wide as long; bright green; each shield marked with 5 parallel black lines; conspicuous lateral, blood-red stripe on each side of head; plastron and bridge marked with black; legs and tail striped with yellow; may reach shell length of 8–9 inches

Note: It is the young of this turtle that are most often found in pet shops, carnivals, fairs, and so on.

Habitat: Most commonly in lakes and river coves with low, swampy shores and some aquatic plant growth; also in large bodies of water—lakes, quiet coves; and in small, open prairie ponds with shallow water

Reproduction: Oviparous; 5–22 eggs deposited April–June

The young of the above turtles are the ones which most often fall into the hands of children. They are easy to maintain in captivity at home or at school. The adults are not so easy to house because of their size and their need for room and freedom. Adults should be kept as pets only in a home with a garden pool available, but the young are the simplest of pets to house and maintain.

HOUSING

ADULT: May be kept in school room for a few days for observation; use cage large enough to allow it to move about freely; release in home garden with pond.

YOUNG TURTLE: Use woodland habitat of small terrarium (see Part II). Cover bottom with layer of coarse sand; top with thick layer of good soil so that pet can burrow. *Retreat*—Required; place sections of moss over soil; across one corner of habitat pile a few pieces of old bark and a few flat rocks. *Moisture*—Necessary; sprinkle soil and moss frequently to keep them slightly damp. *Warmth*—Important; place habitat where it receives some direct morning sunlight; avoid too much sun, exposure for long periods. *Hibernation*—In fall, pet shows intention to hibernate by refusing food and remaining buried several days at a time; set habitat away in cool, protected place; continue to keep soil slightly damp during period of hibernation; warm days of spring will bring pet out again for food.

FOOD

In the wild, cooters and sliders feed on aquatic insects, aquatic plants, small fish, aquatic snails, and tadpoles; adults feed more heavily on plant life than do turtle young. Offer aquatic plants, fresh, *green* vegetable tops, fruit in season, especially melon rinds, bits of raw meat. Try hamburger and meal worms. Keep piece of fresh, *green* lettuce on water at all times.

WATER: All cooters and sliders feed under water; food must be dropped on water of pool or dish. Pet must have large dish of water deep enough for it to submerge in completely and move about in freely. Push dish down into cage soil so that its rim is even with surface of soil. Arrange a few stones stair-step fashion from bottom to top of dish, so that turtle can crawl out of pool at will.

MAP TURTLES AND SAWBACKS: Genus *Graptemys*

MAP TURTLE: *Graptemys geographica*

Range: Mississippi and St. Lawrence basins, from Iowa through southern Wisconsin, Michigan, and Ontario to Lake George, New York, and Vermont; southeastern Kansas, Missouri, Illinois, Indiana, Ohio, and Pennsylvania; eastern Virginia, West Virginia, and eastern Tennessee, eastern Oklahoma, and Texas

Description: Shell moderately low and flattened with central keel; carapace smooth, olive-brown with netlike pattern of light lines; plastron yellow to almost white, may be marked with simple pattern;

head large; head and legs olive to brown with light stripes; usually longitudinal spot behind eye; reaches shell length of 10–11 inches

Habitat: Strictly aquatic; found in quiet back waters of rivers, sloughs, and lakes; hibernates in mud at bottom of lakes and rivers

Reproduction: Oviparous; 10–16 eggs deposited May–July

FALSE MAP TURTLE: *Graptemys pseudogeographica*

Range: Mississippi Basin; Louisiana, Mississippi, Alabama, Tennessee, Kentucky, Ohio and Indiana; Illinois, southern Wisconsin and Iowa; eastern Kansas, Missouri and eastern Arkansas to eastern Oklahoma

Description: Carapace high with knobby keel, rear edge notched; olive to brownish with variable pattern; plastron yellow with or without dark pattern; head and legs greenish-black with greenish-yellow stripes; conspicuous greenish-yellow mark on head is broad neck stripe that crosses nape at mid-point, then turns forward and downward at edge of eye; reaches average shell length of 5–7 inches

Habitat: Aquatic; found in lakes, streams, sloughs, and backwaters with abundance of aquatic vegetation; not found in clear, strong currents with little or no vegetation; in northern part of range, hibernates in mud at bottom of habitat and remains until ice goes out; in southern part of range, does not hibernate

Reproduction: Oviparous; 7–13 eggs deposited June–July

Only young map turtles should be used. They are often found among other baby turtles sold commercially. They are not hardy in captivity, but are worth keeping temporarily for observation.

HOUSING

Use woodland habitat in small vivarium box (see Part II). Cover bottom with layer of charcoal. Next add layer of sand. Top all with thick layer of loose, loamy soil. Provide basking surfaces: Across one end of habitat, pile pieces of old bark; at opposite end place large sections of moss. Sprinkle moss and soil frequently to keep them slightly damp—but *not* wet.

FOOD

In the wild, map turtles feed on small water snails, baby crayfish, aquatic insects, small fish, some carrion, and some plant life. Give small water snails, aquatic insects, baby top minnows, small earthworms, and fresh, green lettuce.

WATER: Map turtles feed under water; food must be dropped on water. Pet must have dish or small pan of water deep enough for it to submerge in completely and move about in freely. Push dish down into soil so that its rim is even with surface of soil. Cover bottom of dish with thick layer of coarse sand. Arrange a few stones stair-step fashion from bottom to top of dish so that pet can crawl out of water at will.

PAINTED TURTLES: Genus *Chrysemys*

EASTERN PAINTED TURTLE: *Chrysemys picta picta*

Range: Nova Scotia to Alabama
Description: Carapace low, elongated-oval, unkeeled and widest at rear. Adult: Shell smooth, unkeeled; scutes of carapace form straight rows across back (only one of painted turtles in which this occurs); front edges of scutes olive, together form light band across carapace; shell margin marked with red and black; plastron plain or yellow; may or may not have 1 or 2 dark spots; head with 2 bright spots on each side. Reaches shell length of 4½–6 inches. Young: Carapace keeled; olive with red margins; plastron plain yellow; neck and sides of head striped with yellow; red stripes on legs
Note: Not hardy in captivity but young will live for some time; not recommended as satisfactory pet material
Habitat: Aquatic; found in quiet waters of ponds, protected lake shores, ditches, slow streams, and marshes; hibernates in mud or trash at bottom of habitat; in southern ranges may not hibernate at all; known to wander in large numbers from one body of water to another
Reproduction: Oviparous; 3–11 eggs deposited May–July

MIDLAND PAINTED TURTLE: *Chrysemys picta marginata*

Range: Southern Quebec and southern Ontario to Tennessee
Description: Adult: Shell smooth, unkeeled; carapace with scutes that alternate with scutes along sides; no light anterior borders on

cross seams; usually dark figures in center of plastron; red markings on shell margins and legs; head with yellow stripes; resembles eastern painted turtle; reaches shell length of 4½–5½ inches. Young: Carapace keeled; margins red; plastron with long, narrow blotch along center; head and neck striped with yellow; legs striped with red

Note: Hardy in captivity and fairly long-lived; becomes gentle and learns to take food from one's hand

Habitat: All kinds of quiet water, sometimes in streams; partial to shallows with dense vegetation; extremely tolerant to industrial pollution of habitat; appears more tolerant of low temperatures than other species as it has been reported more or less active every month of year; generally hibernates in mud or debris under water; sometimes moves overland from one body of water to another

Reproduction: Oviparous; 3–11 eggs deposited June–July

Southern Painted Turtle: *Chrysemys picta dorsalis*

Range: Mississippi Basin, northward to southern Illinois
Description: Adult: Shell smooth, unkeeled, carapace plain yellow with broad red stripe down back; stripe sometimes may be yellow; plastron with 1 or 2 small black spots; sometimes plain; reaches shell length of 4–5 inches. Young: Carapace keeled, otherwise marked as adult

Note: These turtles often sold in pet shops.
Habitat: Almost exclusively in quiet waters of ponds, overflow ponds, backwaters of larger rivers and shallow ponds with much vegetation; also in sloughs

Reproduction: Oviparous; 4–6 eggs deposited June–July

Western Painted Turtle: *Chrysemys picta belli*

Range: Western Ontario and Missouri to Vancouver Island; scattered colonies in the southwest
Description: Adult: Shell smooth, unkeeled; carapace with light, irregular lines, sometimes forming netlike pattern; very little red on margins; plastron with large dark figure that branches out along seams of scutes; largest of painted turtles—reaches length of 5–7

inches. Young: Carapace keeled; plastron with irregular red design around margin; head and neck with yellow stripes

Note: Hardy in captivity. Becomes gentle and learns to take food from one's fingers

Habitat: Variety of situations such as lakes, streams, ditches, ponds, roadside pools, shallow quiet waters with soft bottoms and an abundance of aquatic plants

Reproduction: Oviparous; 5–8 eggs deposited May–June

Only young painted turtles should be used as pets. They may often be found among other baby turtles sold commercially.

HOUSING

Use woodland habitat in handmade vivarium box (see Part II). Cover bottom with layer of charcoal; top with layer of sand, then with thick layer of loose, loamy soil. *Basking surfaces*—Pile a few pieces of old bark at one end; at opposite end place large section of moss. *Moisture*—Sprinkle moss and soil frequently to keep them slightly damp, but *not* wet. *Warmth*—Important; place habitat where it receives some direct morning sunlight; protect it from overheating and chilling. Be sure pet can retreat under moss or pieces of bark.

FOOD

In the wild, painted turtles feed on larvae of aquatic insects, such as caddisfly, dragonfly, aquatic flies; water beetles, water fleas; fairy shrimp, baby fish; small water snails, tadpoles; aquatic plants, such as duckweed, algae, milfoil, elodea, etc. Give bits of raw fish, small earthworms, meal worms cut in pieces, young of top minnows, small water snails, aquatic insects, small strips of raw liver, pieces of aquarium plants if available, cut-up bits of fresh, green vegetable tops, cut-up bits of waterlily pads. Keep piece of fresh, *green* lettuce on water at all times.

WATER: Painted turtles feed under water; place all food in water. Pet must have dish or small pan of water deep enough for it to submerge in completely and move about in freely. Push dish down into soil so that its rim is even with soil surface. Arrange a few stones stair-step fashion from bottom to top of dish so that pet can crawl out of water at will.

POND TURTLES: Genus *Clemmys*

Spotted Turtle: *Clemmys guttata*

Range: Eastern North America from Quebec and Maine westward through Ontario, Michigan, and Wisconsin; in the east to West Virginia, and in the west through Ohio, Indiana, and Illinois

Description: Carapace broad, low, and usually smooth; 1 yellow spot in each shield of carapace; legs and tail with yellow spots; yellow bar behind ear; plastron yellow in center surrounded by black, reversed in young; reaches average shell length of 4½ inches

Habitat: One of most aquatic members of genus; found in small bodies of water, most often in meandering meadow brooks, little bog holes, and ponds

Reproduction: Oviparous; 1–4 eggs deposited in June

Wood Turtle: *Clemmys insculpta*

Range: Eastern North America from Nova Scotia to Virginia, westward through central Michigan, and central Wisconsin to Iowa

Description: Shell broad and low, very rough, keeled, with edges widely flared; carapace brown, usually with black and yellow radiating lines; plastron yellow with dark blotches on outer edges; head dark; upper jaw notched at tip; underparts of head and legs orange; reaches shell length of 7 inches

Note: Wood turtles have become rare due to man's depredations. Some states have laws to protect them. Check state laws before seeking a specimen for a pet.

Habitat: Both aquatic and terrestrial; during warm parts of year found in all types of country—woods and meadows; at nesting time during extremely dry, hot weather and at hibernation time found in or near water

Reproduction: Oviparous; 4–12 eggs deposited May–June

Western Pond Turtle: *Clemmys marmorata*

Range: Western United States, west of Cascades and the Sierra Nevada

Description: Carapace low, broad, and smooth; varies from brown color to almost black; no distinctive markings on head and legs; plastron tends to be yellowish; reaches average shell length of 7 inches

Note: Excellent pet both for school and for the home garden.

Habitat: Aquatic; frequents ponds, lakes, and quiet streams, especially quiet, muddy waters; wanders about on land during nesting season; hibernates during winter, probably in muddy bottom of habitat

Reproduction: Oviparous; 3–11 eggs deposited May–August

Adult pond turtles are a little too large to maintain with comfort in the average-sized terrarium, but make wonderful pets for a home garden. Only small turtles should be used for school specimens. Young are sometimes found among baby turtles sold commercially.

HOUSING

ADULTS: *Must have freedom;* if kept as pet, needs home garden and pool. May be kept for short while at school for observation; use large terrarium with woodland habitat (see Part II); give freedom of room daily.

BABY TURTLE: Use woodland habitat in handmade vivarium box (see Part II). Cover bottom with layer of charcoal; top with layer of sand; finish with thick layer of loose, loamy soil. *Basking surface—* Pile a few pieces of old bark at one end of habitat; place large section of moss at opposite end. *Moisture—*Important; sprinkle moss and soil frequently to keep slightly damp, but not wet. *Warmth—* Important; place habitat where it receives some direct morning sunlight; protect it from overheating or chilling; be sure pet can retreat under bark or moss.

FOOD

In the wild, pond turtles feed on both plant and animal matter; consume larvae of aquatic insects such as dragonfly, caddisfly; water fleas, fairy shrimp; small snails, tadpoles, small fish, small crayfish; earthworms; carrion; water plants—algae, moss, willow leaves, duckweed, coontail, sometimes pods of wild yellow water lily, and wild berries. Give aquatic insects, earthworms, meal worms, bits of raw fish and raw beef, snails; water plants such as algae, young, tender willow leaves, fresh, tender young vegetable greens. Also offer fresh fruits in season, such as berries, apples, and melons.

WATER: Pond turtle feeds under water, although pet often learns to come out and take food from owner's fingers. Drop food in water and on soil. Provide large container of water deep enough for pet to submerge and move about in freely. Push dish down into soil so that its rim is even with surface of soil. Cover bottom of dish with layer of sand. Arrange a few stones stair-step fashion from bottom to top of container so that pet can crawl out of water at will.

Tortoises

The members of this group of strange-looking turtles are terrestrial inhabit. They have come down through the centuries from ancient geological times and in their somewhat grotesque appearance and habits seem to carry the weight of these centuries with them. Only three small, closely related members of this group are found in North America. All three are interesting creatures and make gentle pets, but their life span in captivity is short.

HIBERNATION: All three native tortoises hibernate, the desert tortoise to a much greater degree than the others. They dig their own holes or burrows for this purpose. Digging is carried out by the forelegs; the loose soil is then shoved out by pushing it with the forward part of the shell.

CAPTURE: Tortoises are not difficult to capture, as they are slow-moving and do not appear to be easily frightened. However, a gopher tortoise close to its burrow can escape quickly enough. Otherwise, their means of defense is to withdraw into their armorlike shells where they remain until they feel all danger has passed.

LIBERATION: All three native tortoises are too large to maintain comfortably in a school terrarium, but they can be kept for a few weeks for observation by giving them the freedom of the room plus a warm place in which to crawl for the night. They should be released shortly in the area where they were captured.

It is an easy matter to maintain tortoises at home, especially if one lives in the range of these interesting creatures.

PARASITES AND DISEASES: Almost every wild animal is afflicted by diseases and parasites and the tortoises are no exception, in spite of their hermetically sealed appearance. There are both internal and external parasites. The gopher tortoise appears to be the greatest sufferer among the three native tortoises. A large blood-sucking mite and a species of tick attack it. These pests work their way in between the scales of the skin where they attach themselves and cause great difficulties.

BODY CHARACTERISTICS: *Shell:* The shell of all three of our native tortoises is high and domelike. The plastron is firmly joined to the carapace by heavy sutures.

SKIN: The skin is dry, scaly, and wrinkled.

EYES: Tortoises have movable eyelids.

EARS: It is assumed that tortoises have some structure that serves as a functioning ear.

TONGUE: There is nothing unique about tortoise tongues.

TEETH: Tortoises do not have teeth but the heavy, bonelike claws can cut sharply. There is a ridge on the upper jaw that runs parallel to the cutting edge, which no doubt makes the bite more effective.

FEET: The forelegs of the tortoise are adapted for digging. The toenails are heavy, broad, and short. The hind legs are cylindrical and columnar. When the creature walks, it is like an elephant. The legs, with the head, are retractable, although in one species the forelegs are drawn together in front of the head.

AGE: Very little is known about the life span of the three native tortoises.

FOOD: All three are vegetarians. Food consists of wild plant growth, grasses, herbs, blossoms, and wild fruits.

SEX: The males of all three species are larger than the females. The plastron of the male is concave and the tail is longer.

REPRODUCTION: All North American species are oviparous, but little else is known about their breeding habits.

CARE IN CAPTIVITY: Tortoises may be maintained in captivity for some time when given plenty of room, warm sleeping quarters, and a quantity of fresh food.

GOPHER TORTOISES: Genus *Gopherus*

DESERT TORTOISE: *Gopherus agassizi*

Range: Southern California, western Arizona, and southern Nevada

Description: Shell high and domelike; carapace dull brown or gray brown, sometimes, with yellowish centers in shields; plastron yellow shaded with brown; forward projection of plastron usually not bent upward; head small, rounded in front; hind feet very large; reaches shell length of 12–13 inches

Note: Excellent pet; responds readily to human advances, but short-lived in captivity

Habitat: Hot, dry desert areas with sandy flats, or rocky hillsides, and canyon beds; during cold snaps congregates in dens, apparently for warmth and protection; during extreme summer heat crawls into burrows to avoid heat and dryness; Basks only when sun's rays weak (tortoises, along with all other reptiles, die in few minutes when forced to remain in hot sun); hibernates October–November; remains until March; burrow penetrates sandy hillside to depth of 2–3 feet; tortoise makes no effort to fill burrow after it crawls in

Reproduction: Oviparous; 1–6 eggs deposited in May

TEXAS TORTOISE: *Gopherus berlandieri*

Range: Southern Texas and adjacent Mexico

Description: Quite similar to desert tortoise in general appearance, but shell shorter and head more pointed; carapace brown, sometimes with light yellow centers in shields; head, legs, and plastron dull yellow; reaches length of little more than 8 inches

Habitat: Open woods, chaparral, and mesquite with well-drained, sandy soil; often under near-desert conditions; digs burrows but never deep enough to cover self completely unless it burrows under decayed stumps and piles of rubble

Reproduction: Oviparous; 3 or more eggs

GOPHER TORTOISE: *Gopherus polyphemus*

Range: Coastal plain from South Carolina to Florida, westward to Mississippi River northward into southern Arkansas

Description: Carapace high and domelike; brown or tan with or without light centers in shields; plastron yellowish; head large and blunt; hind legs small; reaches shell length of 11 inches

Habitat: Areas of sandy ridges, sand dune country; in high pine woods of peninsular Florida; digs extensive, well-made burrows in colonies; width and depth of burrows vary with size of tortoise; enlarged as tortoise grows; each burrow ends in small chamber; sometimes 2 tortoises occupy the same burrow; burrows furnish homes for many other animals also, such as opossums, raccoons, snakes, rabbits, gophers, and frogs

Reproduction: Oviparous; 5–6 eggs deposited April–July

HOUSING

IN SCHOOLROOM: Tortoise must have freedom of room. Needs retreat and sleeping quarters to use at will. Knock out most of 1 end of barrel big enough for pet to fit in; leave just enough board to keep bedding material from spilling out. Place barrel on its side. Provide with thick layer of sandy soil covered with thick layer of dry leaves and grass. *Warmth*—Most important; allow tortoise to bask in sun at will; when maintained outside its natural range, its sleeping barrel must be placed near heating unit. Quarters must be dry and warm at all times; must not become chilled at night.

AT HOME: If pet is kept in house, maintain as in schoolroom. When placed in yard, conditions should represent, as closely as possible, native conditions; must have areas where soil is loose enough for pet to dig under grasses and low herbs. Advisable to use sleeping barrel, described above, until pet adjusts.

FOOD

Native tortoises feed on wild plant growth—grasses, herbs, blossoms, hard wild fruits. In captivity, give fresh grasses, alfalfa, clover, dandelion leaves, fresh green lettuce, melon rinds, apples, berries, sweet potatoes. *Water*—Tortoise drinks infrequently; when it does, takes large amount; water must always be available, especially in hot weather; place shallow container near retreat or sleeping quarters; keep water fresh and clean.

ALLIGATORS AND CROCODILES (CROCODILIANS)

Alligators and crocodiles are lizardlike creatures belonging to the family Crocodilidae. They are extremely large animals found in many of the warmer parts of the world. Only two members of the family occur in the United States—the American alligator and the

American crocodile. Neither makes a good pet and neither is recommended. They are most difficult to maintain in captivity out of their natural habitat. In addition to suffering from lack of warmth, they refuse food and soon die. Information on housing and feeding is given in case a specimen is brought into a classroom, and interest becomes aroused in this group of reptiles.

Alligators have been so persistently hunted in times past for commercial use of their skins that few, if any, now ever reach the size of the original giants, which have been recorded at nineteen feet in length.

In addition to commercial use of the skins, there was formerly a busy trade in the sale of baby alligators for so-called pets for children. The ruthless capture and sale of these small creatures naturally reduced the number of adults to the point where they were approaching extinction. It became necessary to protect them by law, and no more of the native young of the United States species can now be sold commercially. However, so-called baby alligators are still sold, especially in Florida, but they are baby caimans, which are a species of crocodile native to South America that are imported for sale here.

The skin of both alligators and crocodiles is thick and horny, and forms heavy, ridged scales over their backs and tails. They do not shed their skins as do the greater number of reptiles. Scales that become old and worn are replaced by new growth from underneath.

When alligators and crocodiles move rapidly on land, they stand with their bodies raised so that they actually run along on their toes. When frightened or angered they can move with lightning speed and run so fast that a man cannot keep up with them.

In the water they lie submerged or nearly so with only the nostrils and eyes visible. When they completely submerge, valves close the nostrils, flaps cover and close the ears, and a valve in the throat closes the windpipe so the mouth may be opened to grasp food without water being taken into the lungs. When moving under water they hold their legs close to the body and swim by wiggling the entire body and propelling themselves with the tail.

The long jaws of both alligators and crocodiles are well supplied with sharp teeth. When food is grasped, the creatures roll and twist their bodies and often lash about with their powerful tails.

WARNING: Neither alligators nor crocodiles normally attack humans, but it is wise to be wary. It is especially dangerous to approach an alligator's nest when the female is guarding it. It is also dangerous if either alligator or crocodile has been wounded, especially the crocodile as it is vicious—extremely so when fighting. Above all, avoid the powerful tail of the creatures, one blow of which can easily break a man's bones.

The word alligator was derived from the Spanish name of the large American crocodile native to Cuba—*el lagarto.*

ALLIGATOR: Genus *Alligator*

AMERICAN ALLIGATOR: *Alligator mississippiensis.*

Range: Atlantic and Gulf coastal plains, from Tyrell County, North Carolina, to the Texas coast to Corpus Christi; formerly to the lower Rio Grande; northward in Mississippi Basin to Arkansas and southern Oklahoma

Description: Head has broadly rounded snout; large, 4-inch tooth on lower jaw not visible when mouth closed; ground color black; young have yellowish cross bands on black background; average length now, when full grown, 10–12 feet

Habitat: Rivers, swamps, lakes, bayous, and marshes; young and old bask in sun for long hours; when in water only eyes, snout, or part of head seen above surface; rarely leaves fresh water

Reproduction: Oviparous; 20–70 hard-shelled eggs about size of goose eggs deposited in center of nest made of mud and masses of vegetable debris piled to height of 3 feet; warmth produced by decaying vegetation incubates eggs; mother guards nest until young hatch in 9–10 weeks; when ready to emerge, young make loud peeping sound; mother tears nest open and liberates them; young may remain with mother until following spring

Food: Food changes as creature grows; young feed almost entirely on aquatic insects and crustaceans; later take frogs, snakes, and fishes; then fishes, young pigs, muskrats, and some waterfowl; adult takes fishes, pigs, and larger animals that stray too close to water's edge, such as cows, calves, and deer.

Voice: Both young and old alligators hiss; female grunts like a pig in calling young; young make moaning sound, with mouth closed, in high key; male makes deep, bellowing roar heard throughout swamp

CROCODILE: Genus *Crocodylus*

AMERICAN CROCODILE: *Crocodylus acutus*

Range: Southern Florida and the Florida keys; recorded from Volusia, Palm Beach, Collier, Dade, and Monroe counties. Native also in Hispaniola, Jamaica, and Cuba, swimming freely to off-shore cays from main island; along Pacific coast of the Americas from Sinaloa, Mexico, to Guayaquil, Ecuador, and on the Caribbean coast from Yucatan to northern Colombia and the Magdalena Basin

Description: Head tapers markedly so that snout seems long and narrow; large 4-inch tooth on lower jaw visible from side when mouth closed; gray or tannish-gray with dusky markings; young gray or greenish-gray with narrow black crossbands or rows of spots; known to reach length of 23 feet; this size probably rare now

Habitat: Confined to Everglades National Park, Biscayne Bay, and the Florida Keys; works way into salt or brackish water from Miami southward along the keys

Reproduction: Oviparous; probably same number of eggs as alligator; buried in sand scooped up into low mound; nest usually left unguarded but female may return from time to time

Food: Probably much the same as that of alligator

Voice: Young have high-pitched grunt similar to that of young alligators; male has low rumble or growl-like voice but lacks penetrating qualities of alligator

The feeding and housing directions below also apply to baby caimans.

HOUSING

Use a 10- to 20-gallon aquarium. Cover bottom with several inches of sand, mounded high at one end so specimen can crawl out of water at will. Add 3–4 inches of water at lower end. Press several strands of aquarium plants into sand and allow them to float out in water. *Warmth*—Essential; constant temperature required; place aquarium where it receives direct sunlight for as long as possible during day. By night, temperature may be regulated to some extent by placing an electric light over habitat.

FOOD

Offer food during warmest part of day when specimen is most active. Food must be alive. Give aquatic insects and aquatic snails. Try tadpoles, baby frogs, and top minnows. Place all food in water.

SPIDERS AND OTHER ARTHROPODS

ARTHROPODA, which means jointed foot, is a large phylum of the animal kingdom. It comprises more than three-fourths of all the named animals in the world. The chief characteristics are jointed legs and bodies that have several sections. The bodies are covered with a hard, sometimes shell-like, skin called an exoskeleton, i.e., an outside skeleton. This exoskeleton protects the soft, inner body tissues and furnishes attachments for muscles.

The exoskeleton cannot grow as do the bones of a true skeleton, so when the animal grows, the exoskeleton is shed or molted. The new skin is soft at first and able to stretch enough to accommodate the increase in size. The new skin soon hardens and becomes again the protective body covering. The molting process occurs at intervals until the arthropod reaches full growth.

The majority of arthropods have the ability to regenerate appendages which have become damaged or lost through injury or as the result of a fight. The new appendage grows as the creature molts. In most cases it does not form as perfectly as the original appendage, but it does develop into a completely functional structure.

The most important classes of arthropods are the arachnids, the insects, and the crustaceans. The class Arachnida includes the spiders, scorpions, mites, ticks, and their relatives; the class Insecta includes insects only; while the class Crustacea includes crabs, lobsters, shrimps, and their relatives.

This chapter discusses some of the more common arthropods

169

that would not commonly be thought of as pets. These are the spiders and scorpions, centipedes, millipedes, and the crayfish, each of which belongs to a different Class. We begin the discussion with the order Araneae, to which the spiders belong.

SPIDERS

Spiders, naturally, belong to the class of arachnids, a name not difficult to remember when one knows the lovely old Greek myth from which the name was taken. The legend tells us that in the days of ancient Greece there lived a beautiful Lydian maiden named Arachné. She was famous for her great skill in weaving, and especially for her exquisite tapestries. She had been so praised by people from far and near that she felt herself an equal with the gods. To prove her perfection, she challenged Athene, the goddess of handicrafts, to compete with her, and Athene accepted. Arachné's tapestry proved to be much more exquisite than that of Athene. Athene was unable to accept such a defeat and flew into a divine rage, turned Arachné into a spider, and bade her spend the remainder of her days in spinning.

Spiders are found all over the world in almost any situation and any location.

Spiders are benefactors to man as they consume innumerable destructive insects. There is but one species of spider in the United States which to date has been *proven to* be deadly poisonous to man. This is the black widow spider.

Spiders cannot be thought of as pets in the same sense as a pet dog or cat, since they are unable to respond to human attentions. But they are interesting creatures, on the whole most helpful to man, often excite the curiosity of children, and are easily maintained in captivity.

Body characteristics: *Divisions:* Spiders have but two divisions to the body. The head and thorax are fused into one structure called the cephalothorax, which means head and thorax. The forward portion of the cephalothorax bears the eyes, the mouthparts, and the pedipalps; the remainder bears the eight jointed legs. The cephalothorax is joined to the abdomen by a stalklike pedicel, which means little foot, and bears no appendages.

Eyes: The eyes of a spider are usually near the front or anterior end of the head, but some are directly on top. They are single facets, hence are called simple eyes. They may number two, four, six, or eight; eight is the usual number. However, the cave spiders lack eyes entirely. Regardless of the number, the eyes are always placed in a definite arrangement. Often some pairs are much larger than others.

Mouthparts: The mouthparts consist of the chelicerae and the pedipalps: The chelicerae are a pair of heavy, jawlike structures with which the spider seizes and crushes its prey, and terminate in fangs. Usually the fangs are folded inward and upward when they are not in use. It is through the fangs that the spider ejects poison into its prey. The pedipalps are a pair of footlike appendages which are used in chewing and manipulating the prey.

SPIDER SILK: Spider silk is produced by a number of glands located in the abdomen of the spider. These glands send out a liquid through small tubes called spinnerets which are located at the tip of the abdomen. As this liquid is drawn out of the body, it hardens into silk thread.

There are usually six spinnerets. These are flexible as fingers, and in a way are used like fingers, as the spider manipulates the strands of silk.

Spider silk is used in a variety of ways and takes many forms. It is not only used for the construction of webs, but single threads are combined in different thicknesses to be used for snares in capturing prey; as a "drag line" to protect the spider; to enable the spider to drop quickly out of sight; for support; to wrap prey in; to live in; for a retreat during hibernation, molting, and mating; for ballooning lines; to line underground homes; for egg sacs; and nurseries for spiderlings.

The thread mentioned above as the "drag line" is a most important strand in the life of a spider. Regardless of where the spider goes, this line reels out behind it from the spinnerets, a true "life line." The drag line is also important in the construction of a web.

Webs are constructed in a variety of ways and patterns, many so distinctive in their design that they are used to designate families of spiders, such as the orb weavers and the funnel weavers.

A variety of silk with many threads making up a strand goes into a web. Some strands are used as guide lines, some as drop lines, some very interesting ones, which look like strings of beads, for capture of prey. The "beads" are drops of a sticky substance which makes it impossible for an insect to extricate itself when caught by these strands.

Most webs are damaged during the day as insects struggle for freedom. During the night the spider repairs the damage and begins the day with a new web.

Spider silk is used commercially in astronomical instruments, in gun sights, and in engineers' levels.

LIFE SPAN: Most spiders have a life span of a year or less, depending upon the species, but some among the larger species may live for many years.

COURTSHIP: Courtship is unique among many species of spiders. It begins by the male wandering about in search of a female. When he finds one he announces his presence by tweaking a snare line of her web. Then he proceeds to go through various maneuvers which might be called a dance, such as swinging his palps and legs about, and raising a leg or two on one side along with the abdomen. Sometimes he simply strikes peculiar attitudes. No doubt all this impresses the female with the fact that she has a suitor at her door and not the offering of a meal! Mating eventually takes place, after which the male goes on his way. He may search for other females with which to mate, or on occasion he may be eaten by the female.

REPRODUCTION: Spiders reproduce by laying eggs. There is a great difference in size between the sexes. Males are usually very small compared to the females. This is natural since the eggs develop within the abdomen of the female.

POISON: Most spiders are provided with poison sacs in the large basal segment of the chelicerae. The chelicerae end in a distal fang through which the poison is ejected. The poison is used to subdue enemies and prey and is rarely injurious to man.

FOOD: Spiders are exclusively carnivorous. Food consists entirely of insects and other spiders. Most spiders can survive for long periods without food but few can survive for long without water.

THE GIANT SPIDERS: Genus *Dugesiella*

TARANTULA: *Dugesiella hentzi*

Range: South central United States; other species found throughout drier areas of the West

Description: Bodies black or brownish; covered with thick furlike hairs; 8 eyes, placed in group on top and to front of cephalothorax; eyes with but a single facet; 8 legs, also covered with furlike hairs; largest of all spiders in United States—may reach body length of 3 inches

Habitat: In burrows, covered with thin web of silk; in cracks in old logs or stumps; in debris under stones and old logs; along open areas on hillsides, in mixed desert growths, or along edges of cultivated lands

Reproduction: Tarantulas mate September–October; following summer female deposits 600–700 eggs in thick-walled cocoon, which she often places near entrance to her burrow to be sunned; she guards the nest; if disturbed at this time, she may assume her striking attitude or she may turn and devour eggs and young.

Life span: Tarantulas are especially interesting because of their long growth period before maturity; believed to be 10 years old before they mature; at this time males leave their burrows in search of mate; after mating, male's function seems to have been completed; if he does not die, female may kill him; she may live on to the age of 25 years

Handling: Experiments on native tarantulas have shown their bites to be no more harmful than a bee sting, but since man experiences individual idiosyncrasies, it is wise to be cautious when first handling a tarantula; fangs are long and can inflict a deep wound; a captive tarantula seldom tries to bite, but if teased by children, it may be tempted to do so

Capture: Tarantulas are seldom found except September–October when they are in search of mates; as they do not move rapidly, they can be easily guided into large-mouthed jar or box

HOUSING

As tarantulas need plenty of room to move about in and to hunt food during the night, use small aquarium or handmade vivarium box with screen cover (see Part IV). Fill container two-thirds full of loose soil. Construct retreat by piling a handful of dry leaves mixed with scraps of old, dead bark across one end of habitat; pile up several flat rocks in a way that provides hiding space underneath; place piece of old log with wide crack or deep hole across rocks and leaves.

FOOD

In the wild, tarantulas feed on a large variety of insects. Food in captivity must be alive. Give grasshoppers, crickets, large beetles, cockroaches. When large insects are difficult to obtain, offer larval and adult meal worms. Sometimes, smooth-skinned caterpillars such as tomato worms are accepted; offer occasionally (see Part III). Tarantulas are nocturnal; place food in habitat in late afternoon; be sure to cover terrarium with screen. Feed every 4–5 days during spring, summer, and fall. Offer food only occasionally during winter, if spider remains active. *Water*—Most essential; must be fresh and available at all times; use small, flat, shallow container; push container into soil so that top edge is level with surface of soil.

TRAP-DOOR SPIDER: Genus *Bothryiocyrtum*

TRAP-DOOR SPIDER: *Bothryiocyrtum californicum*

Range: Restricted to southern and western states

Description: Smaller replica of tarantula; stockily built; legs short; body dark brown, thickly covered with hairs; 8 eyes placed in group on top and to front of cephalothorax; chelicerae with rows of large spines used for digging; reaches diameter of 1–2 inches

Habitat: In tunnels dug in moist banks; tunnels are lined with silk and closed by tightly fitting lid also lined with silk and hinged to one side; lids are usually covered with bits of vegetation from surrounding area for camouflage; spider is able to hold lid closed with surprising strength

Reproduction: Trap-door spiders mate September–October; following summer female deposits 600–700 eggs in thick-walled cocoon which she places near entrance to her burrow; she guards nest; if disturbed at this time, she may assume her striking attitude or she may turn and devour eggs and young

Handling: Trap-door spiders also possess poison which is used to subdue their prey and is not harmful to man; seldom attempts to bite, so it may be handled with confidence

Capture: Walls of trap-door spider's tunnel are coated with combination of soil and saliva before spider lines passage, making walls very firm so that the entire nest may be dug from bank without crumbling; surrounding soil must be removed carefully so as not to damage nest; spider will not attempt to escape but will hold firmly to its door; collect a quantity of the surrounding soil as it will be needed in the captive habitat

Trap Door: Doors on trap-door-spider tunnels vary according to the kind of spider making them; "wafer" type door covered with nothing more than silk; "cork" type is made of silk combined with soil; spider sits with door partially open and grasps any unwary insect that comes along

The trap-door spiders are hardy in captivity when their tunnels are properly placed in soil and they are properly fed.

HOUSING

Use small aquarium or hand-made vivarium box (see Part IV). Fill container with soil brought from bank where spider was captured. Build soil up at one end to represent a sloping bank, and firmly pack soil into place. Dig out pocket in soil and place spider nest at same angle as in original location. Carefully pack soil about nest, taking care not to crush nest by pressing too hard. During winter, sprinkle soil heavily to simulate winter rains. *Retreat*—Necessary for live food which is placed in habitat and hides there during the day; plant a few patches of thick-growing mosses on bank of soil; lay 2–3 small, flat rocks and pieces of rotted bark among mosses.

FOOD

In the wild, trap-door spiders feed on a large variety of insects and other arthropods. All food must be alive. Give quantity of any available insects; also give sow bugs, pill bugs, other spiders. Trap-door spiders do not forage for food; lie in wait at night with door slightly raised and grab prey as it crawls by. In captivity, teach specimen to feed before night by gently dragging food along close to trap door at same time each feeding. *Water*—Not as essential as to other spiders, but must be offered occasionally; use small, flat container; place close as possible to trap door.

HUNTING SPIDERS: Genus *Lycosa*

WOLF SPIDER: *Numerous species*

Range: Throughout United States

Description: Great variation in color and markings from black to gray or brown; all have long, slender legs covered with short hairs; body covered with shorter hairs which give velvety appearance; 4 small eyes on cephalothorax, in a row in front, and 4 larger ones on top forming a square; reaches 1 inch or more in body length depending upon species

Habitat: Simple burrows under logs or stones; some dig tunnels several inches deep; always lined with silk and surrounded by little wall of soil, sticks or stones; some species build a sizable turret about mouth of burrow

Reproduction: Females of all species spin tough, silken sacs in which eggs are placed; mother attaches sac to her spinnerets and drags it with her for a week or so, often sunning it; when eggs hatch, spiderlings break out of sac and cling to hairs on mother's back where they are carried for 2–3 more weeks

Handling: Harmless; may be maintained without fear

Capture: Most species move too quickly to be caught by hand; instead locate tunnel, pour water into it, and have small jar with large mouth ready to place quickly over the spider as it gives signs of darting out

Wolf spiders can be maintained for some time in captivity when they are given the proper habitat and live food.

HOUSING

Wolf spider needs soil deep enough for tunneling; use large, rectangular or round battery jar provided with tightly fitting screen top. Fill jar to within 3 inches of top with soil of same texture and consistency as that of area where spider was captured. Keep soil moist; push glass tube with large bore down between soil and wall of jar; as soil begins to dry out, add water through tube. If spider is turret builder, scatter *tiny* bits of broken twigs, straw, glass, and tinfoil on soil surface; spider will work these into turret.

FOOD

In the wild, wolf spider feeds on a large variety of insects. Give live insects of all kinds—flies, soft-shelled beetles, crickets, grasshoppers, cockroaches, adult and larval meal worms. Drop food on soil of habitat; wolf spider chases after prey. *Water*—Essential; must be fresh, clean, and available at all times; use small, flat container; push container down until its top edge is level with soil surface.

GARDEN SPIDERS: Genus *Argiope*

Orange Garden Spider: *Argiope aurantia*

Range: Common throughout United States

Description: Female is large, with vivid orange and black or deep yellow and black design on large abdomen; legs long and slender; weaves large, beautiful orb-shaped web; body 1 inch long; male is small (¼ inch long); cephalothorax brown; abdomen with broad, brown band down middle of back; white zigzag band on each side; palps large

Habitat: Found in the fall, usually resting head downward in hub of web, which may be among herbaceous plants and grasses of meadows and pastures, or in garden shrubs close to habitation

Reproduction: In early fall spins pear-shaped egg sac which is suspended firmly on nearby shrub or weed; dies soon after; eggs hatch shortly but spiderlings remain in sac during winter

Handling: Never attempts to bite, but not necessary to handle; remains quietly in web

Capture: Easy to capture; use a large-mouthed jar which can be held under web; shake the branch and make spider drop into the jar, or place the jar over it as it rests in the web, and with a card or piece of stiff paper tap it from the opposite side to force it into jar

An orange garden spider that is captured in September will carry on its natural activities when housed in a roomy cage and properly fed. It will construct egg sac, suspend it somewhere in the cage, and soon after refuse to eat and then die.

HOUSING

As orange garden spider needs a great deal of space in which to construct web, use small animal cage (see Part IV). Cover cage bottom with thin layer of sand. As web attachments, provide 2–3 thinly sprawling, sparsely leaved branches; set them upright so that twigs touch sides and top of cage.

FOOD

Spider feeds on large variety of insects, most of them pests; often swaths food in silk until it looks like mummy; may bite, then drag it to hub of web to be eaten later. Offer live grasshoppers, cockroaches, beetles, large flies, wasps, bees, and any other insects spider will take.

CARE OF EGG SAC

Egg sac will be placed high in some corner of cage. Keep it over the winter. If sac was fastened to a twig, cut loose portion with sac and firmly attach it to some shrub outside. Choose a place where it is not likely to be destroyed.

When no safe place is available outside, set egg sac aside in glass jar. *Keep sac moist*; during winter, dip sac in water once a week to provide moisture sac would normally receive out of doors.

When warm spring days come, bring sac indoors. Watch for appearance of spiderlings, which begin feeding on each other as soon as they emerge.

COMB-FOOTED SPIDERS: Genus *Latrodectus*

BLACK WIDOW SPIDER: *Latrodectus mactans*

Range: Throughout United States

Description: Female is shiny, jet black, with large, round abdomen, small cephalothorax, and long, slender legs; usually has characteristic red hourglass pattern on under surface of abdomen; occasionally this mark is missing; sometimes a series of red patches along back; body length ½ inch; male is very small with narrow abdomen marked with red and yellow, plus 4 pairs of stripes along sides

Habitat: In old logs, at bases of tree trunks, under large stones or loose bark, in shrubbery, corners of little-used buildings, dark corners of basements, attics, barns, sheds, outdoor toilets; solitary creature; battles to kill any others that come within range

Reproduction: Egg sac placed high up in ragged web; usually several sacs; eggs hatch in few weeks and spiderlings emerge soon after

Handling: Poison is *sometimes fatal* to man, but does not bite readily; timorous; bites only when cornered, pressed, or squeezed; however, should be housed in jar with tightly fitting lid to prevent any possibility of escape; jar should be handled by experienced adult only

Capture: Spider never jumps; when disturbed, it retreats to farthest corner of its ragged web; push broom into web against spider, which usually remains quietly among bristles; with small stick gently push it from broom into quart jar

The black widow spider is included in this discussion, first, because it is the only spider that is, to date, known to be deadly to man; second, because it is so common across the country that children should be taught to recognize it (knowledge is necessary for protection); third, because it can be easily maintained in captivity without fear, and its habits observed.

The black widow spider is often called the hourglass spider because of the red mark on the abdomen. Again it may be called the shoe button spider because of the shape of the shiny, black abdomen. Black widow is the most common name and the one most generally used.

Regardless of common names, the black widow belongs to the comb-footed spiders which possess a row of strong, curved bristles on the last pair of legs. These bristles or combs are used to throw spider silk about the body of any prey that becomes entangled in the ragged webs.

A black widow spider may be maintained in captivity with little difficulty. It requires no care other than food.

Note: If a person is bitten call a doctor immediately. The victim may need injections of calcium gluconate, and other medication to alleviate the intense pain. The symptoms are not only local but systemic, e g., abdominal cramps, nausea, profuse sweating, and sometimes difficulty in breathing. About the only home remedy is to bathe the small wound with alcohol or some other disinfectant to minimize the possibility of bacterial infection. The poison acts on the nervous system, and the usual treatment for snakebite—to incise the wound, promote bleeding or suck out the poison—is generally ineffectual, and may do more harm than good.

HOUSING

Black widows must be housed alone; otherwise, they kill each other. Quart jar sufficient, as spider needs little space for movement. Keep top screwed on, but punch air holes. Spider adjusts itself to captive quarters and carries on normal activities; spins web from sides of jar to lid; rests on undersurface of lid.

FOOD

In the wild, black widow feeds on a large variety of insects, many of them pests. Give live flies, bees, wasps, beetles, small grasshoppers, crickets, and any other insects available (see Part III). Place one insect at a time in jar. Disturb spider by tapping on lid; this causes it to drop to bottom of jar and delay feeding; quickly drop insect in and screw on lid. *Warning*—Black widow does not readily bite, but for the sake of safety, only an experienced adult should feed it.

CARE OF EGG SAC

Egg sac will be placed close to lid of jar; should be left in jar with adult spider. Hatching of spiderlings can be observed in jar; they gradually emerge and begin feeding on each other. *Warning*—When spiderlings hatch, air holes in jar lid must be covered. Spiderlings should not be allowed to escape; they can bite and are dangerous to humans. After hatching has been observed, it is wise to destroy both adult and spiderlings.

SCORPIONS

Scorpions are true arthropods and belong with the spiders to the class of arachnids. But they are so distinctive in other characteristics that they are placed in an order all their own, that of Scorponida.

Scorpions do not occur in great number nor are they as widely distributed as the spiders. They are secretive in their habits and active only at night, so they are not commonly seen by man.

Scorpions are much restricted in their range. They occur primarily in the southwestern United States.

Scorpions destroy a great many injurious insects, and most are harmless to man. Their sting causes severe pain and a little swelling, but the average person experiences no lasting difficulty. *However, there are species that possess a poison which is fatal to humans.* These occur in western Texas, New Mexico, Arizona, and southern California. One must know them in these areas in order to be protected.

It cannot be said that scorpions make attractive pets. However, since some are so dangerous to man, it is well to become acquainted with them when the opportunity arises.

BODY CHARACTERISTICS: *Divisions:* Scorpions have two body regions —the cephalothorax, and a broadly attached abdomen of seven segments with a long narrow tail that ends in a poison sting.

LIFE SPAN: Scorpions have been known to live for several years, but their maximum life span is unknown.

COURTSHIP: The courting "dance" of many species of scorpions is strange and interesting. A male sets out to find a female. When she is found he grasps her pedipalpal claws with his own, then walks sideways and backward while she follows. Often this movement is preceded by the two facing each other, straightening their bodies with the abdomens flat on the ground, then extending their tails upward and continually entwining and disengaging them. A sort of promenade follows this movement, with the tails raised and the female placidly following the male. This may last for several hours. Finally the pair disappears to some retreat where mating takes place, which often ends by the female consuming the male.

REPRODUCTION: Fertilized eggs develop within the body of the female. The young are born alive.

POISON: Poison is located in the bulblike terminal segment of the tail with its sting. The poison is used to subdue or kill prey and for defense. For attack, the tail is thrown forward and down, which places the stinger in a position for striking the prey or enemy.

FOOD: Food consists of ground insects and small animals.

SCORPIONS: Various Genera

SCORPIONS: *Numerous Species*

Range: Southern states, the Southwest, and from eastern Washington south

Description: Long, flat-bodied; some species very slender; cephalothorax joined to abdomen by wide segment; abdomen made up of 7 wide segments followed by long, narrow tail of 5 segments which terminates in bulblike structure with sting; pedipalps large, bearing pair of strong pincers; 1 pair of eyes near midcephalothorax; on each side, near edge of body, group of 2–5 simple eyes; some species have no eyes; 4 pairs of legs attached to thorax, fitted for walking; exoskeleton smooth, shiny, varying from pale yellowish to reddish brown; when scorpion runs, pincers carried horizontally in front and tail curved up over back; length varies from 2–6 inches according to species

Habitat: Under rocks, pebbles, in dry grass, piles of leaves, and any other objects that afford shelter; often enters houses and crawls into old shoes and clothing; lies concealed during day; comes out at night to hunt

Reproduction: Eggs hatch just before emergence from body of female; young immediately climb on mother's back and hold on by pincers; remain attached for day or 2 after first molt, then scatter on their own

Handling: Since there are some species of scorpions deadly to man, it is wise *not* to handle any specimen unless it can be identified as a harmless one

Capture: Look for scorpions under objects, or go out with a flashlight at night when they are active; use jar or can with lid punctured for air; gently push or guide scorpion into container; if specimen is harmless, pick it up by its tail which renders it helpless at once

Scorpions are easily maintained in captivity when properly housed and fed.

HOUSING

Keep no more than 2–3 scorpions together at a time. Watch to see if they fight. Sometimes they destroy each other. As they need conditions typical of natural habitat, establish desert habitat in large vivarium with screen cover (see Part II). Cover bottom with thick layer of loose sand; top with inch of fine sand mixed with some soil. Construct retreat by piling several large, flat rocks about; place handful of dry leaves or other dry vegetation across one end of habitat; place a few more small rocks among leaves and grass. Scorpion must have warmth to carry on normal activities; protect from chilling during winter; keep in warm room.

FOOD

In the wild, scorpions feed on spiders, centipedes, flies, cockroaches, grasshoppers, crickets, mantids, butterflies, ants, adult and larval beetles, myriapods. Give as much native food as possible; must be alive when dropped into vivarium. Use adult and larval meal worms (see Part III). Some owners have been successful in using small bits of juicy, raw meat dragged slowly about within vision of scorpion; try when other food is difficult to obtain. *Water*—Not necessary.

MILLIPEDES

Millipedes, most commonly called thousand-legged worms, are not worms but are wormlike creatures which are slow-moving, secretive, and not commonly seen by humans. These more or less harmless creatures are members of the class Diplopoda, meaning double-footed.

Millipedes occur everywhere throughout the United States, and nearly all are considered nondestructive. However, some species, small in size, can become a real pest in vegetable gardens.

Millipedes are considered harmless to man since they have no structures for producing poison. They make up another group among the members of the vast phylum of arthropods which cannot be considered as pets but often create curiosity among children who find them. They are extremely easy to maintain in captivity and offer hours of interesting observation.

BODY CHARACTERISTICS: *Divisions:* There are but two divisions to the body—a distinct head, followed by a long, segmented, wormlike body. When it is time for a millipede to molt, it usually builds a nestlike chamber for protection. If another millipede enters this chamber before the skin of the newly molted creature hardens, the invader will eat the helpless millipede. After molting, the millipede usually eats the cast-off exoskeleton.

REPRODUCTION: Eggs are fertilized within the body of the female. Some species coat the eggs with excrement and earth, then place them in crevices in soil. Others may construct a nest of soil particles moistened with saliva and placed together to form a hollow sphere. The inside of the sphere may be lined with excrement and be very smooth; the outside will be very rough. Sometimes a female will remain curled around the nest for a few days. The incubation period may take several weeks.

FOOD: All millipedes are vegetarians and feed on soft and decomposing plant tissues.

MILLIPEDES: Various Genera

COMMON MILLIPEDE: Numerous Species

Range: Throughout United States

Description: Head distinct from body; 1 pair short antennae; body may be flattened or cylindrical depending upon species; body segmented; each segment represents 2 segments fused, hence each segment bears 2 pairs of legs; first 4 or 5 segments *not* fused so bear single pair of legs; exoskeleton very firm; chestnut brown to blue-black depending upon species; when disturbed, some coil tightly like spring and may emit offensive brown fluid; length ½–2 inches depending upon species

Habitat: In soil, old damp and decaying wood, and on garden vegetables

Handling: Harmless; may be handled without fear

Capture: Pick up with fingers

Millipedes are hardy in captivity, require little space, little care, and little attention, but must have an abundant supply of food.

HOUSING

Millipedes need little space; use small glass vivarium box (see Part IV). Cover bottom with thick layer of sand; top with thick layer of loam; keep *damp*. Construct retreat by covering soil with pieces of decayed wood and soft rotted wood pulp brought from spot where millipedes were caught; pile pieces up and over each other.

FOOD

In the wild, millipedes feed on damp and decaying wood and other vegetable matter. Keep well supplied with pieces of damp, well-rotted wood; also give 2–3 small pieces of raw potato; from time to time, renew rotted wood and raw potato. *Moisture*—Essential; wood, potato, and loam must be kept damp (not wet) at all times.

CENTIPEDES

Centipedes are fairly common creatures but so inconspicuous that they are less familiar than many other arthropods. It is the centipede that should be called thousand-legged as its many legs appear to be more numerous than those of the millipedes. The word centipede means hundred-footed, but the class to which centipedes belong is the Chilopoda, meaning thousand-footed.

Centipedes are found throughout the world, especially in warm, temperate countries.

They are of great benefit to man because of the number of insect pests they destroy. There are a few in the United States whose poison affects humans, but not seriously.

Centipedes are so secretive and so quick in their movements that they may be difficult to observe in captivity. They cannot be considered as pets, but they are easily maintained in captivity, are interesting creatures, and are worth keeping for any observations children may be able to make.

BODY CHARACTERISTICS: *Divisions:* Centipedes have but two divisions to the body—a head, followed by a segmented body.

LIFE SPAN: Centipedes are apparently long-lived. There are records of some species living from five to six years.

REPRODUCTION: Eggs are usually deposited throughout the spring and summer, though mating may have taken place the previous autumn. The eggs are usually laid in a loose mass and left in the soil. Some species brood the eggs and if disturbed will either eat the eggs and young or abandon them. Some species curl about the eggs and young, making a basketlike framework with their legs to hold them. Development requires about three years.

POISON: Centipedes possess poison with which to subdue prey. Those in the United States are not dangerous to man, although there are a few species whose poison does affect humans sometimes, but not seriously. Some tropical species are deadly to man.

FOOD: Centipedes are carnivorous, feeding primarily on insects; some species also feed on snails and earthworms. On occasion some species may feed on plant tissues and can injure crops.

CENTIPEDES: Genus *Scolopendra*

GIANT DESERT CENTIPEDE: *Scolopendra heros*

Range: All over the world, greatest number occurring in warm tropical and temperate countries

Description: Flat-bodied with many somites; 1 pair legs to each somite; head with 1 pair many-segmented antennae and 3 pairs mouthparts; first somite of body just behind head bears 1 pair appendages with poison claws to capture and kill prey; ducts at tips of poison claws from poison glands; head sometimes with cluster of simple eyes; some species may have compound eyes; number of legs varies from 15 to more than 100 pairs; regardless of pairs, number is always odd; extremely swift in movement; secretive; colors vary from pale buff through reddish-browns, even greenish or bluish; sizes vary from less than 1 inch to 8 inches, depending upon species

This oddity in the number of legs brings to mind a few lines composed many, many years ago by the scientist Ray Lankester:

> A centipede was happy quite
> Until a toad in fun
> Said, "Pray which leg moves after which?"
> This raised her doubts to such a pitch,
> She fell exhausted in the ditch,
> Not knowing how to run.

Habitat: In soil, under old boards, stones, old logs, fallen leaves, in houses, and in dark and obscure places

Reproduction: Eggs laid during spring and summer months; often deposited in soil; female broods eggs, usually coiled about them, her threadlike legs forming a basket; when disturbed, she usually eats both eggs and young

Handling: Centipedes bite in self-defense, but the poison is usually harmless, although painful; if bitten by the large desert centipede, one should seek medical attention at once to reduce the discomfort; advisable to avoid picking up centipedes by hand unless wearing gloves

Capture: Use wide-mouthed jar with perforated lid; try to guide centipede into jar with stick or pair of forceps, or grasp it quickly but firmly with forceps and drop into jar; one must be agile

HOUSING

Centipede needs little room; use small glass vivarium box (see Part IV); house alone. Cover bottom with 1–2 inches of soil topped by materials resembling habitat where centipede was caught; for example, if caught between damp old boards, that is what should be placed on soil. Keep habitat slightly damp at all times.

FOOD

In the wild, centipede feeds on all kinds of insects, worms, and slugs. Give native food; place alive in habitat. Feed once weekly. *Water*—Necessary; use small, very flat container; push down into soil near where centipede hides.

CRAYFISH

The arthropods which make up the class of crustaceans are a most interesting group. The members of this class are the sow bugs and pill bugs, which are terrestrial; the crabs, lobsters, shrimps, and their relatives, which are all marine animals; and the crayfish, or crawdads as children call them, which are fresh water inhabitants. The hard, shell-like body covering of the crustaceans is due to lime which is derived from their food and water. The word *crustacea* means hard and shell-like.

Crayfish occur throughout the world. They are used as food in many countries where the flesh is considered a great delicacy. In such countries there are open and closed seasons, and the "take" is limited. In many areas in the United States, crayfish cause a great deal of damage by burrowing in stream banks, which contributes to erosion, and by tunneling in damp meadows where they raise mounds of dirt and feed on young crop growth.

BODY CHARACTERISTICS: The crayfish has two divisions to the body —cephalothorax and segmented abdomen.

REPRODUCTION: Mating takes place during early spring or fall, depending upon geographical location. Eggs are laid several weeks to several months after mating, depending upon the season.

POISON: Crayfish do not possess poison. They use their pincers in self-defense.

FOOD: Crayfish are omnivorous feeders; they possess a series of appendages developed into mouthparts which are used to crush, to pick up food, and to tear it to pieces. It is then strained, further crushed, and finally all juices are sucked into the body.

CRAYFISH: Genera *Cambarus, Astacus*

COMMON CRAYFISH: *Numerous Species*

Range: Most of North America where suitable conditions occur

Description: Eastern specimens have short, quadrangular rostrum, in western specimens rostrum is elongate, carapace depressed; body more or less cylindrical; compound large eyes placed on movable stalks; head and thorax fused to form large cephalothorax covered by shieldlike structure termed carapace; forward end of carapace forms an elongated rostrum which terminates in a short spine; one short pair of antennae called antennules, with 2 filaments each; second pair of antennae bear 1 long filament each; 5 pairs of appendages make up mouthparts; abdomen made up of 6 distinct segments, first 5 bearing swimmerets; last segment forms broad tail fan; 5 pairs of legs, first 3 pairs bearing claws; claws on first pair greatly enlarged; color ranges from browns, reds, orange, and greens, with many intermediate shades; may reach length of 6 inches

Habitat: Some burrow in wet meadows only; some live in muddy ponds, or ditches; some live in lakes or sluggish streams; other species found only in shallow but swift streams with stony bottoms; most are commonly found in shallow streams

Reproduction: When eggs ready to be laid, female thoroughly cleans under side of her abdomen and the swimmerets, rubbing and combing them with her claws; when eggs emerge they are stuck to swimmerets with a gluelike substance and are carried about for many weeks; when eggs hatch each tiny crayfish clings firmly to a swimmeret with pincers and is carried about for another week before it takes off on its own

Handling: Can give sharp pinch with pincers, but if grasped with thumb and forefingers on each side of carapace, crayfish cannot nip because pincers are out of range

Capture: Easily captured with piece of cooked meat tied to end of string; drag bait slowly through water near crayfish; it will quickly grasp the meat with its pincers and hold on so firmly that it can be jerked from the water onto the bank; capture may also be made at night with a flashlight when they are out on stream bank foraging for food

Crayfish may be maintained in captivity for any length of time *only* when in their natural range and when the water of the habitat is similar in oxygen and mineral content to that from which they were obtained.

HOUSING

One or two crayfish may be housed together; if more than one, watch carefully at first; they may fight when maintained in close quarters. Use 5- to 10-gallon aquarium. Cover bottom with 2 inches of sand and pebbles; try to reproduce stream bottom from which creature was taken. Add enough stream water to more than cover specimen. Place fairly large, flat rock in habitat so that it extends above water surface, permitting crayfish to climb out of water at will. Pile several smaller rocks near large one to provide hiding places. *Water*—Change daily; use water from stream or pond where pet was captured. Water must be at constant temperature; sudden changes lower vitality of crayfish, and it soon dies.

FOOD

In the wild, crayfish feed on small fish, worms, aquatic insects, and decomposing organic matter. Give bits of raw or cooked meat, chopped raw fish, earthworms, water insects, prepared fish food, and soybean meal; do not overfeed; crayfish tend to overeat. Prevent pollution at all times; clean out leftover bits of food soon after feeding.

INSECTS

INSECTS, which make up the largest group of animals in the animal kingdom and the largest class in the phylum Arthropoda, occur in untold numbers throughout the world. This is, in reality, the age of insects as today they are the most successful creatures in the common struggle for existence. Insects not only make up the largest class in the animal kingdom but they present man with his most difficult problems. A great many insects are beneficial to man but the majority are harmful. They cause immeasurable discomfort with their bites and their stings. They are among the chief carriers of disease; and they are major factors in the damage and destruction of crops. Much of their success in this struggle is due to their small size, their amazing capacity for reproduction, and their ability to adapt themselves to almost any environmental condition. They have had long centuries in which to develop these abilities as they have been in existence since the carboniferous period, more than sixty million years ago. Fossil specimens of cockroaches have been found from this period, and cockroaches are still abundant today.

Insects may be microscopic in size to many inches in length and breadth. They occur in all manner of shapes, forms, and sizes. They may be aquatic, terrestrial, aerial, or parasitic on plants, other animals, and upon themselves.

There is no locality in which some interesting insects do not exist. Many are attractive to children and arouse a great deal of curiosity. Many are easily captured and can be maintained easily in captivity, but it is important to know what the creature is, what it feeds upon, and how it should be maintained in order for it to carry out its life activities. This section deals with those insects which most commonly occur throughout the United States and are most often captured or noticed by children.

BODY CHARACTERISTICS: *Divisions:* A typical insect is characterized by three divisions to the body—the head, the thorax, and the abdomen. Attached to the thorax are six jointed legs, three on each side, and sometimes wings.

Eyes: The eyes, when present, are placed somewhere upon the head and are of two types: simple eyes, called ocelli, which are found in insect larvae and in many adults; and compound eyes, which are found in adult insects and in the immature stages of types which resemble the adult during growth.

Mouthparts: The mouthparts of some insects are constructed especially for biting. In others they are used only for piercing and sucking, and in still others they may be completely nonfunctional.

Abdomen: The abdomen is made up of a series of segments. All are without appendages with the exception of the last two or three segments which may bear the ovipositor of a female, or the sting, or the mating claspers of a male.

Wings: Most insects have wings although there are many that do not. However, wings are such a characteristic feature that many insect orders have been named according to wing types, viz: butterflies and moths belong to the order Lepidoptera, which means scale wings; beetles belong to the order Coleoptera, which means sheath wings; and flies belong to the order Diptera, which means two wings; and so on.

Cuticle: The outer body covering of insects is firm or hard, as it is in all arthropods. This is caused by a substance in the skin called chitin (ᴋɪ′-tin). Such an external chitinized body covering is called an exoskeleton—outer skeleton—and is a protection for the soft inner structures.

Poison: Many insects have well-developed poison which is ejected through a sting; others have a saliva that may act as a poison; but few insects in the United States are known to be seriously dangerous to man so far as poison is concerned. Due to individual idiosyncracies, some people may become ill from a sting or bite such as that of a mosquito or bee. Also, many diseases are transmitted by insects.

METAMORPHOSIS: All insects, with the exception of the most primitive forms, pass through several stages in their development from the egg to the adult. This is called metamorphosis, meaning to transform. If there are four stages, viz: egg, larva, pupa, adult, the metamorphosis is said to be complete. If but three stages occur, viz: egg, nymph, adult, the metamorphosis is said to be incomplete.

MOLTING: Most insects increase in size by shedding the skin as a new skin develops underneath it. This usually takes place during the larval or nymphal stages so that once the adult stage is reached, the insect does not molt again.

SEX: The presence of an ovipositor at the end of the abdomen designates a female. This structure may be bladelike, swordlike, extremely long, hard, and needlelike, short and curved, cyclelike, and so on. Ovipositors are not present in all kinds of insects, however.

LIFE SPAN: Many insects live for short periods only—no more than a few hours—while others may live for many years.

MIGRATION: Some species of insects follow a definite pattern of migration.

HIBERNATION: Those insects that live more than one season hibernate in some protected spot out of doors or in old buildings, as well as in inhabited homes. In some species only the female lives through the winter in hibernation, the male dying in the fall.

RANGE: Insects may be found anywhere and everywhere—in, on, and near water; in and on the ground; in the air; at high altitudes; in old buildings; at low altitudes; in occupied houses; in gardens; in and on vegetation; in and on other animals; and so on.

FOOD: Insects are amazing in their taste for foods. It ranges all the way from blood to plant juices; from carrion to plant tissues; from starchy seeds to dry wood; from hair and feathers to woolen cloth; and even tobacco, the food choice of cigarette beetles.

COLLECTING: To collect flying insects a net, a large-mouthed jar with screw lid punched with air holes, and a pair of forceps are needed. For water insects a dip net, a large-mouthed jar, and a pair of forceps are needed. Caterpillars may be transferred in jars but should be released in larger quarters as soon as possible.

TRUE BUGS

The true bugs make up a very large order of insects which are characterized by a difference in the structure of the two pairs of wings. The front or fore pair of wings is thickened at the base while the rest of the wing is thin and transparent. The hind wings of all are transparent The structure of the forewing has given the name Hemiptera, meaning half-wings, to this order of insects.

True bugs may be aquatic or semiaquatic, but the great majority are terrestrial. The aquatic and semiaquatic forms feed on small animal life such as other insects, but the majority of terrestrial forms feed on plants, and a number are predaceous.

All the true bugs have mouthparts formed into a piercing or sucking beak for use in taking only liquid food. The piercing beak is made up of the various mouthparts which have become elongated and fitted snugly together to form a tube. Plant tissues are pierced and juices sucked in through this tube. The structure is usually folded back under the body when not in use.

Many of our most destructive pests are found among the true bugs.

Metamorphosis of true bugs is incomplete. The young looks like the adult but is without wings; the wings develop with each molt as the nymph grows.

GIANT WATER BUG: Genus *Lethocerus*

GIANT ELECTRIC LIGHT BUG: *Lethocerus americanus*

Range: Throughout United States

Habitat: At bottom of shallow water; leaves water only to find a mate or a new pool; at this time is attracted by bright street lights

Economic position: Destructive to small fish in some areas; otherwise harmless

Adult: Body broad, flat, elongated, leathery-looking, brown; 2 large compound eyes; forelegs developed for grasping and held in grasping position; second and third pair of legs adapted for swimming; 2 short breathing tubes at tip of abdomen; average length 2¾ inches; 1¼ inches wide

Eggs: Metamorphosis incomplete; eggs deposited on vegetation above water

Nymph: Eggs hatch into creature which resembles adult with wing pads only; wings develop as nymph molts and grows

WATER BUG: Genus *Abedus*

TOE-BITER: *Abedus macronyx*

Range: Throughout United States

Habitat: In soft sediments at bottom of shallow streams; children have named this bug because of the pinching bite it gives when stepped on by barefoot waders.

Economic position: Destructive to small fish in some areas; otherwise harmless

Adult: Body oval, flat, leathery-looking, brown; first pair of legs developed for grasping; third pair adapted for swimming; length averages 1½ inches; width close to 1 inch

Eggs: Pale brown, elongated, and cemented to back of male by female; male carries them until they hatch

Nymph: Eggs hatch into nymphs which resemble adults with wing pads; wings develop as bug molts and grows

Both the electric light bug and the toe-biter are capable of inflicting severe bites. They have a poison that is used to subdue and kill their prey. The poison can be most painful to humans but is not otherwise harmful. Pick up these insects by placing thumb and forefinger on each side of bug between second and third pair of legs; this prevents their grasping forelegs from functioning.

HOUSING

Use rectangular or circular aquarium jar or tank. Cover bottom with half-inch of aquarium sand. Cover sand with thick layer of sediment brought up from stream or pond where bugs were captured. Pile a few flat rocks in one corner to make hiding places. Place a few small aquatic plants brought from stream, or use a few strands of common aquarium plants. *Water*—Water from native pool or stream preferred; pour gently into container; fill half full; allow water to settle before adding bugs.

FOOD

In the wild, bugs feed on tadpoles, snails, young fish, aquatic insects. Feed native food; also feed top minnows (see Part III).

BUTTERFLIES AND MOTHS

Butterflies and moths are probably the most conspicuous of all the insects and the most interesting to children, especially in the larval stages. For rural and village children the collection of butterfly caterpillars and chrysalids is often an all-consuming interest. The magical transformation of the caterpillar into the chrysalid and the final emergence of the adult butterfly is a never-to-be-forgotten experience. The classroom seems the only place where the city child may have this exciting experience.

The bodies of butterflies and moths are covered with a soft, powderlike substance which comes off on one's fingers all too easily. This powder is simply microscopic scales of various shapes and sizes which determine the color pattern of these insects. Because of these scales, the name Lepidoptera, meaning scale wings, has been given to the order to which butterflies and moths belong.

Although butterflies and moths belong to the same order and have many characteristics in common, there are very real differences between them, as follows:

Butterflies	*Moths*
1. Day fliers only.	1. Fly mostly at night.
2. Hold wings up or spread them at right angles to body when at rest.	2. Usually hold wings parallel to body when at rest.
3. Antennae (feelers) threadlike with swelling or knob on end.	3. Antennae commonly featherlike, never enlarged at tip.
4. Pupa has no extra covering; is encased only in hard covering called chrysalis or chrysalid.	4. Pupa frequently encased in some sort of extra protective covering called a cocoon.

MONARCH or MILKWEED BUTTERFLY: Genus *Danaus*

MONARCH BUTTERFLY: *Danaus plexippus*

Range: North and South America, in the islands of the Pacific, and in Europe

Habitat: Woods, fields, gardens, plains

Economic position: Harmless in every way

Adult (butterfly): Wingspread 4–5 inches; wings rich red-brown bordered with black; white spots scattered through the black; veins of wings outlined with black; body black with white spots

Egg: Large, white, cone-shaped, sculptured, deposited singly; usually placed on underside of leaves of food plant; easily seen with naked eye but details require magnification

Larva (caterpillar): Green with circular bands of black and light yellow; toward anterior end carries pair of long, black, whiplike filaments; on posterior end a second but shorter pair of black filaments; when caterpillar disturbed, filaments twitch in peculiar manner

Pupation: When caterpillar reaches full growth, it ceases to feed, crawls to some well-supported part of plant, spins a small patch of silk which it grasps with its last pair of false feet, then hangs head down like an inverted question mark; several days thereafter, depending on temperature, the larval skin is cast off and the lovely chrysalid formed in a rapid and dramatic fashion

Pupa: (chrysalid): Beautiful and jewellike; pendant-shaped, pale jade-green sprinkled with gold dots; suspended by black stalk—the cremaster. Adult emerges 12 to 15 days after pupation

Immunity: Not injurious in any of its stages but is obnoxious to all insectivorous animals because of its acrid taste which makes it inedible in all of its stages; is preyed upon by some parasites, however, the most common of which is a tachina fly

Parasites: Presence of parasites is recognized by appearance of caterpillar soon after it suspends itself preparatory to developing into the chrysalid; it will hang limp and straight with several long strings of mucous hanging from it; the tachina fly larvae, which have been living on tissues of the caterpillar, have reached their full growth just as the caterpillar is ready to pupate; fly larvae bore their way through skin of caterpillar and drop to the ground, leaving strings of mucous behind them; they pupate in the ground and finally emerge as adult flies; parasitized monarch caterpillars brought into a classroom may be used as an example of one of nature's ways of maintaining a balance between all living things: When a species becomes too numerous, then a parasite comes along and reduces its numbers

Migration: Monarch butterfly famous because of its habit of migration; in the fall, throughout Canada and the United States east of the Rockies, monarch butterflies gather in great numbers and begin a mass migration southward along very definite routes; along these routes there are certain fixed places, always the same, where the butterflies collect and rest until the temperature lowers, when they again take off and fly on farther south where the temperature is still warmer; west of Rockies pattern is identical in that tree locations are always the same year after year, but butterflies remain throughout the winter; do not move on farther south after they are once settled; in spring, the monarchs, both east and west, fly north individually, not in mass migration.

Scientists are learning more about insect migration each year. Many monarchs are banded each season with a marker which is fastened to one wing. The statement on the marker instructs persons who find them to report their find in much the same method as that used in bird banding. In time, it is hoped, complete information may be gained about the migration habits of monarch butterflies.

MOURNING-CLOAK: Genus Nymphalis

Mourning-cloak: Nymphalis antiopa

Range: Throughout temperate regions of world
Habitat: In open woods, gardens, and open fields
Economic position: Does not occur in sufficient number to cause destruction
Adult (butterfly): Wings with light yellow margin; just inside margin row of blue spots; remainder of wings dark brownish to black, in some lights almost midnight blue
Eggs: Laid in masses encircling twigs of food plants
Larva (caterpillar): Velvety-black with orange-red spots and black spines
Pupation: Caterpillar crawls to some protected spot on twig or fence where it suspends itself and pupates
Pupa: Yellowish-brown, with dark markings and red-tipped tubercles

The mourning-cloak butterfly hibernates in the adult stage and may do so in the pupal stage, since there are two broods a year. This is frequently the first butterfly to appear in the spring in many localities.

SWALLOWTAIL: Genus Papilio

Tiger Swallowtail: Papilio glaucus

Range: Throughout North America
Habitat: Usually found in woodlands and savannahs, but city flower gardens also attract them; regular visitor at mud puddles, manure droppings, and on carrion, presumably for moisture

Economic position: Do not occur in sufficient numbers at any one time to become destructive

Adult (butterfly): Large with long "tail" on hind wing; yellow with black patterns; hind wings with little blue just within wing margin; underwings duller in color

Eggs: Deposited on leaves of food plants

Larva (caterpillar): Smooth, green; anterior end enlarged, with double stripe of yellow and black across back; pair of yellow-black and greenish eye spots in front of stripe followed by several rows of turquoise dots; pair of orange-colored scent glands back of head which can protrude and give off strong offensive odor for protection

Pupation: Larva hangs self, usually horizontally, by a silk-thread girdle as well as by the cremaster

Pupa: Rough, brown, and greenish mottled, depending upon what surface pupation takes place; some parts of adult butterfly identifiable on pupa

There is no difficulty in capturing the larvae. Break off portions of the plant upon which they feed. Drop in a cardboard box to transfer to captivity.

HOUSING

Use screen-wire insect cage constructed with pie pans (see Part IV); should be tall enough for food plant to fit. Fill bottom pan with moist sand; stick a few stems of food plant into sand. Keep no more than 6–8 caterpillars at a time, as they are difficult to feed adequately if crowded. Caterpillar protects itself by rolling up and falling to the ground; do not let it remain on wet sand; place it in branches of food plant where it cannot roll off when it begins to move again.

FOOD

Use the kind of plant upon which caterpillars were found. Keep plant sprays from wilting by wetting sand from time to time. Keep a constant supply of fresh food as long as caterpillars feed. In the wild, monarch larva feeds upon varieties of milkweed plant; mourning-cloak larva, upon leaves of willow, poplar, and elm; swallowtail larva, upon leaves of wild cherry and related species.

METAMORPHOSIS

Life cycle from egg to adult is completed in about 30 days. Caterpillars eat voraciously and molt several times during growth period. When full-grown, they cease to feed; crawl about in search of a free surface from which to suspend; make sure ends of food plants do not brush against pan over top of cage as caterpillars need hanging surfaces. Caterpillars slip off larval skin, and pupa or chrysalid takes form. Pupal stage lasts about 2 weeks. When adults are ready to emerge, pupal case becomes transparent, and all parts of body of adult butterfly become visible.

Adult may be kept captive for a day or two, but should then be liberated. Place nectar-bearing flowers in cage for adult to feed upon or use sweetened sponge. Saturate piece of sponge with sweetened water placed in small, flat dish. Butterfly feeds readily from sponge; gives opportunity of seeing its use of long, coiled tongue.

MOTHS: Genus *Bombyx*

DOMESTIC SILK MOTH: *Bombyx mori*

There are many species of silk moths which occur in the wild state, a number of which are found in the United States. These are the cecropia moths, the luna moths, the promethia, and the regal walnut moths. Many of these produce silk of excellent fiber, but the species have not responded to domestication. It is the Chinese or mulberry silkworm which has been domesticated for so long that it is no longer found in the wild state. It has lost all its wild instincts and will starve while waiting to be fed. The adult moths have fully developed wings but cannot fly as the wing muscles have degenerated from centuries of disuse.

The silkworm is hardy in captivity and very easily maintained. It requires only cleanliness and a constant supply of fresh, clean mulberry leaves.

The eggs may be purchased at a nominal cost from any reliable supply house, such as General Biological Supply Company, Turtox Division, Chicago; or perhaps there may be someone in a community who is rearing silkworms and will supply the eggs.

HOUSING

Container must be easy to clean; use any cardboard box about 12″ × 14″. Cover bottom with sheet of paper toweling. Place eggs on paper.

MAINTENANCE

EGGS: Silk moth eggs are no larger than flattened pin heads. When just laid; they are yellow; later turn grayish or bluish-white; just before hatching become black.

LARVA: Eggs hatch into black, hairy caterpillars about ⅛ inch long. Keep only 12–14 caterpillars in habitat at a time; difficult to feed a larger number. To feed, pluck youngest and most tender mulberry leaves; must be free of all dust and moisture; lay over hatching eggs. Worm eats its shell, then climbs on leaves and feeds on epidermis only of leaf until first molt takes place. After that, larva feeds on whole leaf.

GROWTH: Caterpillar molts 4 times during growth period; first molt occurs 4–5 days after hatching. Caterpillar ceases to eat at molting time, but feeds voraciously between molts. To feed after first molt, continue to offer young mulberry leaves; cut leaves into small pieces until larvae reach a good size; supply fresh leaves several times daily; give extra supply before leaving at night.

CLEANING: Box must be cleaned daily to maintain hardiness of larva. Each morning place fresh leaves over worms; shortly they will crawl from old leaves to fresh ones; lift out fresh leaves with caterpillars, place on clean paper, and return all to box, first discarding old leaves and paper in box.

SPINNING

When larvae are full grown, they cease to feed and begin nervously to crawl about box. Provide spinning nooks—tie arrangements of twigs or coarse straw together or provide egg cartons. Lift larvae out of feeding box and place on objects provided for spinning. From 3 to 5 days after cocoon is completed, larvae pupates within cocoon. To observe pupation process, cut cocoon open with sharp scissors.

EMERGENCE

Adult moth emerges about 3 weeks after spinning. Moth ejects a fluid against one end of cocoon which moistens and softens silk fibers. Fibers spread and break as moth pushes out. Adult moths possess nonfunctional mouthparts; require no food. Moths mate soon after emerging, deposit eggs shortly thereafter, and die a few days later.

EGG STORAGE

Place eggs in box with tightly fitting lid to protect them from mice. Place box in refrigerator for week or more; then store it in some cool place for remainder of winter. In southern portion of temperate zones, even temperature during winter lowers vitality of eggs and prevents many from hatching the following spring. In mild, warm climate, eggs often hatch soon after being laid; the refrigerator storage prevents this premature development.

TIGER MOTHS: Genus *Isia*

ISABELLA TIGER MOTH: *Isia isabella*

Range: Widely distributed throughout United States
Habitat: In gardens as well as open fields
Economic position: Harmless
Adult (moth): Dull orange-yellow; few dusky spots on forewings; 2 spots on hindwings; 3 rows of dark spots on abdomen; wing expanse of 1½ inches; closely related species—*Diacrisia virginica*—is all white, with black discal spot on each forewing; often submarginal spots on hind wings; abdomen yellowish-brown with black spots on back and sides; may be the more common species in your locality
Eggs: Spherical, slightly flattened, white; deposited late spring and early summer in masses on under sides of leaves or on stems of food plants
Larva (caterpillar): Thickly covered with hair; may be bright cinnamon-red in middle, black at both ends; or all brown; caterpillar of *Diacrisia virginica* may be yellow or straw-colored with black interrupted line along each side
Pupation: Caterpillar spins thin-walled cocoon of silk and hairs from own body, held together with saliva; may hibernate in cocoon during winter and not pupate until spring, or may pupate at once and remain in pupal state until emergence in spring
Pupa: Not visible through cocoon; cocoon may be carefully cut

open to expose oval, glossy, dark-brown pupa, which is capsulelike in shape

There are several species of tiger moths. Probably the most common one in the United States is the Isabella tiger moth. The tiger moths are the adult forms of the familiar wooly-bear caterpillars which are among the most common and most conspicuous fall insects. It is not an uncommon sight in the fall months to see these plump pieces of red-brown plush scurry across a roadway in search of some protected spot in which to spin a cocoon. They arouse the curiosity of children, with the result that many find their way into captivity but seldom reach the adult stage.

HOUSING

Tiger moths need little space; use cardboard box or glass vivarium box (see Part IV). Cover bottom with paper toweling.

FOOD

In the wild, moths feed on a great variety of plants, including garden crops, forage crops, grasses, and weeds. Offer alfalfa, plantain, dandelion, burdock, corn, bean leaves, pea leaves, and chrysanthemum leaves; concentrate on the 1 or 2 kinds the caterpillar eats most readily. Lay food on paper; replace with fresh supply each day. Clean box daily as long as caterpillar feeds. A caterpillar collected in late fall may feed only a day or two or not at all. This indicates it is ready to spin its cocoon.

SPINNING

Caterpillar chooses some corner of box in which to spin. When cocoon is completed, clean out box and set it aside in a cool room or place it in a protected spot out of doors; leave outdoors throughout winter. Bring box in the following spring and watch for emergence of adult moth.

SPHINX MOTHS: Genus *Pholus*

ACHEMON SPHINX MOTH: *Pholus achemon*

Range: Common in United States where grapes are grown commercially

Habitat: Wherever there are nectar-bearing flowers

Economic position: Destructive to vineyards

Adult (moth): Wingspread 3–4 inches; brownish-gray with well-defined spots on forewings; hind wings colored with rich shades of rose, dark brown borders, and few dark spots

Eggs: Pale green and spherical; deposited usually on upper surfaces of older leaves of food plants

Larva (caterpillar): Reddish or rose-colored although sometimes dull green phase; "eye spot" on rear end of body instead of horn; grows to length of 2½ inches

Pupation: Caterpillar crawls down from food plant and digs into soil many inches below surface; rounds out cell which it seals with secretion from salivary glands, making cell impervious to water; pupates in cell and remains throughout winter

Pupa: No jug-handle present since mouthparts develop within pupal case.

SPHINX MOTHS: Genus *Phlegethontius*

Tobacco Sphinx Moth or Tobacco Fly: *Phlegethontius quinquemaculata*

Range: Throughout United States; common where tomatoes, tobacco, and potato plants are grown commercially

Habitat: Wherever nectar-bearing flowers are common

Economic position: Destructive to crops

Adult (moth): Difficult to distinguish from tomato moth; characteristic feature is number of yellow spots on each side of abdomen; 5 spots only on tobacco moth

Eggs: Green and spherical; deposited singly on under sides of leaves of food plants

Larva (caterpillar): Either light green or black; 7 oblique white stripes on each side of body with longitudinal white stripe forming V with each oblique stripe; black horn on posterior end; grows to length of 4 inches

Pupation: Worm drops from food plant and digs into soil many inches below surface; rounds out cell which it seals with secretion from salivary glands, making cell impervious to water; pupates in cell and remains throughout winter

Pupa: Pupa resembles that of tomato worm except that jug-handle extends *beyond* middle of wing cases; is distinguishing feature of tobacco sphinx moth pupa

TOMATO SPHINX MOTH: *Phlegethontius sexta*

Range: Widely distributed across country; especially common in areas where tomatoes grown commercially

Habitat: Wherever there are nectar-bearing flowers

Economic position: Destructive to crops

Adult (moth): Large; wingspread of 4–5 inches; body length 2 inches; general color brownish-gray which harmonizes with bark of trees upon which adult rests during day; distinguishing mark of tomato moth is row of 6 orange or yellow spots on each side of abdomen

Eggs: Green and spherical; deposited singly on under sides of leaves of food plants

Larva (caterpillar): Light green; 7 oblique white stripes on each side of body; rear segment bears purplish-red horn; grows to length of 4 inches

Pupation: Caterpillar crawls down from food plant and digs into soil many inches below surface; rounds out cell which it seals with secretion from salivary glands, making cell impervious to water; pupates in cell and remains throughout winter

Pupa: Glossy brown; all parts of adult discernable through pupal skin; proboscis develops outside main body; gives jug-handle appearance to pupa; "handle" does not extend to middle of wing cases; this is characteristic of tomato worm pupa

SPHINX MOTHS: Genus *Celerio*

WHITE-LINED SPHINX MOTH: *Celerio lineata*

Range: Throughout United States; especially common through entire West

Habitat: Wherever there are nectar-bearing flowers

Economic position: Destructive when in great numbers

Adult (moth): Wingspread 3½–4½ inches; dull brown with white lines on head and thorax; white and darker brown spots on abdomen; forewings with white-lined veins and broad, buff stripe from bases to tips; midwings dark brown with wide, rosy band across middle

Eggs: Spherical; deposited on leaves of food plants

Larva (caterpillar): Occurs in various color phases; 2 extremes are bright green and black; in green phase ground color green; head and horn on tail yellow; little to each side of middle (stripe) line is row of pale spots outlined above and below with black; in black phase ground color black; head and horn on tail either yellow or orange; 3 yellow lines extend along back from horn to head; between these 2 extreme color phases is wide range of variations; grows to length of 3 inches; very slender

Pupation: Caterpillar leaves food plant and digs into soil many inches below surface; rounds out cell which it seals with secretion from salivary glands, making cell impervious to water; pupates in cell and remains throughout winter

Pupa: No jug-handle present since mouthparts develop within pupal case

Caterpillars of the various sphinx moths are among common fall insects. The species include such familiar worms as the tomato worm, the tobacco worm, and the grape worm. The adult moths are primarily night fliers. They come out at dusk to feed on nectar from various kinds of trumpetlike flowers, such as nasturtium, evening primrose, petunias, moon vine, and jimson weed.

The mouthparts are formed into a long tubelike tongue called the proboscis. With this long tongue the moths are able to obtain nectar from deep-throated flowers. When the proboscis is not in use, it is coiled under the head like a watch spring.

The caterpillars of sphinx moths are larger than most caterpillars. As they are slow-moving, they may be easily collected from their food plants. They feed largely at night and remain inactive and concealed during the day. The markings of the caterpillars are distinct with each species so it is easy to determine which kind is to be carried through its life cycle. All of the caterpillars feed readily in captivity and will complete their cycle when given the proper habitat.

HOUSING

Use tightly built wooden box with screened top section (see Part IV); must be large enough to hold 6 inches of soil. Fill box to this depth with firmly packed moist soil. Cut piece of screen wire and lay over top if caterpillars crawl over top of wire sides.

FOOD

As sphinx moths are voracious feeders, keep no more than 6 caterpillars at a time; supply constantly with plenty of fresh food. Since they feed more heavily at night, provide abundance of fresh food each evening. Give native food. Force stalks of food plant down into soil; moisten soil about stalks to keep plants fresh. In the wild, tomato and tobacco worms feed on leaves of tomato, tobacco, potato, ground cherry, jimson weed; achemon sphinx moths, on wild and cultivated grape leaves and Virginia creeper; white-lined sphinx moths on leaves of apple, azalea, beets, buckwheat, currant, bitter dock, elm, evening primrose, fuchsia, gooseberry, grape, melon, pear, plum, prune, and tomato.

METAMORPHOSIS

When caterpillar is ready to pupate, it ceases to feed, the skin becomes dull, and the large blood vessel along back pulsates visibly. Soon after, it crawls from plant and begins to burrow into soil. Keep soil damp all through, but *not wet*. When all caterpillars have burrowed, remove screen wire and clean away old food plants.

STORAGE

Completely bury box in garden; leave outdoors all winter. If no garden space is available, place box in a cool spot; cover with piece of glass to help retain moisture; sprinkle soil in box monthly during winter. Moths may emerge in spring even if soil has not been kept sufficiently moist through winter. However, wings will be too dry to develop, and moths will die shortly.

SOCIAL INSECTS

Bees and ants are members of the largest and most specialized order of insects, the Hymenoptera, meaning membranous-winged. In this order are found the social insects that live together in highly organized communities. The adults have biting, lapping, or sucking mouthparts. The wings, when present, are four in number, with the hind pair hooked to the forward pair; thus the two pairs of wings function as one. On the tail there is a stinglike structure which may be used to insert eggs into foliage, hardwood, or the bodies of other insects or as a weapon of offense or defense.

Although many species in this order of insects are injurious, a great many more are beneficial. For instance, the wild bees are vital pollinating agents, while the domestic bee is not only a pollinator but also supplies man with food and beeswax. Ants, although they are constantly thought of as pests, are in reality more beneficial than injurious since they dispose of enormous numbers of dead and decomposing organisms.

The metamorphosis of bees and ants is a complete cycle—egg, larva, pupa, and adult.

Bees and ants adapt themselves readily to captivity when properly housed and cared for throughout the year.

BEES: Genus *Apis*

HONEY BEE: *Apis mellifera*

Origin: Honey bee, like silkworm, has been domesticated for centuries; is not native to America but was introduced to this country by early explorers; so-called wild bees, which are found in hollow trees and elsewhere in the wild, are swarms which have escaped from domestic hives

Economic position: Excellent as pollinators and producers of honey and wax

Colony: Social insects; live in colonies and have highly specialized organization; 3 kinds of individuals in normal hive: queen, worker, and drone

Queen bee: Usually lighter in color than the other bees of the hive; has slender body with long abdomen; a long, curved sting in tip of abdomen is never used except on another queen; is cared for and fed by the workers of the hive; only function is to lay eggs which queen places at bottom of brood cells; mates but once, but lays eggs throughout life span; may be fertile or infertile at will; lives 4–5 years

Workers: Smallest bees in the hive; are undeveloped females; legs have special structures to carry pollen and cut wax; mouthparts are constructed to obtain nectar and to mold wax; stings are short, curved, and barbed, and are used in defense of hive; when sting is used, the worker bee loses its life; life span varies with seasons of the year; in spring, when there is great activity in hive, worker lives only about 6 weeks; in fall, when activities in hive are more or less dormant, lives through entire winter season

Drones: Drones, the male bees, are the largest members of the hive; early in the year there are several hundred in a hive; have broad, heavy bodies with excessive covering of hairs on thorax; none of the specialized structures of the workers; even lack the sting; take no part in any work of hive; are cared for entirely by workers; only function is to mate with new queen when old queen leaves hive with a swarm to establish new colony; only one drone out of the few hundred carries out this function; after mating drone dies; before winter comes remaining drones are killed by workers and thrown out of hive

A hive of bees is one of the simplest habitats to establish and maintain, especially for a schoolroom. The essential requirement is to obtain the correct type of demonstration hive. The hive should be constructed on the plans of a commercial hive since this type is the most easily maintained.

HOUSING

Use observation-type commercial beehive, which can be purchased from the same firms that provide other beekeepers' supplies. The distinguishing feature of these hives is that they have glass sides to permit observation of the bees' activities. As bees fly out from hive on a line with the hive—a "beeline"—hive used in schoolroom should be placed at a window above the ground floor, so as to avoid interference with children in schoolyard. When too much light enters hive, bees cover glass with wax, preventing observation of their activities. To avoid this, keep glass sides and end of hive covered at all times except when bees are being observed.

FOOD

If hive is established at a time of year when there are few flowers and nectar is not abundant, bees must be supplied with food. Mix 2 parts granulated sugar with 1 part water or purchase feeding honey from an apiary. Put sugar solution or feeding honey in deep, large-mouthed container placed near entrance to hive.

CLEANING

Observation hive must have annual cleaning; smoker and head
screen are used as protection against bee stings; the hive top is taken
off and the oldest and darkest-looking brood frames are removed
and replaced with new frames. Unless one is experienced in handling
bees, a professional beekeeper should be engaged to do this. Many
county agricultural departments employ bee men, and it is often
possible to obtain their services and professional advice.

PESTS

Bee moth is a common pest in hives that are not kept thoroughly
clean; larvae of this moth bore through and feed on wax of comb.
To control, see that hive is thoroughly cleaned once a year. Watch
for bee moths in April and May when they begin to deposit eggs
in hives. Strengthen bees with additional food at this time. Bees
will kill bee moths if they find them, but usually abandon hive if
bee moths become well established. If this happens, thoroughly
clean hive by burning it out with blow torch or by fumigating
with carbon disulphide. Then new swarm may be established. Best
to obtain professional bee man to do this.

ANTS: Genus *Formica*

Common Red Ant: *Formica rufa*

Range: All over the world; many species live undisturbed and un-
noticed by man and perform untold amount of good; other species
are pests in houses and gardens and require constant efforts to eradicate them

Habitat: In the ground, in dry hard soil, under rocks, between
cracks of cement sidewalks, in decaying wood, and in leaf mold
found on floor of forest

Economic position: Can be house pests, but on whole are more
beneficial than destructive

Description: Characterized by small nodule on stemlike part of
abdomen which attaches it to thorax; males and females have 2 pairs
of long, delicately veined wings which are lost immediately after
mating; strong biting mouthparts are tools used for all activities

Colony: Live in colonies and have developed highly specialized social organization; colony always includes wingless workers and 1 or more queens, and at certain times of year winged males and females

Winged members: Winged males and winged females leave colony when they are mature and mate; males then die; females bite or rub off their wings, seek a secluded spot, and start new colony

Wingless workers: Feed and care for queens, take care of eggs, larvae, and pupae, and forage for food

Queen ant: Function is to lay eggs; queen is largest ant in colony; extremely long-lived; when colony is young there is only 1 queen, but with some species a large, healthy colony may have from 2–25 or 30 queens

An ant colony will remain active and healthy for months when established in the proper kind of artificial nest. A well-established colony lends itself readily to close observation and to simple experimentation. It is interesting to place a few ants of one species in the colony of another and observe the results. It is equally interesting to isolate a queen with plenty of food and watch to see if she can start another colony by herself. It is both interesting and instructive to isolate a few workers with some eggs and a few young ants, but without a queen, to determine whether they can produce another queen.

HOUSING

Provide artificial nest (see Part IV), or ant nest can be bought at some pet shops.

COLLECTING

A large-mouthed quart jar, small bottle, small pail, and a trowel are needed. Dig gently into ant nest; collect a large number of adults, larvae, and pupae; place in quart jar with some soil from nest. Queen is essential; easily recognized by her large size; dig deeply into nest until she is uncovered; place alone in small bottle for protection during transportation to new nest. Fill small pail with soil from nest.

ESTABLISHING THE COLONY

Partially fill nest with soil from pail; add queen; gently pour contents of jar into glass nest until it is about two-thirds full. Place a little food on the soil, replace nest top, and leave ants to adjust to new home. Artificial colony takes 24 hours to adjust; may be maintained for many months if supplied with food and water.

Ants prefer darkness but soon adjust themselves to short periods of light; keep glass parts of nest covered except when ants are under observation. From time to time, moisten soil; push glass tube with half-inch bore down into soil; pour a little water into tube to be absorbed by soil.

FOOD

In the wild, ants feed on other insects, decaying vegetation, crumbs, and "honeydew," which is secreted by aphids. Give sugar, honey occasionally; bits of sweet fruits, dry bread and cake crumbs in small amounts; small pieces of lean, cooked meat, dead insects, such as flies and meal worms; and any other food ants seem to like; usually a preference is soon indicated. Place food on top of soil. *Water—* Necessary in artificial habitat; use small, flat container, such as bottle top; press into soil.

SHEATH-WINGED INSECTS

Out of the vast number of insects known today, probably the most successful of all in their struggle for existence are the beetles, the sheath-winged insects, in the order Coleoptera. Their highly specialized body structures as well as their habits make this possible. Their bodies are usually short and robust; their forewings or elytra are horny and serve as a protective shield for the membranous hind or true flight wings; the heavy, hard, thick chitinized cuticle forms an excellent protective body cover; and the strong, heavy jaws seem able to chew into almost any kind of matter.

Many kinds of beetles are familiar because of their destructive habits both to farm crops and plants in home gardens. Others are well known because of their beneficial habits, while some are merely interesting creatures that commonly appear in our environment.

Beetles live in and on both living and dead wood, in water, on plants, and on other animals including themselves. Their metamorphosis is a complete cycle with the usual four stages: egg, larva, pupa, and adult.

There are numerous kinds of beetles, common in various localities, which lend themselves readily to captivity and are fascinating for children to watch and care for.

LADYBIRD BEETLES: Genus Rodolia

VEDALIA: *Rodolia cardinalis*

Range: Native to Australia but introduced into United States in 1888

Habitat: Orchards and ornamental gardens

Economic position: Beneficial both in adult and larval stages, as feeds on scale insects, aphids, and larvae of other injurious insects; vedalia is no doubt the most famous ladybird beetle as it became the standard example of a striking case of biological control; was introduced for specific purpose of controlling cottony-cushion scale which was destroying California citrus industry

Adult: Small, quite round (hemispherical), red with irregular black markings on elytra; in females red predominates; males show more black

Eggs: Tiny, oblong, bright red; deposited singly or in small clumps; usually placed on host if it is cottony-cushion scale

Larva: Small, pinkish, with black markings, and sometimes bluish bloom

Pupation: Larva attaches self to host plant; pupates within larval skin

Pupa: Parts of adult not visible; when touched wiggles vigorously

LADYBIRD BEETLES: Genus *Hippodamia*

CONVERGENT LADYBIRD BEETLE: *Hippodamia convergens*

Range: Common throughout North America

Habitat: Found on all kinds of vegetation where aphids occur; also where Colorado potato beetle and alfalfa weevil occur

Economic position: Beneficial both in adult and larval stages as feeds on scale insects, on aphids, and on larvae of other injurious insects

Adult: Hemispherical; elytra yellow, orange, or red with 12 small oval or round black spots; pronotum with 2 oblique white lines

Eggs: Elongate, pointed at 1 end; deposited in clusters on any convenient object

Larva: Long-bodied, flat, velvety black or gray, with 4 large orange spots on back

Pupation: Larva attaches self to some firm surface, splits skin as pupa forms

Pupa: Red and black

In fall in some parts of the United States, especially the West, the adults of some species of ladybird beetles begin to gather for the winter. They mass in swarms over each other and seek certain spots, usually hollows or small canyons along stream banks, where they crawl among the leaves and twigs of plants and hibernate. In high altitudes they often become buried under deep snows, but with the return of spring and warm weather they all disperse over wide areas.

When the weather is warm and food is plentiful, the life cycle of most species of ladybird beetles is completed in an average of three weeks. Broods begin to appear in early spring, and there is a succession of them throughout the summer.

Ladybird beetles will complete their entire life cycle in a small cage when established in the proper habitat and given an abundance of food. It is best to obtain beetles when they first appear in the spring since they are about ready to deposit eggs at that time.

HOUSING

Use screen-wire insect cage constructed with pie pans (see Part IV); allow plenty of room for plant branches. Fill bottom pan with soil; place cuttings of plants infested with aphids or plant lice in soil; place screen over plants and invert pan over cage top. Keep only 6–8 beetles at a time; care not difficult when beetles not crowded.

FOOD

Beetles feed on aphids and scale insects. Keep constant supply of aphid-infested plants in cage; keep plants fresh by moistening soil.

CARE OF LARVAE

As soon as eggs are deposited, release adults. As soon as eggs hatch, supply larvae with plenty of aphids. The more abundant the food, the more rapidly the larvae grow. When they are ready to pupate, larvae usually crawl from plants and hang on sides of screen. When adults emerge, they should be liberated.

WATER BEETLES: Genus *Dytiscus*

PREDACEOUS WATER BEETLE: *Dytiscus marginicollis*

Range: United States west of the Great Plains; similar species in eastern states

Habitat: In ponds with abundant vegetation; often under street lights during warm summer evenings

Economic position: Larva often destroys young fish, sometimes destructive in fish hatcheries

Adult: Large (1½ inches long); body oval, smooth, dull green; entire margin of prothorax (forward section of thorax) and sides of elytra (wing covers) yellow; third pair of legs long, strong, flattened, and adapted for swimming (used as oars); rests head downward from surface of water; flies readily

Eggs: Deposited in slits cut in stems of aquatic plants

Larva: Called "water tiger"; predaceous and a real killer; head large, flat, with pair of long, slender, curved, sharp, pointed, hollow jaws; prey grasped, body pierced, and juices sucked out through these jaws; 6 slender legs; rests head downward with tip of tail thrust through water surface to obtain air

Pupation: Larva leaves water when full-grown, makes cell in mud bank, and pupates; in midsummer, adult emerges in 3 weeks; in fall, remains in pupal stage through winter months

Pupa: Mummylike appearance; all parts of adult beetle visible; appendages folded forward onto undersurface of body

The adult beetle obtains air as it projects the tip of its abdomen through surface film of water. It lifts the tips of the elytra slightly, which allows air to rush under them. Fine hairs which cover the back of the beetle hold the air which can then readily be taken into the body through the spiracles or breathing pores. In this manner the beetle is able to carry a supply of air that will last for some time.

WATER BEETLES: Genus *Hydrophilus*

GREAT WATER SCAVENGER BEETLE OR
GIANT WATER SCAVENGER BEETLE: *Hydrophilus triangularis*

Range: Throughout United States

Habitat: Ponds and pools with abundant vegetation; often with predaceous water beetle; also found under electric lights on warm summer evenings

Economic position: Larva destroys young fish; sometimes troublesome in fish hatcheries

Adult: Large (2 inches long); shiny black; second and third pair of legs adapted for swimming; rests head downward from water's surface; flies readily

Eggs: Deposited in smooth, brownish case with curved, tapering stem; may be attached to some floating plant or other object, or left to float alone on water's surface

Larva: Long, but body thick as well as tapering; head flat; rests head downward with pair of spiracles at tip of abdomen projected through surface of water to obtain air

Pupation: Larva leaves water, burrows into bank, and makes rough cell in which it pupates

Pupa: Mummylike appearance; all parts of adult beetle visible; appendages folded forward onto underside of body

Both adult and larvae feed on dead and living animal matter. The adult beetle obtains air by piercing the water's surface with the antennae, which permits a thin, silvery layer of air to spread over the underside of the body where it is held by very fine hairs; sometimes called "silver beetles."

Species of water beetles are found wherever there are streams and ponds which abound in plant life. Many are familiar to children, who find them in their natural habitats. Those discussed here are the ones that occur most commonly throughout the country. However, they are seldom thought of as interesting creatures in captivity.

Both adult water beetles and their larvae may be maintained in an aquarium. Both will carry on their normal activities freely. As they are vicious and voracious, they cannot be maintained with other aquarium inhabitants.

HOUSING

Beetles need "balanced" aquarium (see Part II); use 2- to 5-gallon aquarium or aquarium jar. Cover bottom with 2 inches of clean aquarium sand; anchor 6 strands of common aquarium plants with a few clean rocks. Let water stand 24 hours; then drop adult beetle or larvae or both in habitat.

FOOD

PREDACEOUS WATER BEETLE: In the wild, beetle feeds on every kind of aquatic life, such as small fish, tadpoles, worms, other aquatic insects. Needs quantities of food. Give native food plus top minnows and their young; tadpoles and earthworms. Also drop cubes of raw or cooked meat into the water. Always remove surplus food as soon as feeding is over.

GIANT WATER SCAVENGER BEETLE: In the wild, beetle feeds on decaying plant and animal matter plus living water plants and aquatic animals. Feed as predaceous water beetle. In addition, give young aquatic plants.

LACEWING INSECTS

The group of lace-winged insects belongs to the small order Neuroptera, meaning nerve wing. The members of this order are, on the whole, rather small and fragile creatures. The wings may be fairly strong and somewhat leathery and held flat along the back as in the Dobson fly, or very delicate, lacelike, and held rooflike over the back as in the ant lion. Many are day fliers, but may be attracted by bright night lights. Many of the adults are predaceous.

The larvae (called doodlebugs by children) are largely terrestrial, although some are aquatic; but all are predaceous and are vicious creatures both in appearance and habits. Because of this they are truly beneficial to man since they kill many destructive insects.

ANT LIONS: Genus *Hesperoleon*

ANT LION: *Hesperoleon maculosus*

> **Range:** Throughout United States
> **Habitat:** In foliage in gardens

Economic position: Beneficial both in adult and larval state

Adult: Body long and slender; antennae short, clubbed, or knobbed; 2 pairs of long, thin, delicate, many-veined wings; may have many or few dark spots in them; fly with hesitating gait; spend little time on the wing

Eggs: Eggs deposited directly in sand

Larva: Short, plump-bodied; head and prothorax narrow; long, piercing jaws; surface of body covered with long, stiff, spine-like hairs which help to hold body in sand; reaches length of half-inch or more

The pit: The moment egg hatches, larva begins to dig its pit, a funnel-shaped structure at bottom of which larva lies buried with only its sickle-shaped, toothed jaws extending upward; any unwary insect that gets too close to edge usually slides in; it is grasped immediately by jaws of doodlebug, body juices sucked out, and the carcass cast out of the pit with a flip of the jaws

Pupation: When larva reaches full growth it spins a round, silken cocoon to which are glued grains of sand or dust; if cocoon is made in fall, larva rests in it and pupates in spring; if made early in season, larva pupates at once and adult emerges in about 3 weeks

Pupa: Not visible through cocoon

Since the ant lion larva, or doodlebug, must rely entirely on chance to obtain its food, it is adapted to live for many weeks without food. The rate of growth, naturally, depends upon the quantity of food obtained. In captivity the more food it is given, the more quickly it will reach full growth and complete the cycle.

Doodlebugs are extremely easy to capture and equally easy to maintain in captivity. Use an old tea strainer or piece of screen wire, a spoon, and an old box or can. After locating a pit, with a quick motion of the spoon dip up the entire pit or crater. Drop pit in strainer and gently shake until sand or dust is sifted through. Dusty-colored, chunky doodlebug will be left in the strainer.

HOUSING

Use any flat dish or pan that will hold 2–3 inches of sand or dust; keep only 2–3 bugs in one container; too many bugs interfere with each other's pits. No cover is necessary until larva pupates; then cover container with piece of screen wire to prevent escape of adult.

FOOD

In the wild, doodlebug feeds on any small, ground-crawling insects that may fall into pit. In captivity, give ants, flies, and any other small, crawling insects (see Part III); clip fly's wings; gently drop fly into pit. When doodlebug consistently refuses food, it has reached full growth and is ready to pupate.

STRAIGHT-WINGED INSECTS

The katydids, crickets, grasshoppers, cockroaches, and locusts belong to a very large order of terrestrial insects called Orthoptera. The members of this order are on the whole fairly large, usually with two pairs of well-developed wings. The fore pair is well-veined and leathery; the hind pair, well-veined but membranous. When not in use, both pairs lie folded longitudinally. This gives the back of the insect the appearance of being very straight, hence the name of the order, *Orthoptera*, meaning straight wing. These insects also have very well-developed mouthparts for biting and chewing. Cerci (slender structures projecting from the tip of the abdomen) are usually present also. Many members of the order are injurious to farm crops and orchard trees.

The life cycle of the Orthoptera is not complete. There are but three stages of development: egg, nymph, and adult.

KATYDIDS: Genus *Microcentum*

Angular-winged or Common Katydid:
    Microcentum rombifolium

Range: Throughout United States
Habitat: In trees and shrubs with heavy foliage
Economic position: Sometimes destructive to fruit trees and vineyards
Adult: Usually green; folded wings resemble leaves of plants; antennae extremely long and threadlike; hind legs similar to those of grasshopper but much more slender; abdomen short and stocky; female with bladelike ovipositor at top of abdomen; eastern species have voice out of all proportion to size—supposed to say "Katy did,

Katy did, she didn't," over and over; western species have sharper voices, sometimes chirping or clicking notes, which do not sound like "Katy did"

Eggs: Deposited in late fall and hatch during following spring; placed on smaller twigs of various trees and shrubs; oval, flat, and gray; usually laid in 2 rows overlapping somewhat like shingles

Nymph: Frequently resembles adult but lacks wings; active, feeding stage; grows by successive molts during which wing pads develop; wings not fully developed until nymph full grown; adult emerges after last molt

Female katydid captured in fall and properly housed and fed may deposit eggs on branches of food plants in cage; usually eggs are fertile. Female lives for some little time after depositing eggs if weather remains warm and she is given sufficient food.

HOUSING

ADULT: Use screen-wire insect cage constructed with 2 pans (see Part IV). Fill bottom pan with moist soil.

EGGS IN SPRING: Use lamp chimney cage (see Part IV). Fill flower pot with loose, damp soil. Push geranium or rose branch down into soil. Slip lamp chimney over plants and push firmly into soil. Place twig with eggs among branches of plants. Cover chimney top with small piece of cheesecloth and tie securely. Moisten soil from time to time to keep plants fresh. Newly hatched nymphs are very small; wingless, but have small wing pads; antennae exceedingly long and threadlike; transfer nymphs to screen-wire cage after they grow too large to crawl through screen wire.

EGGS IN FALL: When twig covered with eggs is brought in during the fall, tie twig to some shrub out of doors and leave through the winter. Hot, dry air indoors lowers vitality of eggs so that few hatch in spring. Moisture and changing temperatures out of doors are necessary for normal development of eggs.

FOOD

ADULT: In the wild, katydid feeds on variety of plant leaves; rose leaves always acceptable. Push rose branches with younger leaf growth into soil. Moisten soil to keep plants fresh.

NYMPH: In the wild, feeds on youngest and tenderest growth;

keep supply of young, tender rose or geranium leaves in cage as soon as eggs hatch. As nymphs grow, give older and larger leaves. Continue to keep nymphs well supplied with fresh, green food after they are transferred to screen-wire cage.

CRICKETS: Genus *Gryllus*

FIELD OR COMMON CRICKET: *Gryllus assimilis*

Range: Throughout United States; especially abundant during summer, when it makes itself conspicuous by its cheery, chirping song

Habitat: Under old boards, under stones, in cracks in ground, crevices in trees, in dry grass about houses, under outdoor electric lights, and even in houses; on warm spring evenings they are attracted by strong outdoor electric lights and often collect under them in great masses

Economic position: Often destructive to trees and garden crops

Adult: Body low, flat; blackish-brown; female possesses long, spear-shaped ovipositor at tip of abdomen; male wing covers much coarser and heavier; when wings of male raised and rubbed together, produce familiar chirping song

Eggs: Deposited in ground or under protectively covered debris

Nymph: Similar to adult but without wings; wings develop in wing pads as nymph grows

Crickets may be easily captured. The equipment necessary is a large-mouthed jar with a screw top punched with holes for air and either an insect net or just the bare hands. Locate crickets under outdoor electric lights or look for them under old boards, stones, or in dry grass. Cover cricket quickly with hand or with net, and drop it in jar. They are easily maintained in captivity when properly caged and fed, and are a never-ending source of interest to children.

HOUSING

Use glass vivarium box with screen top (see Part IV); make large enough to hold materials making up habitat and for creature to move about in comfortably. Cover bottom with 2 inches of soil; place thick section of grassy sod at one end; moisten sod occasionally to keep grass from drying out completely; replenish sod as grass dies down. Place dry sand and soil at opposite end. Make many retreats; scatter several pieces of old, flat wood over sandy area; add 1–2 irregularly shaped, broad rocks.

FOOD

In the wild, crickets feed on various kinds of vegetation. Give lettuce, fresh fruits in seasons; apples at all times, as crickets are especially fond of them; also give dry crackers, whole wheat bread crumbs, cake and cookie crumbs. Place food on dry soil of habitat; feed often and generously.

DRAGONFLIES AND DAMSELFLIES

Dragonflies and their smaller, narrow-winged counterparts, damselflies, are common insects throughout the summer in all parts of the country where there are streams and ponds about. All are strong-winged, often brightly colored, and extremely graceful creatures. They remind one of an airplane as they skim over the water's surface in zigzag lines and sweeping curves. Often they stop in midair, then dive at an angle and are off again. These brightly colored, graceful creatures belong to the order Odonata, from the Greek word *odontos*, meaning tooth. The reason for the name is unknown.

The members of this order have well-developed biting and chewing mouthparts. They feed on all kinds of winged insects, including their own relatives, which they capture out of the air in their legs, held basketlike. The front legs then hold the prey while it is devoured.

Dragonflies, which are the larger members of the order, are strong, steady fliers which hunt great distances from their aquatic breeding areas. Damselflies, on the other hand, are much smaller in size, are weak fliers, and are seldom seen far from their aquatic areas. Their nymphs are also small and difficult to maintain in captivity.

The life cycle is incomplete: egg, nymph, and adult. Eggs are usually laid during spring and summer. Some species insert them into plant tissues; others drop them in the water or push them down in the mud or sand of shallow bottoms of ponds.

The nymphs are entirely aquatic. They are grotesque creatures that spend their lives in the mud or sand at the bottom of ponds, lakes, and streams. They feed upon all kinds of small aquatic animals: crustaceans, young of stone flies, mayflies, other dragonflies, salamanders, frog and toad tadpoles, fish, and so on.

All the members of this interesting order are among man's best friends as they consume large quantities of noxious insects.

DRAGONFLIES: Genus Anax

GIANT DRAGONFLY: Anax junius

Range: Throughout North America, Asia, and Hawaiian Islands

Habitat: Flies far afield in open country as well as near vegetation around bodies of water

Economic position: Beneficial in every way to man

Adult: Large; 2 pairs clear wings with spread of over 2 inches; head and thorax bright green; top front of head with round black spot surrounded by yellow; yellow outlined by dark blue; head very large, composed mostly of 2 enormous compound eyes, mouthparts, and a pair of very short antennae

Eggs: Tiny; dropped in water

Nymph: Egg hatches into grotesque creature with robust body, flattened abdomen, broad head with pop-eyes and a "mask" over face; mask is lower lip adapted for capturing prey; prey usually ambushed, then captured by lower lip thrust out and extended like arm; when not in use, folded back over face like mask; Nymph grows through process of molts; wings develop within pads with each molt; when adult emerges, wings quickly become fully developed

Emergence of Adult: Nymph crawls out of water onto stem of some aquatic plant where it clings until skin dries in sun; in due time skin splits along back of head and thorax; very gradually adult body pulls its way slowly out of nymphal case; new creature is delicate and transparent-looking, its wings damp and compressed; remains clinging to old case until new skin hardens and colors, and wings dry and unfold and become strong enough for flight

Adults of dragonflies and damselflies cannot be maintained in captivity but the nymphs can, especially those of the giant dragonfly. When properly maintained they will develop normally, reach full growth, crawl from the water, and demonstrate the manner in which the adult emerges.

In order to obtain dragonfly nymphs one needs a small rake, a bucket, a dipnet or old strainer, and a quart jar. Gently rake surface sediment from bottom of pond or stream, or dip or scoop it up with net or strainer and place it on the bank. Do not dig deeply; just scoop surface sediment. Allow water to drain, then gently rake about in sediment. Nymphs usually make themselves visible by darting about rapidly. Fill jar half full of water and drop nymphs into it. Fill pail with quantity of surface sediment and algae, then fill with water to help establish habitat for nymphs.

HOUSING

As nymphs need some room for movement and are best observed in a glass container, use a 9-inch aquarium jar, a small aquarium, or a balanced aquarium from which fish have been removed (dragonfly nymphs attack small goldfish and tropical fish). Cover bottom with an inch of sediment from pond or stream. Push 4–6 strands of water weed (anacharis) into sediment and anchor with small rocks. If using balanced aquarium, drain water from it until it is half full. Plant something that extends above water line, such as either sagittaria or "parrot feather" for nymph to rest on when its growth is completed; place plant against side of container and allow to extend above top. Let sediment settle. When water becomes clear, gently pour in nymphs and water from quart jar. Nymphs must all be same size; otherwise, larger ones devour the smaller.

FOOD

In the wild, dragonfly nymphs are predaceous and feed on small aquatic life, such as mosquito wigglers, small water beetles, young of fish, other nymphs, tadpoles, and so on. In captivity give flies from which wings have been cut off; small worms; small tadpoles; small fish, such as young of top minnows. Drop all food in water; must be alive.

PART II

THE VIVARIUM

THE term vivarium has come to mean any sort of place where live animals are housed. The place may be as large as a zoological garden with hundreds of animals or as small as a tumbler of water in which a single tadpole is living. Present usage, however, has divided the vivarium into two types: the terrarium, in which terrestrial animals are maintained, and the aquarium, in which aquatic animals are housed. This chapter deals with both the terrarium and the aquarium, and describes the habitats which may be established in each. It also suggests the kind and number of animals which are suitable for each habitat.

Vivaria of all types may be purchased at biological supply houses for almost any price one wishes to pay, but many smaller ones may be homemade or constructed to order.

TERRARIUMS

Three kinds of habitats may be established in a terrarium: the woodland habitat, the swamp or marsh habitat, and the desert habitat. Any one of these habitats, properly set up with plants and animals, makes a lovely and interesting spot in a home or a classroom and provides a source of never-failing interest.

The custom-made terrarium, shown in Part IV, is large enough to set up attractively and can house a variety of small animals. Ready-made terrariums, of glass in metal frames, are also available. These may have a screen top or a removable glass cover. Some commercial terrariums have a slanted front; moisture that condenses on the glass drops onto the vegetation. As a result, a near-tropical atmosphere can be maintained in this type of terrarium.

It is desirable to have a smaller habitat to house small specimens, such as tiny turtles or small lizards. A small aquarium, smaller all-glass aquarium jars, or the small handmade vivarium boxes are most practical for these little creatures.

Limit the number of animals placed in a terrarium. One or two of a species will be comfortable in any terrarium if the total number is kept to a minimum; feeding is also less of a problem. Consider the size of the specimens too. More smaller specimens can be maintained together than if they are large. The habits of the animals must also be understood. For example, many of the small turtles and some salamanders are burrowers. Two burrowers are enough; otherwise, the habitat becomes completely disorganized. It is also important to know which specimens are cannibalistic, which hibernate, which can be maintained for short periods only, and which can or cannot be placed together. For this information, refer to the chapters in which your captive specimens are discussed.

Woodland Habitat

MATERIALS

For the bottom, you will need wood charcoal; sand; and loose, rich loam (soil), preferably leaf mold from the forest floor. If commercial leaf mold is used, mix peat moss or coarse compost with soil in the proportion 1 part peat moss or coarse compost to 3 parts leaf mold. A glazed flower pot saucer, deep glass dish, or a pan is used to fashion a pool.

From the woods, obtain an old log or large limb that has a good hole or two and is beginning to decay. Also obtain old and decayed-looking pieces of bark and lichen- or moss-covered rocks. In addition, bring moss from a stream bank or other moist area, and collect small, hardy plants that grow near a stream. If woods are not available, rocks and moss may be obtained from the garden. You may use a weathered, gnarled fireplace log, preferably one with a hole, and pieces of bark pulled from firewood. Use small garden plants, such as wandering jew, Kennilworth ivy, ajuga, wild bleeding heart, ferns, hardy begonia, coleus, and so on.

ESTABLISHMENT

Use standard terrarium, aquarium, or handmade vivarium box with cover (see Part IV); size selected depends upon inhabitants. Cover bottom with half-inch layer of wood charcoal followed by thin layer of sand. Top sand with 3–4 inches of soil. Pile more soil at one end or in corner to make a slope. Scatter old log and pieces of bark over soil. Place 1–2 jagged rocks near or against pieces of wood. Set out plants as you wish. Place sections of moss over soil and over and around log, pressing them firmly into place. Make a pool by sinking the glass dish or glazed flower pot saucer into soil in low corner of terrarium. Cover bottom of dish with layer of coarse sand. Pile a few small, flat rocks against one side of dish in stair-step fashion. Stick spray of water plant in sand, and fill dish with water. Place moss and ferns on soil around dish in attractive manner. Change water often; must always be fresh and clean. *Warmth*—Place terrarium where it receives some direct sunlight each day, preferably during the morning. On extremely warm days, shade terrarium from sun or roll it into shade. *Moisture*—Moderate amount necessary; lightly sprinkle plants and moss each morning unless terrarium is commercial slanted-front type (see Part IV); never allow soil to become wet as drainage is incomplete and too much water causes soil to sour.

ANIMALS SUITABLE FOR WOODLAND HABITAT

Amphibians: Frogs, newts, salamanders, and toads.

Reptiles: Lizards— Anolis, gerrhonotus, glass, skinks. *Snakes*— Black, garter, water. *Turtles*—Florida cooter, map, painted, pond, red-eared, yellow-bellied.

Marsh or Swamp Habitat

MATERIALS

Coarse sand is needed for the bottom of the terrarium. As acid soil is required to top sand, obtain sediment from bottom of marsh or, if marsh is not available, from bottom of garden pool. If neither marsh nor pool is available, use ordinary garden soil, but habitat will remain established for short time only. Gently pull small plants, which adjust better to indoor temperature than large specimens, from marsh sediment. Marsh-type plants may also be purchased at aquarium supply houses; varieties may include *Callitriche* (water fennel), floating heart, *hippuris* (mare's tail), *myriophyllum* (parrot feather), *Sagittaria sinensis* (giant arrowhead), spatterdock, water hawthorn, water hyacinth, water lily, and water poppy. Collect mosses and pieces of old, dank wood from marsh area as well as 1–2 flattened rocks. *Water*—Best to bring from outdoor marsh; otherwise, use water from garden pool; as a third choice, use tap water that has been allowed to stand for 2–3 days to become well aerated and to reach room temperature.

ESTABLISHMENT

Use 10-gallon or larger aquarium with cover; the larger the aquarium, the more effective the habitat (small tanks and glass vivarium boxes may be used but are satisfactory for a short time only). Cover bottom with inch of the coarse sand; pile up 2 inches higher at one end. Cover raised area with moss; scatter rocks and pieces of damp wood on the moss. Top sand at lower end with sediment. Place marsh plants of varying sizes and heights around attractively. Use mosses, bits of old wood and rocks. Plant a few small aquatic plants in sediment at low end for retreats. Cover sediment with 1–2 inches of water. *Warmth*—Moderate temperature needed; place habitat where it receives direct sunlight during early morning only; never place near heating unit at any time. *Pollution*—Do not overfeed animals; when water becomes murky or odorous, siphon it off at once and replace with fresh water.

ANIMALS SUITABLE FOR MARSH HABITAT

Amphibians: Frogs, newts, salamanders.

Reptiles: Snakes—Garter. *Turtles*—Florida cooter, map, painted, pond, red-bellied, red-eared, yellow-bellied.

Crustaceans: Crayfish.

Desert Habitat

MATERIALS

Charcoal, broken bits of pottery and small pebbles, fine-grained sand, and soil are needed for the bottom of the habitat; sand from American deserts may be used, contains much rich soil. Also collect several rocks. Obtain succulents and small cacti, both tall growing and low growing. Collecting permits are now usually required to gather succulents and cacti in most desert areas of the United States. Check regulations before attempting to collect in these areas. However, nurserymen now grow and carry large stocks of these plants, and a fine selection may easily be obtained at nominal cost.

ESTABLISHMENT

Use standard terrarium, aquarium, or handmade vivarium box (see Part IV); the larger the better. Cover bottom with layer of charcoal, followed by layer of small broken bits of pottery and pebbles. Top with inch of loose, rich soil. Cover soil layer with 2 inches of mixture of 4 parts sand combined with 1 part soil. Scatter a few rocks over sand; use desert types with soft colors. Set plants in soil, pushing roots firmly into place. Place low, flat plants against rocks. Arrange pieces of weathered cholla cactus (obtainable at nurseries) and rocks to provide hiding places. For touch of true desert color, add small pieces of broken glass that have become lavender from long exposure to sun. *Water*—Small amount beneficial; sprinkle base of plants every 2–3 days; avoid too much water, as it causes roots to decay. *Warmth*—Required; place terrarium where it receives a maximum of direct sunlight daily.

ANIMALS SUITABLE FOR DESERT HABITAT

Arthropods: Scorpions.
Reptiles: Lizards—Chuckwalla, collared lizard, horned lizard. *Snakes*—Coastal rosy boa, desert rosy boa.

Some Special Problems of Animal Care

Captive animals often suffer from vitamin deficiencies, since their food in captivity is almost invariably different from that to which they are used in the wild. Common symptoms are listlessness, loss of appetite, trembling, or partial paralysis, particularly of the hind limbs. Administration of multiple vitamin preparations often results in prompt recovery. A liquid preparation such as the Stuart formula, obtainable at drug stores without prescription, may be mixed with the food or administered with a dropper. There is also a preparation known as Avitron vitamin drops that is especially intended for pets and is easily administered, as it appears palatable to many animals; even lizards will literally lap it up. It should be sought for at pet stores.

Fleas, mites, and ticks can be controlled by the use of insect powders that can be purchased at any pet shop; the insecticide must of course be of a type nonpoisonous to the pet itself, but this can reasonably be assumed if the preparation is intended for dogs or cats. Remember that the cage must be treated, as well as the animal, or the latter will quickly become reinfected.

Ticks, of course, which are slow-moving and large enough to be easily seen, can be picked off with a pair of forceps. Pull slowly and steadily; make sure that the head does not break off and remain in the skin where it will cause a festering sore. It is wise to swab the area with 70 per cent alcohol after the tick has been removed.

Ear mites, which get inside the aperture of the ear and cause intense itching, can be controlled by injecting baby oil in the ear with a medicine dropper. Hold the animal so the oil will stay for a few minutes; then swab with cotton on an applicator.

Snakes are often parasitized by mites. The treatment here is a thorough dusting with insect powder, which may be applied even to the eyes, because snakes lack movable eyelids and have the eye covered by a transparent scale that protects it from irritation by foreign bodies. It is important to remove water from the cage during treatment because the mites will take refuge in the water to escape the powder.

For treatment of cuts or other open wounds, about the best that can be done by the amateur is to clean the wound with warm soapy water and let nature take its course. Bandages are likely to be chewed off, and the animal will lick the wound, thus removing and probably ingesting any antiseptic that might be applied.

Broken legs (or tails!) can be splinted. The broken member can be straightened so that the ends of the bone are in line. A splint can then be placed on each side. The splints are held in place with several small bandages tied tightly enough to prevent the ends of the bone from grinding together as the animal moves. Bandages are less likely to be removed by the animal from a splinted limb than from an open wound.

A prized pet that is ill or injured should always be taken to a veterinarian. Any animal that does not respond to simple home treatment should either be taken to a veterinarian or painlessly disposed of.

Some animals can carry diseases transmissible to man. If in doubt, consult a veterinarian or a physician.

AQUARIUMS

The aquarium is usually considered the indoor habitat for goldfish, but this is but one of its many uses. The aquarium is also a suitable habitat for various kinds of native or tropical fish, a large variety of aquatic insects, some mollusks, and tadpoles.

The kind of habitat and the animals to be established in it determine the type and size of aquarium to be used. Small fresh water life such as aquatic insects and tadpoles may be established in various kinds of battery jars, aquarium jars, or small aquarium tanks. These may be obtained in different sizes from pet shops, aquarium companies, tropical fish dealers, and from scientific supply companies.

Never use a fish bowl or globe for any kind of fish. The usual goldfish bowl contradicts all principles for setting up a balanced aquarium because of its shape. It does not hold sufficient water for one fish; the bottom surface is not large enough for the sand required by plants; the water requires constant changing; the glass usually distorts the image of the contents and often breaks with changes in temperature.

The most practical size of aquarium to use is one that holds from ten to twenty gallons of water.

"BALANCED" AQUARIUMS

An interesting experiment is to try to set up what is called a "balanced" aquarium. All green plants manufacture carbohydrates from carbon dioxide and water, using energy supplied by sunlight, and giving off oxygen as a by-product (a process known as photosynthesis). Animals either eat plants directly or eat other animals which feed on plants. Animals require a constant supply of oxygen which they can obtain from the excess oxygen produced by plants. (Plants also require some oxygen, but not nearly as much as they produce.) Animals excrete nitrogenous wastes which plants require as fertilizer. In an aquarium that is "balanced" the plants supply the animal life with plant food and oxygen. The animal life in turn supplies the plants with carbon dioxide and the necessary nitrogen compounds. This cycle goes on indefinitely when all conditions are correct; it is then that the aquarium becomes a "balanced" habitat. Thus, perfect aquarium conditions have been obtained: (1) pure, well-aerated water; (2) constant temperature; (3) correct number of plants in relation to animals; and (4) right amount and kind of food.

The aquarium cannot remain balanced if there are too many plants, or too many fish, or both. And if the light is insufficient, both plants and animals suffer for want of the proper amount of oxygen. The same is true if the temperature is not properly regulated. Restraint must be used in the number both of plants and of animals placed in the tank. It is advisable for a prospective aquarium owner to visit a shop or a museum where aquariums are maintained professionally to observe how the various sizes of tanks are established, especially the number of animals compared to number of plants, the position and spacing of the plants in the tank, and the use of thermometers, thermostats, and aerators in case these are to be used.

Water absorbs a certain amount of free oxygen from the air, but this amount is so small as compared with what the plants produce that it is not important. To cover the aquarium with glass does not reduce the oxygen supply. It does, however, prevent a film of dust and oil from collecting on the water and disturbing the established balance, and it prevents rapid water evaporation.

When the principle of balance between plant and animal life is thoroughly understood, it is possible to establish and maintain an aquarium in a container as small as a tumbler.

Most people want to keep more animals in an aquarium than a balanced aquarium will support. In this case it is necessary to feed the animals (see below) and to aerate the water by artificial means, such as the small air pumps that can be purchased at an aquarium supply shop. Plants are then used largely for decorative purposes.

Fresh Water Aquarium

MATERIALS

For goldfish and native wild fish, use coarse sea sand (called bird gravel or aquarium sand). For tropical fish, use fine grade (called tropical fish sand). Select plants from the list below; they are needed for oxygen, food, protection, and ornamentation. No more than one-fourth of tank's surface should be taken up by floating plants; oxygenators and ornamentals must be pinched back when growth becomes too thick. In addition, every aquarium of 1 gallon or more needs 2 or more scavengers; fresh water choices are listed below. Everything placed in an aquarium should be in keeping with the fresh water habitat. Marine shells, ceramic and plastic castles, and other artificial gadgets are inappropriate. Fish often injure themselves on these unnatural additions.

PLANTS RECOMMENDED FOR FRESH WATER AQUARIUMS

Many of the submerged plants supply food. The roots and the compact growth of many of the floating plants harbor much small animal life which is also food for the fish, at the same time providing protection for small and baby fish. It is possible to obtain a fine variety of plants from aquarium shops, as most of them carry a supply of both oxygenators and ornamentals. Following is a list of plants most commonly used, many of which are known by several names:

Oxygenators

Anacharis—elodea or Canadian waterweed
Cabomba—fanwort
Ceratophyllum—hornwort (floating)
Crystalwort—water net or floating riccia (floating)
Hair grass
Heteranthera
Ludwigia—swamp loosestrife
Moneywort—creeping jenny or herb twopence
Nitella—stonewort
Quillwort
Sagittaria natans—ribbon arrowhead
Sagittaria sinensis—giant arrowhead
Sagittaria subulata—awl-leaved arrowhead
Salvinia—moss fern (floating)
Vallisneria—eel grass or tape grass

Ornamentals

Azolla—water fern (floating)
Callitriche—water fennel
Cryptocoryne
Duckweed, greater—Spirodela, (floating)
Duckweed, lesser—Lemna (floating)
Floating heart
Fontinalis—willow moss
Herpestis—figwort
Hydrocharis—frogbite (floating)
Lace Plant—Madagascar lace plant
Potamogeton—pond weed or dense weed
Spatterdock, Japanese
Spatterdock, southern
Trianea
Utricularia—bladderwort (floating)
Water chestnut
Water hyacinth (floating)
Water lettuce
Water poppy

SCAVENGERS RECOMMENDED FOR FRESH WATER AQUARIUM

European weatherfish: Excellent for any aquarium of ten gallons or more. *Source*—Dealers, who usually carry them in several sizes. *Description*—Smooth-skinned, eel-like fish with number of feelers about mouth; interesting habit of burying self in sand with only head exposed; does this more often on cloudy days. *Food*—Feeds on sediment which collects on sand, but requires supplementary fish food; drop on sand near head.

Fresh water mussel: Excellent for aquarium of ten gallons or more. *Source*—Dealers. *Description*—Shell thin; brown or brownish-green. *Food*—Feeds on algae as it plows through sand; often completely buried. Requires no supplementary food.

Common pond snail: Good in any size aquarium. *Source*—Common and native to our streams but usually carried by dealers. *Description*—Shaped like a bulging whorl; all black; small; hardy. *Reproduction*—Eggs laid in clear lumps of jelly fastened to water plants. *Food*—Supplementary food not required.

Japanese trap-door snail: Excellent for aquarium of ten gallons or more. *Source*—Dealers. *Description*—Turban-shaped; dark olive-green; grows to size of large walnut. *Reproduction*—Young born alive; pea-sized when dropped. *Food*—Hardy feeder; requires supplementary feeding. Give lettuce leaf and tomato as for red ramshorn (see below).

Red ramshorn snail: Excellent for any size aquarium. *Source*—Dealers. *Description*—Curled like ram's horn; transparent; body coral-red. *Reproduction*—Eggs deposited in round, flat mass of pink jelly attached to sides of aquarium. Fish are fond of these eggs and young snails. To rear, remove egg mass with sharp knife or razor blade. Place mass in small balanced aquarium jar. When eggs hatch, keep small pieces of clean, fresh lettuce on water for young to feed on. *Food*—Consists of minute animal life and dead and decaying matter; heavy feeder; keep piece of fresh lettuce leaf floating on water at all times. When tomatoes are in season, place small piece on lettuce leaf once per week.

Spotted African or paper-shell snail: Excellent but extremely short-lived. Body of this snail disintegrates so rapidly after death that it can pollute an aquarium in a short time. Snails should be checked each day and dead ones removed at once. *Source*—Dealers. *Description*—Shell transparent; brown spots on body show through. Grows to fair size. *Reproduction*—Prolific breeder; eggs laid in long, curved strips of firm jelly attached to leaves of water plants. Fish fond of young snails; only a few reach maturity in aquarium. *Food*—Not a heavy feeder but does like a little lettuce now and then.

ESTABLISHMENT

Use any type of aquarium jar or regular aquarium tank; choice depends on animals to be housed. A large aquarium should be placed on a small table with rollers, so that it can be moved about at will. Cover bottom with 1½ inches of bird gravel, aquarium sand, or tropical fish sand; wash thoroughly to free it from all dirt before using it; put in pan or buckets, run water through, and stir constantly until water runs clear.

PLANTING: Space all plants of one kind 1–2 inches apart. Best plan is to plant tall growers at back facing window, shorter ones at sides, leaving front space open for observation. Push roots of plants down into sand (a little water poured over sand makes planting somewhat easier); weight down the plant stems by pushing small rocks into the sand against them; otherwise, animals uproot plants. Take care to leave plant crowns uncovered.

ROCKS: Wash them thoroughly and scrub them free of all foreign matter before placing them in the aquarium. Use large, irregularly shaped rocks of various sizes; pile them on top of each other or scatter over sand; colorful rocks with quartz and mineral deposits in them add attractiveness.

WATER: Fill aquarium with water to within 1 inch of top; pour gently over saucer to break force and prevent stirring up sand and uprooting plants. Cover aquarium with glass and let stand for 1 week before introducing animals; this gives roots chance to take hold and allows water to become properly aerated and of room temperature. Always keep aquarium covered; this keeps water surface free of dust and oil, prevents fish from jumping out, keeps foreign objects from falling in, and prevents rapid evaporation of water.

LIGHT AND HEAT: As plants need some sunlight in order to grow and produce oxygen, place aquarium near window where it receives *diffused* light with about 2 hours of direct morning sunlight. During the winter, keep aquarium out of drafts and away from cold windows and heating units; near-constant temperature is ideal. For tropical fish, which should have constant temperature, use aquarium heater with thermostat set at temperature required by the variety of tropical fish housed. Constant direct light causes microscopic plant life (algae) to grow on glass sides of aquarium nearest light; scrape off growth with razor blade and allow to fall to bottom as food for fish and scavengers; adjust aquarium to control light conditions.

BALANCE: Aquarium may remain in balance for a year or more. Never change water so long as balance is maintained, water is sweet and clear, and animal life is active and healthy. Dark sediment that collects on sand need not be removed; provides some food for animal life.

CLEANING: Sometimes, during the spring, microscopic plants grow so rapidly that water becomes a dense green; this is healthy condition for fish but makes observation difficult. Siphon off half to two-thirds of the green water and replace with fresh water which has been brought to same temperature as aquarium water (sudden changes in temperature can quickly kill fish or make them ill). Let tap water stand at least 24 hours until it reaches room temperature; gently pour it into the aquarium, taking care not to uproot plants. Process may have to be repeated several times, over a period of days, before water clears completely.

POLLUTION: Surplus food can quickly unbalance a tank; condition is indicated by disagreeable odor, fish "bubbling" at surface, and murky appearance of the water. Remove fish with dip net to another container filled with room-temperature tap water and a few water plants. Siphon off all water in aquarium; remove sediment on top of sand; take out all plants, wash them thoroughly, and replant them. Refill tank with well-aerated, room-temperature water and allow to settle 3–4 days before returning animal life. To control pollution, remove all surplus food daily; use long forceps, dip tube, or siphon hose.

ANIMALS SUITABLE FOR FRESH WATER AQUARIUM

Gold fish: Many varieties, such as fan tails, comet tails, shubunkins or calico fish, telescope fish, medakas, and more.

Tropical fish: Many varieties, such as guppies, scalares, blue moons, Mexican sword-tails, and a long list of others.

Native fish: Many varieties, such as baby catfish, top minnows, different species of sunfish, Johnny darters, sticklebacks, suckers, and many others.

Aquatic insects: For information see the chapter on insects. *True*

Bugs—Giant electric light bug, toe-biter. *Beetles*—Predaceous diving beetle, great water scavenger. *Miscellaneous*—Mosquito wigglers, dragonfly nymphs.

FOOD

In the wild, aquarium animals feed on a variety of plant and animal life. Use prepared mixes, which contain dried insects, meat, fish eggs, codfish, dried ground shrimps, or a mixture of various kinds of fish and shrimp, dried and ground (latter especially good for goldfish); or use prepared food made at home (see Part III). Give earthworms and strips of raw liver to native wild fish.

How to feed: In the wild, fish must hunt for food, which keeps them active and healthy. In an aquarium, fish readily overeat because activity is curtailed and food is ready at hand. Feed only the amount that will be eaten at one time; remove surplus. *Goldfish*— Give 1 pinch, dropped on surface of water, twice a week only. *Tropical fish*—Feed as instructed at time of purchase. *Native wild fish*—Feed 3 times weekly.

SICK FISH

When a fish appears out of condition, it must be observed closely. If it appears to be sick, it should be removed at once from the aquarium. This is imperative since many diseases of fish are contagious. In the wild state, when fish are in ill health most of them seek brackish water or saline earth. Knowing this, fish breeders use the salt bath as the first treatment for various ills.

For the salt solution use one heaping teaspoonful of salt to one gallon of water. Sea salt is the best to use, and can be bought commercially. Table salt usually has chemicals in it to prevent it from caking; it can be used, however, if sea salt is not available. The salt solution must be at the same temperature as the aquarium water before the fish is placed in it. The bath should be placed out of the light and the fish left quietly in the solution without food. It is advisable to change the salt solution every two days. If the fish does not show signs of improvement at the end of several days, dispose of it at once.

The most common disease of goldfish is a fungus. This is a whitish scum that appears first on the fins and tail; later it spreads over the body. If the condition is allowed to develop further, the fish becomes ill and dies. It is a contagious disease and spreads rapidly among the fish in the aquarium. If this happens, destroy the fish, empty the aquarium, disinfect it with a strong salt solution, and re-establish.

Salt solution is usually the best remedy for this fungus disease. It is often wholly effective if the treatment is used the moment any fungus is noticed on a fish. It is also effective in the treatment of fish lice, which are external parasites that are easily detected.

The salt solution is good for goldfish and for some, but not all, native fish. Another good fungicide, not as readily available as salt but usually obtainable at a drug store, is the dye methylene blue. This may be used with either fresh or salt water fish. It is completely nontoxic to fish, so the concentration does not have to be regulated very carefully. A common rule of thumb is to add enough of the dye to color the water a rich blue. Fish may be kept in such a solution a week or longer without harm.

A common disease of both fresh and salt water fish is fin rot, which is a bacterial disease easily detected because the fins first become frayed at the edges and then gradually deteriorate toward the base. This may be treated with the antibiotic terramycin, which commonly comes in 250 milligram capsules. It should be applied at the rate of 250 milligrams to every five gallons of water. The capsules must, of course, be opened and the contents put in the water for more rapid solution.

If a fish does not respond to treatment within a week or ten days, the wisest thing to do is to dispense with treatment and dispose of the ailing fish.

Salt Water Aquarium

The salt water aquarium is a "problem child" for anyone who does not live on the seacoast and does not have the means to acquire the necessary equipment to establish and maintain it. Most professional aquarists say that a marine aquarium cannot be kept balanced for a satisfactory length of time by an amateur. Yet there are records of its having been done, so it is possible when one has the patience, the proper equipment, and the ideal situation.

For one who lives on the seacoast or who intends to spend a long holiday on the coast, especially a rocky coast, there is ample opportunity to indulge in the fascinating experience of establishing a marine aquarium and collecting the sea life to go into it.

First of all, the container for a salt water aquarium must be of glass—all glass. If any metal is used in the construction and is placed so that salt water comes in contact with it, defeat occurs before establishment begins. Salt water acts chemically upon metal with the result that substances are dissolved which kill all life as soon as it is placed in the aquarium.

Conveniently sized all-glass containers are available at many shops or from biological supply houses. The best size for a beginner is one that holds from eight to ten gallons.

MATERIALS

A small electric air pump and plastic tubing are needed to provide adequate aeration. Transport sea water in enamel buckets or large glass jars. Be sure there is no dilution of salt water from fresh water stream or sewage disposal. Also collect a few rocks from tide pools and a few oxygenating plants, which grow in lagoons and on rocks of tide pools.

ESTABLISHMENT

Cover bottom with 2 inches of clean, wet shore sand. Study tide pool and try to reproduce portion of it in aquarium. Place rocks on sand piled against one side and one end of aquarium, allowing several to extend above water surface.

PLANTS: No more than 2–3 needed at a time. Use common ulva (the most satisfactory), also called sea lettuce; seaweed or moss, eel grass, and cladophora. Do not use brown or red seaweed, as they pollute water quickly. Avoid large root masses of eel grass; contains small animal life that dies quickly and pollutes water. Locate plants attached to small rocks; cut free and place in aquarium. Small rocks with plants growing on them can also be removed and placed in aquarium.

WATER: Fill aquarium two-thirds full unless shore crabs only are to be housed, in which case fill but half full. Mark water level on glass with pencil or adhesive tape. As sea water evaporates, add fresh water to bring it up to mark; fresh water must be soft tap water, rain water, or distilled water, of the same temperature as aquarium water. As salt content of aquarium water is very important, use hydrometer to keep constant. Reading of natural sea water is 1.025. Add fresh water from time to time to keep reading normal.

TEMPERATURE: Must be between 50 and 60 degrees F.; must be

kept constant. Give very little direct sunlight; keep in cool location; northeast exposure best. Algae that grow on glass sides of aquarium help reduce light; scrape off from front glass only to allow observation.

POLLUTION: Can occur in a brief time. Never allow plant or animal matter to decompose. Remove all surplus food immediately after feeding animals. Use long wooden forceps or glass dip tube.

SOME ANIMALS SUITABLE FOR SALT WATER AQUARIUM

Anemones: Common in tide-pools. Locate one on loose rock small enough to bring in; use knife to remove from rock, taking care not to injure body.

Barnacles: Common along rocky coasts. Grow in colonies on dead shells, on rocks, and on wood. Sometimes found on small loose rocks which can be picked up; otherwise use knife to remove.

Fish: Vary according to habitat. Capture small ones with dip net.

Hermit crabs: Strange, small crabs that live in borrowed houses, usually in broken shells, often much too large or small for them. Captured easily by hand; found most often higher up on beach and quite far from water's edge.

Scavengers: Only the three listed are recommended; all may be captured by hand or dip net. *Young eels*—Found in muddy bottoms of lagoons. *Common snail*—Found on rocks along beaches. *Small shore crab*—Found among rocks on beaches or along shore.

Sea urchins: Small ones suitable for aquarium are often found in tide-pools; may be lifted by hand if done quickly; otherwise must be pried loose.

Shore crabs: Usually common among rocks at water's edge. Capture by hand; use smaller ones only.

Starfish: Many varieties, kinds, and sizes; some suitable for an aquarium, many not. Use small ones found among rocks at edges of beaches; pick up by hand.

FOOD

ANEMONES AND BARNACLES: Native food consists of any small animal or plant life carried across tentacles by waves. Drop finely ground particles of clam and snail meat on tentacles.

CRABS AND SNAILS: Native food consists of dead and decaying organic matter. Give small pieces of fish, clam or snail meat.

FISH AND EELS: Native food consists of small aquatic life, some plant life, decomposing organic substances. Give dried ground shrimp, chopped raw fish, chopped clam and snail flesh. Squeeze juice from clam flesh before feeding.

SEA URCHINS: Native food consists of shell fish and other small sea life. Give bits of ground sea food or freshly chopped clam and snail flesh.

STARFISH: Native food consists of mollusks. Starfish forces shell open by continued pull of its tube feet; then covers flesh with its stomach and digests it. Place rock covered with small clams or mussels in water for starfish to find.

Artificial Marine Aquarium

Biological laboratories in inland schools may obtain equipment, supplies, information, plant and animal life, and food from the General Biological Supply Company, Turtox Service Department, Chicago, Illinois. For a great many years this company has supplied inland high school and college-university laboratories with the wherewithal to establish marine aquariums far distant from the coast. With their permission, the following information is quoted from their Turtox Service Leaflet No. 20. Their first paragraphs give information about collecting and shipping, kinds of tanks to use, kind of sand, how to make synthetic sea water should one desire to do so, salt concentration, temperature, and aeration. The remainder of the information is quoted as follows:

A marine aquarium may, of course, be "balanced" just like a fresh-water aquarium if the oxygen given off by the plants is sufficient to supply the needs of the animals. The green alga, *Ulva*, commonly called sea-lettuce, is helpful as an oxygen producer, as is also *Cladophora*. Marine diatoms are particularly desirable and we now include them in the sand supplied with our larger sets. In general, however, the "balancing" of a marine aquarium comes about gradually and, at the start, it is highly desirable to aerate the water by artificial means.

Light

Salt-water aquaria require much less light than do fresh-water aquaria and they should receive very little direct sunlight. Except when it is desirable to watch the inhabitants, the aquarium should be shielded by cardboard on three sides to keep out very strong light.

The Animals

With the aquarium tank made ready and in its permanent location, the preliminary preparations are completed and the living marine animals may be ordered. Under the ideal conditions existing in very large aquaria, almost any marine forms will live; but the marine-aquarium enthusiast who is experimenting with small tanks should attempt to secure the more hardy animals which will live for awhile, at least, under somewhat adverse conditions. Among the best small-aquarium inhabitants are small marine snails and barnacles. Starfish, sea urchins, sea cucumbers, and sea anemones will usually live for a few weeks and under carefully controlled conditions may be kept in aquaria for much longer periods. Small crabs will often thrive where more exacting forms die, and *Obelia* will often live and reproduce new colonies in very small aquaria. . . .

Feeding the Animals

. . . Twice a week is often enough to feed the various forms. Small pieces of macerated oysters, clams or fish make a fine food and they should be dropped near the mouth of the animal by means of forceps. The juice of oysters and clams also makes a fine food and can be dropped by means of a pipette into the mouths of such animals as the *Metridium*, *Thyone* and *Cucumaria*. Fresh water clams may be used as well as salt-water clams and even small pieces of fresh-water fish will be readily devoured. . . .

Summary

The really essential points to keep in mind are few; but they are *very important*: (1) Use small specimens and few of them; (2) Keep the water temperature low; (3) Aerate the water constantly and (4) Feed sparingly.

PART III

HOW TO GROW
AND PREPARE FOOD
FOR CAGED PETS

IT is usually a problem for the average person to obtain a constant supply of food for some kinds of pets. This is especially true of many of the insect feeders such as toads, frogs, and lizards. It is also difficult to provide enough small rodents for pet snakes when one must depend upon trapping them or upon the ability of children to bring them in. Some pets require fish in their diets, but small, live fish are not always available at the time needed. In order to eliminate semistarvation periods for many pets in a classroom or a home it is advisable to grow the required foods, or prepare those that can be easily prepared, thus ensuring a constant and ready supply at all times.

The following information deals with the rearing of those creatures which are most commonly required as food for caged animals, and the preparation of other foods which are not animal in nature.

Meal Worms

Meal worms are important in the diet of almost every kind of pet. They seem to act as a medicinal agent as they appear to have the effect of a tonic for pets that fall a little below par in vitality.

Meal worms are prolific breeders when they are maintained under proper conditions. Their three requirements are warmth, food, and moisture. Once a meal worm culture is established and properly maintained, it provides an endless supply of food for captive pets.

Meal worms may be purchased from any supply house and sometimes at pet shops. Advertisements in various pet magazines may give sources of supply also.

DESCRIPTION

ADULT: Dark brown, somewhat flat beetle, little more than an inch long.

LARVA: Light golden brown, hard-shelled, about 1½ inches long; resembles wire-worm, a common garden pest.

PUPA: Naked; all parts of adult beetle visible.

CONTAINER

Use heavy-walled, tight-fitting 14-inch square wooden box with hinged top. Tack metal strips over seams of box or cover entire box with sheet metal to prevent worms from working through seams.

Wood is used because it holds warmth, keeps constant temperature, and is lightproof. Glass battery jars let in too much light and are too cold. Earthenware crocks, although lightproof, are too cold.

CULTURE

Start culture with 1 dozen meal worms. Fill box two-thirds full of fresh bran, which can be bought in bulk from feed and fuel dealers. Store surplus bran in mouse-proof container. As meal worms require darkness and carry on all activities on top of bran, lay piece of cardboard carton, cut to exact size of box, over bran. Keep hinged box top open about 1 inch at all times to allow ventilation; prop open with small block of wood.

As bran alone is insufficient for prolific breeding, provide fresh carrots for additional food and for moisture; remove tops; push down 2–3 at a time into bran; add whole, fresh, clean carrots as needed. Also add fresh bran from time to time; bran becomes dustlike as worms work through it.

Clean out entire box annually. Using common wire strainer, sift out and keep stages of beetles; discard debris. Fill box with fresh supply of bran and replace beetles.

WEEVIL PESTS

Nearly every meal worm culture, at some time or other, becomes infested with common small brown beetle called a weevil. Eggs of this pest are introduced into the culture with the bran. Unless watched, weevils make heavy inroads upon bran supply in breeding box.

CONTROL: When weevils first begin to develop, adults appear on inside of box top. Crush them at once with fingers or some flat tool; continue to do so daily. If weevils gain control, entire culture must be thrown out, box aired well for several days, and new culture established.

Cockroaches

Cockroaches provide a splendid food for many of the smaller pets and are especially suitable for spiders. A little time is required for the colony to multiply after it has become established. Once a colony has become sufficiently large, adults may be removed and used as food for pets without danger of reducing the colony too rapidly.

DESCRIPTION

ADULT: Flat, oval-shaped insects, with long legs and extremely long antennae; wings carried folded along back; colors vary from shiny, light yellowish-brown to dark brown depending upon species. Quick and nervous; run with incredible speed; nocturnal. Length from ½–1½ inches.

NYMPH: Like adult but wings not developed. This stage excellent for food.

CAPTURE

As bait, use garbage placed in dishes or pans with smooth sides. Once in this type of container, roaches cannot escape. Place container where roaches are known to come for food.

CULTURE

Use 5- to 10-gallon aquarium with tightly fitting screen top, which *must be escape-proof*. As roaches breed in dark quarters, cover bottom with 2 inches of sawdust. Provide plenty of cover material; scatter many thin pieces of bark over sawdust; pile several over each other. Warmth is essential for normal development; place aquarium where temperature is most constant; put near heater during night. *Food*—Native foods are warm, moist, and starchy; give scraps from table, such as water-soaked bread and cake, sweet fruits, pastes, and some lean, cooked meat; place food on small, flat containers such as tin lids, as these are easiest to keep clean. *Water*—Essential; must be fresh and available at all times; use water bottle partially pushed down into sawdust.

Crickets

Common black crickets provide an excellent food for many pets, especially the large spiders. Details concerning their appearance, method of capture, and maintenance are given in the chapter on insects, above. When they are maintained for prolific breeding, they must be established in large quarters and fed frequently and abundantly. Overfeeding is essential; if they are not given an abundance of food, they dine upon each other.

Bluebottle Flies and Blowflies

Because of the long fight against the house fly as a carrier of disease, it is difficult for one to have a tolerant attitude toward any fly. The habits of a large number of them are unspeakable. However, they have a necessary function, and it is important that they fill it.

Bluebottle flies and blowflies (fleshflies), both as larvae and adults, are one of the best pet foods. They breed prolifically and quickly and can be made to breed through the winter months when other insect food is difficult to obtain.

DESCRIPTION

Adult: Several times larger than house fly; metallic green or blue; busy, annoying buzz; quickly attracted to overripe meat where they deposit their eggs.

Larvae: Soft white maggots or grubs; often headless and footless.

Pupa: Dark brown, oval, somewhat rough object resembling a capsule.

CAPTURE

Adult flies are attracted by the odor of overripe meat. Place piece of raw liver or lean beef in a warm place out of doors; slash liver in several places so that flies can fasten eggs to tissue. After white egg masses have been deposited on bait bring it indoors and place on moist soil of breeding cage; surface of bait must not become dry; moisten if necessary.

CULTURE

Use 9-inch battery jar, vivarium box, small aquarium, or large coffee can. Provide container with tight-fitting screen top (see Part IV).

Cover bottom with 2 inches loose loam. As soil must be kept moist at all times, sprinkle lightly each day.

METAMORPHOSIS: Blowfly eggs usually hatch in 24 hours. Larvae feed on bait for 4–5 days, then burrow into soil, where they pupate. Adult flies emerge about 12 days after pupation. High temperature accelerates stages in development of flies and low temperature retards stages; keep breeding cage in warm room during winter to aid development.

FOOD FOR ADULTS: Give cube sugar, candy, icings, and other sweet substances; place in small flat dish set on soil of breeding cage.

REPRODUCTION: After a few days of feeding, adult flies mate and begin depositing eggs. Again provide piece of overripe meat or liver on moist soil and allow cycle to repeat itself; be sure to slash liver and keep surface moist.

CAPTURE OF ADULT FLIES FROM BREEDING CAGE FOR PET FOOD: Make 1-inch hole in one corner of screen top of breeding cage. Fasten close-fitting metal or wire cap over hole by wire brad or staple so that cap slides back and forth over hole (see Part IV). Carefully push cap aside and invert a bottle over opening. If breeding cage is of glass, cover all of it with dark cloth except region about inverted bottle. Flies immediately dart up into bottle. When required number collected, slip cap back over hole, slip cardboard under mouth of bottle, and turn flies loose in pet cages.

Fruit Flies

Fruit flies, now better known as drosophila, so common around spoiling fruits, make the most excellent food for some of the smaller lizards. The flies feed on the fermenting juices of decomposing fruit and deposit their eggs in the decaying pulp. As the life cycle is completed in ten days, the flies are a means by which food may be produced quickly.

DESCRIPTION

ADULT: Small; eyes red; body plump, yellowish; wings clear.

LARVAE: Maggotlike; live in fruit pulp where they pupate. Larvae and eggs so small they are seldom noticed.

CAPTURE AND CULTURE

Use small fruit jar; moisten bottom. Put in any soft, juicy, partially crushed fruit; overripe banana excellent. Leave jar in exposed spot;

do not allow fruit or bottom of jar to become dry. After fruit flies have swarmed over bait for several days, place jar in cage with animals to be fed. Adults soon emerge and supply pets with food.

Ants

Black ants of many species make excellent food for many small animals, especially horned lizards. Ants are not easily reared in the large quantities required for feeding purposes, but they may be captured by the half pint at a time. Such a quantity supplies a half-dozen lizards with food for two or three days.

DESCRIPTION

ADULTS: Characterized by small nodule on stemlike part of abdomen which attaches it to thorax. Males and females have 2 pairs of long, delicately-veined wings which are lost immediately after mating. Strong biting mouthparts are tools used for all activities.

CAPTURE

Locate ant hill. With a small spade, dig straight down into hill. This cuts through passages; ants become excited, come tumbling out, and fall into pit. Have ready a straight-sided, large-mouthed jar (square-shaped one best). Place jar in pit and fill in any empty space around it with dirt. Ants now tumble into jar. If colony is healthy, ants may be collected in a few minutes; if weak, must visit second nest. Take no more ants than pets will eat in 2 days; ants survive for short time only when piled on top of each other in close quarters and kept without food.

Rats and Mice

The majority of pet snakes must be fed rats and mice, and they should be given frequently to pet crows and magpies. It is advisable to keep a pair of rats or mice for breeding purposes only. Children should not be allowed to handle them or to make pets of them. It is usually an unhappy experience for a child to know that a pet is to be used as food for another pet. The wise thing is to feed when children are absent.

Rats and mice that are to be reared for food must be maintained as for pets (see chapter on mammals). When young are wanted for food only occasionally, the pairs should be allowed to breed only as food is needed.

Top Minnows

Top minnows or mosquito fish are the species used to control mosquitos in abatement programs. They furnish excellent food for many small turtles, are prolific breeders, and are easily maintained. Once well established in an aquarium, they become a constant supply upon which to draw.

DESCRIPTION

ADULT: Small, greenish fish about 1 inch long.
YOUNG: Born alive; large numbers dropped at a time.

CAPTURE AND CULTURE

Using dip net, capture a few specimens (2–3 pairs are sufficient) from some pond where they have been planted (obtain permission if necessary). Place in regular aquarium (see Part II); do not place with other fish.

FOOD: Native food is aquatic life at water's surface. Give live insects, such as small flies, young fly larvae. When this is not available, try granulated fish food and *very small* portions of scraped liver. Drop food on surface of water; feed no more than is consumed at one time; remove excess after feeding.

Indoor Earthworm Culture

Collect worms by digging them out of rich soil. A dozen are enough to start a culture.

HOUSING

Use 4′ × 4′ × 2′ box made of half-inch lumber, or use an old oak barrel or large wooden keg. Thoroughly mix equal parts of light loam, partly rotted leaves, well-rotted leaf mold, and well-rotted cow manure. Fill container two-thirds full of this mixture. Add worms. Cover box with piece of glass to retard evaporation and help maintain even temperature; push cover to one side from time to time if too much moisture condenses on glass. *Moisture*—Essential; mixture must be kept slightly moist; never allow it to become wet or soggy. *Temperature*—Must be kept between 40° and 55°F; place container where temperature can be kept as constant as possible.

FOOD

No special food needed if plenty of dead leaves are added to mixture.

Health Grit

Health grit, essential in the diet of all caged birds, may be purchased at pet shops but is also easy to prepare at home. There are but two ingredients: egg shells and *wood* charcoal.

PREPARATION

INGREDIENTS: 3 or 4 egg shells dried in oven until light brown; small quantity of wood charcoal.

METHOD: Crush egg shells and charcoal to powder with rolling pin; mix together equal parts of each. Place in small container in cage.

Nestling Food

Nestling food, essential in the diet of baby birds and breeding parent birds, may be purchased at all pet shops under the commercial name of "nestling food." It consists of meal worms, ant eggs, wasp grubs, blight beetles, caterpillars, spiders, and flies, which have been dried, ground, and thoroughly mixed. It is not always possible to make this mixture at home because of the difficulty of obtaining the various ingredients.

Fish Food

The best food for goldfish is the commercial food prepared from dried, ground sea animals, but a home-prepared food consisting of oatmeal, fresh spinach, egg, and puppy biscuit may be used as a substitute food for goldfish and native fish as well.

PREPARATION

INGREDIENTS: Oatmeal cooked without salt; spinach cooked and drained; egg scrambled dry; puppy biscuit ground.

METHOD: Mix equal parts of each thoroughly and allow mixture to dry. Use pinches as needed.

Green Growth

Plastic containers planted with seeds ready for sprouting are available at pet shops, but it is more economical and just as easy to grow your own.

Use an 8- to 10-inch flower pot saucer filled with good, rich, moist, soil. Plant bird seed in the soil; keep it moist but not wet. When growth reaches 2 or 3 inches in height, set the saucer in the bird cage.

A constant supply of green growth is possible by planting a series of containers several days apart.

PART IV

DESIGNS FOR CAGES

PET shops have greatly improved designs in cage construction by the use of hardware cloth stapled into required shapes and sizes. The bottoms and doors are efficiently made so that feeding and cleaning are extremely easy.

These cages are excellent for temporary housing and for transportation, but they are not satisfactory for an animal that is to be housed permanently and trained as a pet. For example, those rodents that require soil in which to burrow, dig, or roll are not happy in such a cage. A knowledge of the natural habitat, the habits, and the food of each animal to be housed is essential before a cage is chosen.

Cages may be constructed from many different designs. Since any captive animal is at once placed in an unnatural situation, first by restriction of its freedom, and second by a changed environment, the design of the cage to be used should be guided by the following points:

1. The cage should be large enough to give the animal abundant freedom of movement. Exercise is essential if the pet is to remain healthy.

2. Space must be sufficient to make it possible to reproduce the natural habitat of the pet.

3. Space must be allowed for sleeping or nesting quarters when such are required.

4. Space must be allowed for playthings such as wheels for chipmunks, spinners for mice, ladders for rats, and so on.

5. Doors must be placed so as to allow ease in feeding while at the same time preventing the escape of the pet.

6. The cage must be constructed so that cleaning can be performed quickly and easily.

7. Larger cages should have good rollers so that they can be moved with ease.

Commercial cages with wire bottoms are not desirable for small animals that need a sawdust-shavings mixture, sand, or soil on the cage bottom. The wire floor is uncomfortable. Moreover, variously sized animal cages are manufactured which have removable trays for litter and bedding and no wire bottom. (To clean the cage, simply hold the animal up off the tray and slide it out.) If necessary, a guinea pig can be made comfortable in a wire-floored cage if the wire is covered with plenty of bedding material.

CAGE FOR PRAIRIE DOG

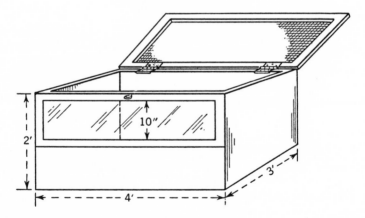

1. Box of wood with 10″ glass panel across front.
2. Top of screen wire hinged at back and provided with a strong hook in front.

LARGE ANIMAL CAGE

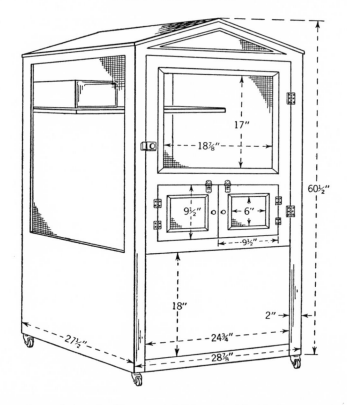

1. Large hinged door facilitates establishment of habitat.
2. Small doors within large door convenient for placing food and water.
3. The 24¾" × 18" front panel slides up and out so soil can be changed.
4. Use half-inch mesh hardware cloth.
5. As this cage, when properly established with soil, etc., is difficult to move, it should be provided with good ball-bearing rollers.
6. When cage is to be used for squirrels, place a 12" × 1" board high up across the back. Many tree squirrels like to sprawl out on a flat surface.
7. Nest box, if required, should be wooden, 12" × 12" × 6", with front end open.

SMALL ANIMAL CAGE

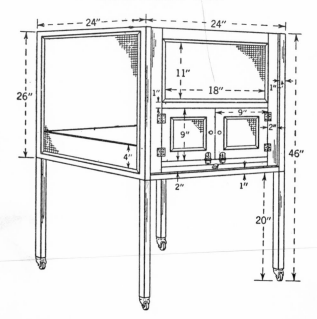

1. Entire front slides up and out for ease in creating habitat and cleaning.
2. The two doors open out.
3. Three panels of sheet metal or plywood placed around sides prevent sand, seeds, etc., from falling through onto floor.
4. Cage is covered with half-inch mesh hardware cloth.
5. Good rollers are necessary.
6. A 2' square sheet metal tray that slides in and out should be provided for bottom of cage; makes cleaning easy.

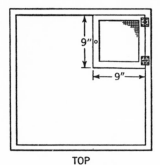

TOP

TOP

1. Door cut in rear right corner facilitates care of nests when cage is used for small birds such as finches.

RAT "APARTMENT"

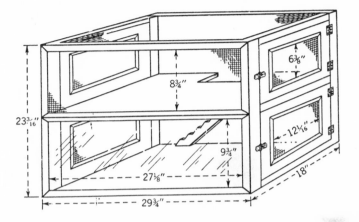

1. Back of wood.
2. Top of screen wire.
3. Front of upper compartment screen wire; front of lower compartment of glass.
4. Screen doors at both ends of each compartment.
5. A 4" × 3" hole cut in floor of upper compartment, with stairlike runway from lower floor.
6. When sexes are to be separated, cover hole with something that may be weighted down to prevent pets from moving it.
7. When cage is to be used for hamster, provide it with a 3" deep metal tray to cover cage bottom. This prevents soil from aging wooden frame and hamster from gnawing it.
8. Cage may be provided with legs if it is to be moved frequently. Legs should be 20" × 2" × 2", with good rollers.

MOUSE CAGE

1. Top of screen wire, hinged along back.
2. Bottom, ends, and back of wood; front of glass.
3. Doors in right end facilitate cleaning.
4. A half-inch dowel is placed across middle of cage 6" below top. Screen wire runway 1½" wide, is fastened to peg on end of cage, draped over dowel and along back of cage on several pegs, then forward across other end of cage and fastened to floor.
5. Use top and bottom of 4½" × 4" fruit can with cylinder of screen wire soldered on to make wheel; cut four 1" holes in each end. Wheel must turn freely on rod bolted through end of cage.
6. Merry-go-round: Cut 7" sheet metal circle; use 11" pencil-sized rod sharpened to point at each end; solder circle to rod half-way up. Cut piece of half-inch dowel 1½" long; fit a metal cap, depressed in center, over one end; fasten other end into 2" × 2½" block of wood. Fasten another metal cap on underside of horizontal dowel. Fit pointed ends of rod into depressions in center of metal caps. Set up merry-go-round about 3" away from wheel; it should whirl freely.
7. Knotted cord must be of heavy twine; tie around dowel but tack in place to prevent slipping. Tie knots at 1–2" intervals and hang an inch or so short of floor.

Right End of Cage
Use the two doors for placing food in cage and to facilitate cleaning.

Jumping Table
1. Cut 3" circle of sheet metal.
2. Use half-inch dowel, 5" long, for pedestal.
3. Fit metal cup to top end of dowel and solder circle to it.
4. Place other end in 1½" × 1½" heavy block of wood. If block is not heavy enough, fasten it to bottom of cage; otherwise it will tip over as mice jump on and off.
5. Place jumping table where it does not interfere with other apparatus.

Teeter Board
1. Use thin plywood.
2. Wooden triangular supports for crossbar have small cradle cut in top of each.
3. Use large nail for crossbar.
4. Use soft wire to fasten board to nail; board must teeter freely.
5. Place teeter board where it does not interfere with other apparatus.

MOUSE CAGE

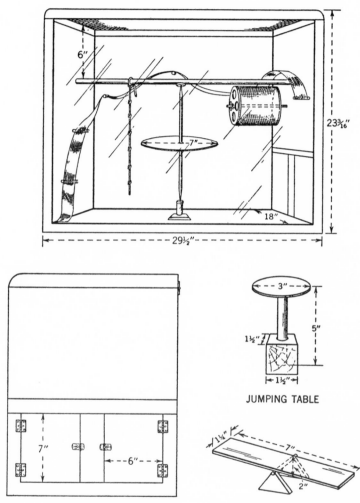

RIGHT END OF CAGE

JUMPING TABLE

TEETER BOARD

WATER BOTTLES AND SEED CONTAINERS

WATER BOTTLE   SEED CONTAINER

Water Bottles for Larger Pets
1. Easy to set up with any size bottle or jar which has wide mouth.
2. Fill container with water within 1" of top; invert glazed flower pot saucer over it; then turn whole thing upside down.
3. Saucer must not be too deep or too large. Pets should not be able to get into it.

Seed Container for Larger Pets
1. Same principle used for seeds and pellets as that for water bottle.
2. Bottle or jar must have wide mouth.
3. Fill and invert in flower pot saucer, dish, or pan.
4. Saucer must not be so large that pets can get into it.

Note: Patented feeders and water bottles of various types can be obtained at pet shops. Many are made of plastic and are very serviceable. When purchasing either water bottle or feeder, tell dealer what pet it is to be used for.

LARGE BIRD CAGE

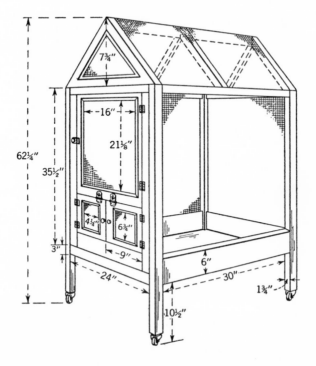

1. Rooflike top provides space for many-branched limb to reach from floor to ceiling (necessary to provide exercise for feet of birds).
2. Entire cage is covered with quarter-inch mesh hardware cloth.
3. Large door is necessary for establishment of habitat.
4. Food and water are conveniently passed through small doors.
5. Ball-bearing rollers on legs are necessary so that cage can be moved about easily.

BOX-TABLE OR SAND-TABLE

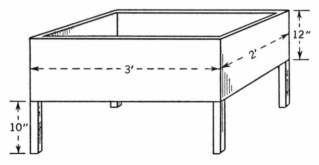

Suggested for temporary housing of ducklings and goslings.

TERRARIUM

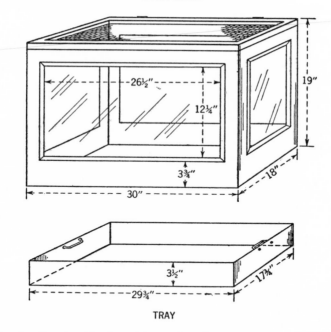

TRAY

1. Wooden frame with glass sides and ends.
2. Top of window screen wire, hinged along back.
   Tray of sheet metal with handle at each end fits snugly into bottom of terrarium, but is easily lifted in and out.

LARGE REPTILE CAGE

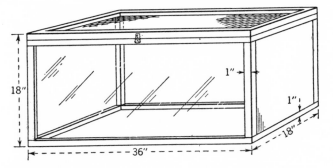

1. Top is of quarter-inch mesh hardware cloth, hinged along back, locked in front.
2. Bottom, back, and ends are of wood; front is of glass.
3. Ends may be of glass if preferred, but remember that glass with sun on it can produce excessive heat.

SMALL REPTILE CAGE

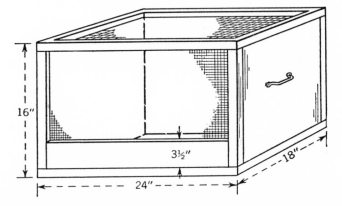

1. Bottom, back, and ends are of wood; front is of quarter-inch mesh hardware cloth.
2. Top is of quarter-inch mesh hardware cloth hinged along back, hooked in front.
3. A 3½" wood panel across front prevents sand and gravel from falling through.
4. Handle on each end makes transportation easy.

CONSTRUCTION OF VIVARIUM BOX

1. Cut 3 pieces of glass 16″ × 9″ for 2 sides and bottom of box.
2. Cut 2 pieces of glass 9″ square for 2 ends.
3. Place pieces on table as illustrated below.

Note: Pieces are placed with space of sixteenth-inch between edges to prevent chipping when pieces swing into position.

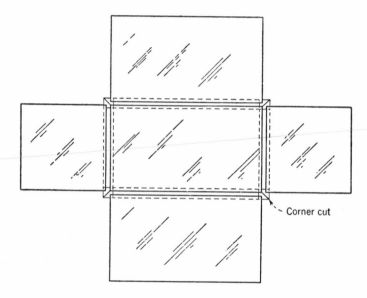

Corner cut

4. Cut 1″ wide strips of waterproof adhesive tape required length and press onto glass pieces as indicated by dotted lines.
5. Cut overlapped pieces of tape at corners as indicated.
6. Adhesive tape sticks more firmly to glass surfaces when rubbed in place with knife handle or rounded edge of scissors.
7. Move entire box out to edge of table so that one hand may be placed under central piece of glass. Lift the whole thing with care and allow pieces to swing down in place.
8. While holding box in this position, with free hand press cut ends of tape firmly around corners.

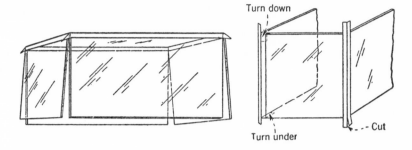

9. Carefully place box on table in upright position. (Brace ends or sides against books.)
10. Cut 4 strips of tape 11" long to seal corners. Leave 1" extra at top and bottom on each strip to turn over. Press tape firmly in place and set box right side up on table.
11. Cut tape at each corner as indicated. Turn under at bottom and on inside at top and press firmly into place.
12. Again rub firmly over all adhesive surfaces to ensure good attachment.
13. Tear tape into narrow strips and cover exposed top edges of box. Rub tape firmly onto glass.

If box is to be used as a terrarium to house small lizards, young turtles, or a water dog or two, it must have a screen cover.
1. Cut piece of screen wire 2" longer and 2" wider than size of box.
2. Cut out a 1" square from each corner.
3. Place wire over top of box; bend down slightly both sides and both ends; then remove and bend wire sharply along same lines. This makes top fit snugly.

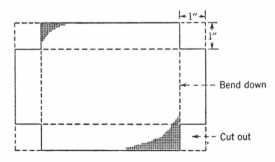

The above vivarium box may be constructed in any size and shape one may desire. Smaller boxes often are more convenient to house such small creatures as millipedes, centipedes, some spiders, and many insects. Note that, in some instances, it may be less expensive to use a ready-made aquarium as a vivarium box than to build one.

If box to be used for temporary aquarium, press aquarium cement firmly and well into all seams; let harden overnight.

Note: Aquarium cement comes in different forms. Probably the easiest to use is the puttylike compound which becomes soft when held near heat or worked in the hands. It may be obtained from glaziers or from companies that manufacture aquariums.

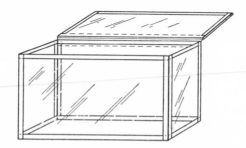

If box is to be a little aquarium, it should be provided with a top.
1. Cut piece of glass 16″ × 9″.
2. Tear 3 narrow strips of adhesive tape and cover exposed edges of glass.
3. Cut 2 strips of tape 10″ × 2″. Press half the width of 1 piece onto the glass along raw edge, leaving 1″ flap.
4. Support glass against some object, then press other inch of tape on inside edge of long side of box. Be sure to leave sixteenth-inch space between two pieces of glass.
5. Turn glass over to cover box.
6. Press second piece of 2″ tape along outside edge at top to form hinge.
7. With knife handle press adhesive firmly against glass.
8. Gently raise and lower lid. If pieces are not too close together, tape acts as hinge and a permanent top is ready for aquarium.

PRACTICAL INSECT CAGES

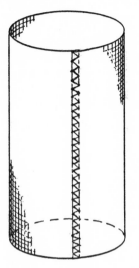 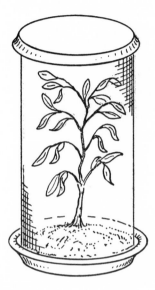

SCREEN WIRE CAGE

1. Use window screen wire 18″ wide.
2. Cut 1 piece 24″ long.
3. Roll piece into a cylinder; lap edges 1″.
4. Clip edges together at top and bottom to hold while sewing.
5. With coarse needle and string, sew edges down; use a wire stapler if available.
6. Use two 9″ pie pans, enamel or tin.
7. Pile mound of well-dampened soil or sand in one pan.
8. Push branches of food plant well down into soil or sand.
9. Set screen cylinder over plants and soil.
10. Turn second pan over top of cylinder. Habitat now ready for occupants.

LAMP CHIMNEY INSECT CAGE

1. Use flower pot and lamp chimney.
2. Fill pot with dampened soil.
3. Stick branch of host plant down in soil.
4. Place lamp chimney over soil.
5. Place insects inside chimney and fasten piece of gauze over top with rubber band.

This type of small cage is especially good for ladybug beetles and for eggs and nymphs of katydids.

HABITAT FOR SPHINX MOTH LARVAE

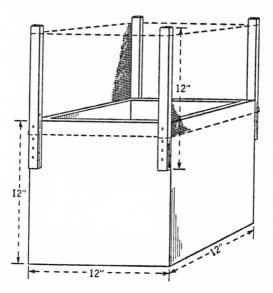

1. Use wooden box.
2. Cut 4 strips of wood 12" × ¾".
3. Nail a strip at each corner of box to make 4 posts.
4. Place screen wire 48" × 16" around top of box, tacking to sides of box and to posts.
5. Fill box with 8" of **damp** soil, firmly packed down.
6. Push branches of food plants well down into moist soil.
7. If cover is required, cut piece of screen and lay over top.

ANT NEST

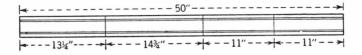

1. Use piece of wood 50″ × 2¾″ × ¾″.
2. Cut half-inch deep groove half-inch from edge on each side.
3. Cut wood into 4 pieces: 1 piece 13¼″, 1 piece 14¾″, and 2 pieces 11″.
4. Nail the two 11″ pieces onto ends of 13¼″ piece half-inch up from bottom, matching grooves.

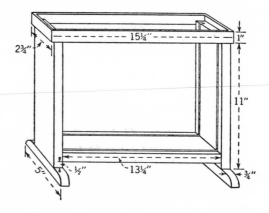

5. Take piece of quarter-inch plywood 36″ × 1″; cut 2 pieces 15¼″ long; cut 2 pieces 2¾″ long.
6. Nail these pieces around top of frame so that they extend half-inch above top.
7. Cut 2 pieces of wood 5″ × ¾″; round off top ends; nail to bottom of end pieces for feet.
8. Cut 2 pieces of glass 14″ × 10½″; slip into grooves.
9. For top, take the 14¾″ piece of wood and cut out a piece 1″ × ¾″ at each end of grooved surface.

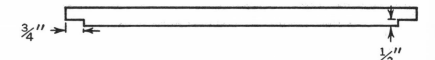

10. Bore 4 evenly spaced 1″ holes down center; tack or staple an 11″ × 1½″ piece of screen over holes. This piece serves as top for nest.

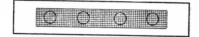

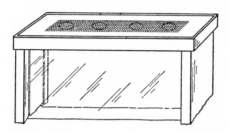

BREEDING HABITAT FOR BLUEBOTTLE FLIES AND BLOWFLIES

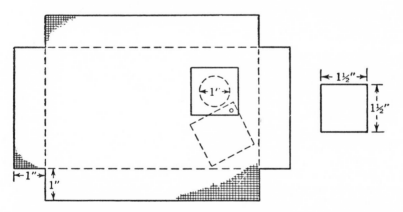

1. Cut piece of screen wire 1″ longer and 1″ wider than top of container tube used.
2. Cut out 1″ square from each corner of screen.
3. Cut 1″ hole near one end.
4. Cut 1½″ square from stiff card; fasten over hole with brad and work back and forth until it moves easily.
5. Place wire over habitat and bend down both sides and ends; remove and bend sharply along same lines to make a tight fit.

TO CAPTURE ADULT FLIES

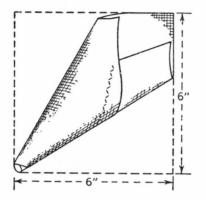 

1. Cut piece of screen wire 6" square.
2. Begin at one corner and roll into a cone with wide flare at top and small hole at bottom, the latter large enough to permit a fly to pass through.
3. Fit cone inside mouth of bottle to be used, with **no space** between cone and bottle.
4. When shape is correct, sew overlapped sides to hold in shape.
5. Place piece of overripe meat in bottle, fit funnel into position, and set trap outside where it will attract flies.

GLOSSARY

ALBUMIN. Any of a class of proteins.

ALBUMINOUS. Pertaining to or containing albumin.

ALGA. (pl. algae) A group of plants containing chlorophyll but having no true root, stem, or leaf, such as seaweeds and pond scums.

ANAL. Of or near the anus.

ANTERIOR. Toward the front, or forward.

ANUS. Opening at the posterior end of the alimentary canal.

BIOLOGICAL. Pertaining to life.

BODY CREST. Ridge along the back of some amphibians.

CANINE. Of or like a dog (canine tooth—like a dog's tooth).

CANINE TOOTH. The pointed tooth next to the incisors.

CANNIBALISTIC. The trait of eating others of one's own kind.

CARAPACE. The bone, or hornlike shield, covering the back of turtles, armadillos, and many crustaceans.

CARNIVORE. A flesh-eating animal.

CARNIVOROUS. Flesh-eating.

CARRION. The decaying flesh of a dead body.

CEPHALOTHORAX. The head and thorax combined in a single part.

CHELICERA. One of the clawlike or pincerlike anterior appendages of a spider or scorpion (pl. chelicerae).

CLOACA. The chamber into which empty the urinary, intestinal, and reproductive systems in various vertebrates, especially birds, reptiles, amphibians and fish.

CONSTRICTION. Contraction by squeezing.

CREMASTER. The spikelike process on the rear end of the pupae of Lepidoptera.

Function of the cremaster: When a butterfly larva is ready to pupate, it first spins a disk of silk from which it suspends itself by its last two prolegs. When last larval skin is shed, it is worked back to the tail end of the larva, is grasped between two abdominal segments, and held while this part of the body frees itself. The cremaster is now able to

279

insert itself into the disk of silk. The pupa is now held firmly in place where it hangs until the adult is ready to emerge. In Lepidoptera that pupate in the ground, the cremaster assists in burrowing.

CREPUSCULAR. Active at twilight.

CUTICLE. An outer noncellular layer produced by the epidermis in arthropods and some other animals.

DIURNAL. Active during the day.

DORMANT. Sleeping, lethargic, or inactive.

DORSAL (dorsum). Pertaining to the upper surface; the back.

DORSOLATERAL. Between the back and the side.

EMBRYO. Young organism in early stages of development.

EPIDERMIS. The outermost cellular layer of the skin of plants and animals.

ESTIVATE. To lie dormant during heat and drought.

EXOSKELETON. The hard, outside supporting structure, as the covering of insects.

FACET. Single small surface of a compound eye.

FORAGE CROP. Food for domestic animals.

FRONTAL. Pertaining to the front, or especially to the forehead.

GRANULAR. Consisting or appearing to consist of grains.

GULAR SAC. The throat pouch that occurs in males of many lizards.

HAMMOCK. A slightly elevated tract of wooded land.

HIBERNATE. To lie dormant during winter months.

INCUBATE. To keep eggs in a favorable environment for hatching or developing.

INVERTEBRATES. Animals without backbones.

JUVENILE. The immature or undeveloped stage, as in some amphibians.

KEELED. With a ridgelike process.

MASK. A cover over the face that conceals it, as in the dragonfly nymph.

METAMORPHOSIS. A change in form, structure, or function, as a result of development.

MIDDORSAL. Middle of the back.

MOLLUSKS. Members of the large phylum that contains the slugs, snails, mussels, clams, oysters, limpets, cuttlefish, etc.

NICTITATING MEMBRANE. A transparent third eyelid hinged at the inner angle or beneath the lower lid of the eye of various animals, and capable of being drawn across the eyeball.

NOCTURNAL. Active during the night.

OMNIVOROUS. Eating everything, especially both animal and vegetable food.

OPAQUE. Not allowing light to pass through; not transparent.

OPERCULUM. A covering flap.

OVIPAROUS. Egg-laying.

OVIPOSITOR. A specialized organ for depositing eggs.

OVOVIVIPAROUS. Egg hatches within the body of the mother, and the young emerge alive.

PEDICEL. A small stem or stalk.

PLASTRON. The ventral portion of the shell of a turtle.

POSTERIOR. The hinder end or the rear.

PREDACEOUS. Preying on other animals.

PREDATOR. One that preys on other animals.

PRIMITIVE. Simple in evolutionary structure or development.

PRONOTUM. The forward and dorsal portion of the thorax, common in insects.

PROTEIN. A large class of organic compounds containing nitrogen, in contrast to fats and carbohydrates.

PROTUBERANCE. That which projects or bulges out.

RESONANT. Resounding.

ROSTRUM. A beak or beaklike process as in the crayfish.

RUDIMENTARY. Imperfectly developed.

RUFOUS. Reddish or rust-colored.

SAVANNA. Treeless plain.

SCULPTURED. Cut or carved with some design.

SCUTES. Heavy, hornlike scales, most commonly the large ventral scales of snakes.

SHIELDS. Hard, protective plates, as on turtles, or the heads of snakes and lizards.

SOMITE. A segment.

SPECULUM. The patch of bright color on the secondary wing feathers of most ducks and some domestic fowls.

SPINNERETS. The organs for producing the threads of silk from the secretions of the silk glands in spiders.

SPIRACLE. A breathing hole; in insects placed along sides of thorax and abdomen.

TERRESTRIAL. Land-dwelling as opposed to aquatic.

TRANSLUCENT. Partially transparent, as frosted glass.

TUBERCLES. Small, knoblike prominences.

VEGETARIAN. Feeding on plant forms only.

VENOMOUS. Poisonous.

VENT. The external opening of the cloaca.

VENTRAL. The belly or underside of the body.

VIVIPAROUS. Bearing young alive.

SUGGESTED READING

Books marked with an asterisk (*) should be especially interesting to children because of the illustrations, because of the text, or both.

AMPHIBIANS AND REPTILES

*BLY, ROBERT, HUASS, HANS. *The Illustrated Book about Reptiles and Amphibians of the World.* New York, Grosset & Dunlap, 1960. 157 pp.

CARR, ARCHIE, and GOIN, C. J. *Guide to Reptiles, Amphibians and Freshwater Fishes of Florida.* Gainesville, University of Florida Press, 1955. 341 pp.

COCHRAN, DORIS M. *Living Amphibians of the World.* Garden City, N.Y. Doubleday, 1962. 199 pp.

CONANT, ROGER. *A Field Guide to Reptiles and Amphibians of Eastern North America.* Boston, Houghton Mifflin, 1958. 366 pp.

*MATHEWSON, ROBERT. *The How and Why Wonder Book of Reptiles and Amphibians.* New York, Wonder Books, Grossett & Dunlap, 1960. 48 pp.

*MERTENS, ROBERT. *The World of Amphibians and Reptiles.* New York, McGraw-Hill, 1960. 207 pp.

OLIVER, JAMES A. *Snakes in Fact and Fiction.* New York, Macmillan, 1958. 199 pp.

*POPE, CLIFFORD H. *The Giant Snakes.* New York, Knopf, 1961. 289 pp.

SCHMIDT, KARL P. *A Check List of North American Amphibians and Reptiles.* (Sixth ed.) American Society of Ichthyologists and Herpetologists, University of Chicago Press, 1953. 280 pp. (Gives *distribution* of species and subspecies.)

SCHMIDT, KARL P., and INGER, ROBERT F. *Living Reptiles of the World.* Garden City, N.Y., Hanover House, 1957. 287 pp.

*SMITH, HOBART M. *Pet Turtles.* Fond du Lac, Wisc., All-Pets Books, 1955. 24 pp.

*————. *Snakes as Pets.* Fond du Lac, Wisc., All-Pets Books, 1958. 80 pp.

*SMYTH, H. RUCKER. *Amphibians and Their Ways.* New York, Macmillan, 1962. 292 pp.

WRIGHT, A. H., and WRIGHT, A. A. *A Handbook of Snakes of the United States and Canada.* Ithaca, N.Y., Comstock, 1957. Vol. I, 564 pp. Vol. II, pp. 565–1105.

THE AQUARIUM

The Aquarium. The Aquarium Publishing Co., 51 East Main Street, Norristown, Pa. Monthly magazine.

AXELROD, HERBERT R. *Aquarium Plant Guide: An Instructive Book for Beginning Aquarists.* Jersey City, T. F. H. Publications, 1954, 34 pp.

*AXELROD, HERBERT R., and VORDERWINKLER. *Color Guide to Tropical Fish* (rev. ed.). New York, Sterling, 1959. 160 pp.

————. *Encyclopedia of Tropical Fishes, with Emphasis on Techniques of Breeding.* Jersey City, T. F. H. Publications, 1962. 763 pp.

*BERRILL, N. J., and BERRILL, JACQUELYN. *1001 Questions Answered about the Seashore.* New York, Dodd, Mead, 1957. 305 pp.

*BURGER, CARL. *All About Fish.* New York, Random House, 1960. 138 pp.

*BURTON, MAURICE. *Under the Sea.* New York, Franklin Watts, 1960. 256 pp.

EDDY, SAMUEL. *How to Know the Freshwater Fishes.* Dubuque, Iowa, William C. Brown, 1957. 253 pp.

*FREY, HANS. *Illustrated Dictionary of Tropical Fishes.* Jersey City, T. F. H. Publications, 1962. 768 pp.

GANNON, ROBERT. *Live Foods for Aquarium Fishes.* Jersey City, T. F. H. Publications, n.d. Pamphlet.

HERALD, EARL S. *Living Fishes of the World.* Garden City, N.Y., Doubleday, 1961. 303 pp.

INNES, WILLIAM T. *Exotic Aquarium Fishes.* Philadelphia, Innes, 1956. 541 pp.

*MANDAHL, BARTH G. *Aquarium Fish in Color.* New York, Dutton, 1959. 138 pp.

STRAUGHAN, ROBERT P. L. *The Salt Water Aquarium in the Home.* New York, Barnes, 1959. 262 pp.

*ZIM, HERBERT S. *Fishes: A Guide to Fresh and Salt Water Species.* New York, Simon & Schuster, 1957. 160 pp.

ARTHROPODS—SPIDERS, etc.

BAERG, WILLIAM J. *The Tarantula*. Lawrence, University of Kansas, 1958. 88 pp.

*BUCKSBAUM, RALPH, and MILNE, LOUIS J. *The Lower Animals*. Garden City, N.Y., Doubleday, 1960. 303 pp.

CLOUDSLEY-THOMPSON, J. L. *Spiders, Scorpions, Centipedes and Mites* New York–London, Pergamon Press, 1958. 228 pp.

COMSTOCK, JOHN HENRY. *The Spider Book* (rev. ed.). Ithaca, N.Y., Comstock, 1948. 729 pp.

EMERTON, JAMES H. *The Common Spiders of the United States*. New York, Dover Publications, 1961. 227 pp.

GERTSCH, WILLIS JOHN. *American Spiders*. New York, Van Nostrand, 1949. 285 pp.

*KASTON, B. J. *How to Know the Spiders*. Dubuque, Iowa, William C. Brown, 1953. 220 pp.

*SHUTTLESWORTH, DOROTHY E. *The Story of Spiders*. Garden City, N.Y., Garden City Books, 1959. 57 pp.

ARTHROPODS—INSECTS

BARKER, WILL. *Familiar Insects of America*. New York, Harper & Row, 1960. 236 pp.

*BUCKSBAUM, RALPH, and MILNE, LOUIS J. *The Lower Animals*. Garden City, N.Y., Doubleday, 1960. 303 pp.

CROMPTON, JOHN. *A Hive of Bees*. Garden City, N.Y., Doubleday, 1958. 180 pp.

DILLON, LAWRENCE S., and DILLON, E. S. *A Manual of Common Beetles of Eastern North America*. Evanston, Ill., Harper & Row, 1961. 884 pp.

*ERLICH, PAUL R., and ERLICH, ANNE H. *How to Know the Butterflies*. Dubuque, Iowa, William C. Brown, 1961. 262 pp.

FROST, S. W. *Insect Life and Insect Natural History* (2d ed. rev.). New York, Dover Publications, 1959. 526 pp.

GAUL, ALBRO T. *The Wonderful World of Insects* (rev. ed.). New York, Holt, Rinehart, Winston, 1960. 289 pp.

*GRAY, ALICE. *The Adventure Book of Insects*. New York, Capitol, 1956. 117 pp.

*KLOTS, ALEXANDER B., and ELSIE B. *1001 Questions and Answers about Insects*. New York, Dodd, Mead, 1961. 260 pp.

*———. *Living Insects of the World*. Garden City, N.Y., Doubleday, 1959. 304 pp.

*KLOTS, ALEXANDER B. *World of Butterflies and Moths.* New York, McGraw-Hill, 1958. 207 pp.

PERSSON, PAUL. *World of Insects.* New York, McGraw-Hill, 1959. 204 pp.

*PHILLIPS, MARY G. *Dragonflies and Damselflies.* New York, Crowell, 1960. 95 pp.

*———. *Makers of Honey.* New York, Crowell, 1956. 163 pp.

*POOLE, LYNN and GRAY. *Weird and Wonderful Ants.* New York, Ivan Obolensky, 1961. 118 pp.

RICHARDS, OWAIN W. *The Social Insects.* New York, Harper & Row, 1961. 219 pp.

ROOD, RONALD N. *The How and Why Wonder Book of Ants and Bees.* New York, Wonder Books, Grosset & Dunlap, 1960. 48 pp.

*———. *The How and Why Wonder Book of Insects.* New York, Wonder Books, Grosset & Dunlap, 1960. 48 pp.

ROSS, EDWARD S. *Insects Closeup.* Berkeley, University of California Press, 1953. 80 pp.

SMITH, ARTHUR C. *Western Butterflies.* Menlo Park, Calif., Lane, 1961. 65 pp.

TEALE, EDWIN WAY. *The Golden Throng.* New York, Dodd, Mead, 1961. 216 pp.

———. *Insect Friends.* New York, Dodd, Mead, 1955. 96 pp.

URQUHART, F. A. *The Monarch Butterfly.* University of Toronto Press, 1960. 361 pp.

WILLIAMS, C. B. *Insect Migration.* New York, Macmillan, 1958. 235 pp.

*ZIM, HERBERT S., and COTTON, CLARENCE. *Insects—A Guide to Familiar American Insects.* New York, Golden Press, 1951. 160 pp.

BIRDS

ALLEN, ARTHUR A. *The Book of Bird Life* (2nd ed.). New York, Van Nostrand, 1961. 396 pp.

*CAYLEY, NEVILLE W. *Australian Finches.* Sydney, Australia, Angus & Robertson, 1932. 256 pp.

DARLING, LOIS, and LOUIS. *Birds.* New York, Houghton, Mifflin, 1962. 261 pp.

DELACOUR, JEAN T. *The Water-fowl of the World.* Vol. 1. London, England, Country Life Limited, 1954. 284 pp.

DUKE OF BEDFORD. *Parrots and Parrot-like Birds*, with COFFIN, DAVID L. *Diseases of Parrots.* Fond du Lac, Wisc., All-Pets Books, 1954. 210 pp.

GILLIARD, E. THOMAS. *Living Birds of the World.* Garden City, N.Y., Doubleday, 1958. 400 pp.

*HART, ERNEST H. *Budgerigar Handbook.* Jersey City, T.F.H. Publications, 1961. 251 pp.

*MANDAHL, BARTH G. *Cage Birds in Color.* New York, Barrows, 1959. 149 pp.

*MATHEWSON, ROBERT. *The How and Why Wonder Book of Birds.* New York, Wonder Books, Grosset & Dunlap, 1960. 48 pp.

PETERSON, ROGER TORY. *A Field Guide to the Birds* (East of Rockies). Boston, Houghton Mifflin, 1947. 290 pp.

————. *A Field Guide to Western Birds.* Boston, Houghton Mifflin, 1961. 366 pp.

MAMMALS

*ALMEDINGEN, E. M. *Kittens in Color: A Studio Book.* New York, Viking Press, 1961. 70 pp.

AMERICAN KENNEL CLUB. *The Complete Dog Book* (rev. ed.). Garden City, N.Y., Garden City Books, 1961. 524 pp.

*BOWRING, CLARA. *Poodles: A Studio Book.* New York, Viking Press, 1960. 64 pp.

*COOK, GLADYS EMMERSON. *All Breeds, All Champions: A Book of Dogs.* New York, Harper & Row, 1962. 120 pp.

DECHAMBRE, E. *The Pocket Encyclopedia of Cats.* Garden City, N.Y., Doubleday, 1961. 166 pp.

DODD, ED. *Mark Trail's Book of North American Mammals.* New York, Hawthorne Books, 1955, 242 pp.

ENGELHARDT, WOLFGANG. *Survival of the Free: The Last Stronghold of Wild Animal Life.* New York, Putnam's, 1962. 257 pp.

*FENTON, CARROL LANE, and CARSWELL, EVELYN. *Wild Folk in the Desert.* New York, John Day, 1958. 128 pp.

*FOX, CHARLES PHILIP. *Mr. Stripes, the Gopher.* Chicago, Reilly & Lee, 1962. 32 pp.

GAY, MARGARET COOPER. *How to Live with a Cat: A Practical Manual.* New York, Simon & Schuster, 1961. 267 pp.

GREER, MILAN. *The Fabulous Feline.* New York, Dial Press, 1961. 241 pp.

INGLES, LLOYD G. *Mammals of California and Its Coastal Waters* (rev. ed.), Stanford University Press, 1954. 396 pp.

KINNEY, JAMES R., and HONEYCUTT, ANN. *How to Raise a Dog in the City and Suburbs.* New York, Simon & Schuster, 1953. 209 pp.

LEEDHAM, CHARLES. *Care of the Dog.* New York, Scribner's 1961. 243 pp.

MACKENZIE, COMPTON. *Catnip.* New York, Taplinger, 1962. 104 pp.

McCOY, J. J. *The Complete Book of Dog Training and Care.* New York, Coward-McCann, 1962. 308 pp.

McNULTY, FAITH, and KEIFFER, ELISABETH. *Wholly Cats.* Indianapolis, Ind., Bobbs, Merrill, 1962. 208 pp.

*MURIE, OLAUS J. *Field Guide to Animal Tracks.* Boston, Houghton Mifflin, 1954. 374 pp.

*PALMER, E. LAURENCE. *Fieldbook of Mammals.* New York, Dutton, 1957. 321 pp.

*SACKVILLE-WEST, VICTORIA. *Faces: Profiles of Dogs.* Garden City, N.Y., Doubleday, 1961. 45 pp.

*SANDERSON, IVAN T. *Living Mammals of the World.* Garden City, N.Y., Doubleday, 1961. 303 pp.

*SHUTTLESWORTH, DOROTHY E. *The Story of Dogs.* Garden City, N.Y., Doubleday, 1961. 56 pp.

*SWEDRUP, IRAN. *Dogs in Color.* New York, Barrows, 1961. 146 pp.

GENERAL

*BORLAND, HAL. *Beyond Your Doorstep.* New York, Knopf, 1962. 400 pp.

*PARKER, BERTHA MORRIS. *The Golden Treasury of Natural History.* New York, Golden Press, 1952. 216 pp.

*ROEDELBERGER, FRANZ A., and PHILLIPS, MARY (English version by Mary Phillips): *The Wonderful World of Nature.* New York, Studio Publications, 1962. 212 pp.

INDEX

Format by Katharine Sitterly
Set in Linotype Electra
Composed, printed and bound by The Haddon Craftsmen, Inc.
HARPER & ROW, PUBLISHERS, INCORPORATED